F R A M E

Family Law

Tony Wragg

Senior Lecturer in Law
University of Derby

FINANCIAL TIMES
PITMAN PUBLISHING

FINANCIAL TIMES

MANAGEMENT

LONDON · SAN FRANCISCO
KUALA LUMPUR · JOHANNESBURG

Financial Times Management delivers the knowledge,
skills and understanding that enable students,
managers and organisations to achieve their ambitions,
whatever their needs, wherever they are.

London Office:
128 Long Acre, London WC2E 9AN
Tel: +44 (0)171 447 2000
Fax: +44 (0)171 240 5771
Website: www.ftmanagement.com

A Division of Financial Times Professional Limited

First published in Great Britain in 1998

ISBN 0 273 63404 6

British Library Cataloguing in Publication Data
A CIP catalogue record for this book can be obtained from the British Library

10 9 8 7 6 5 4 3 2

Typeset by Land & Unwin (Data Sciences) Ltd, Northampton
Printed and bound in Great Britain by Bell and Bain Ltd, Glasgow

The Publishers' policy is to use paper manufactured from sustainable forests.

Financial Times Pitman Publishing books

We work with leading authors to develop the strongest ideas in business and finance, bringing cutting-edge thinking and best practice to a global market.

We craft high quality books which help readers to understand and apply their content, whether studying or at work.

To find out more about Financial Times Pitman Publishing books, visit our website at:

www.ftmanagement.com

F R A M E W O R K S

Each book in the Frameworks series is a
comprehensive and concise introduction to
the subject. The books are well structured
and provide a step-by-step guide to essential
principles. They develop a basic framework
of understanding to underpin further study
of core business, financial and legal subjects
in the higher education curriculum.

Contents

Preface   vii

Table of cases   viii

Table of statutes   xii

Abbreviations   xvi

1   Introduction   1

Part One
MARRIAGE AND ITS BREAKDOWN

2   **Marriage**   7
Statutory formalities under the Marriage Acts 1949–1994 •
Recognition of foreign marriages

3   **Void and voidable marriages**   13
Void marriages • Voidable marriages • Bars to a decree •
Marriages with a foreign element

4   **Divorce**   26
Divorce under the Matrimonial Causes Act 1973 • Adultery and
intolerability • Respondent's behaviour • Desertion • Separation
• Bars to a decree • Divorce under the Family Law Act 1996 •
The statement of marital breakdown • Orders preventing divorce

5   **Domestic violence**   47
The Family Law Act 1996 Part IV • Occupation orders • Non-
molestation orders • Injunction proceedings • Harassment

Part Two
FAMILY PROPERTY AND FINANCIAL PROVISION
ON DIVORCE

6   **Financial obligations during marriage**   61
Duty to maintain • Maintenance and separation agreements •
Financial provision in Magistrates' courts • Failure to provide
reasonable maintenance • Maintenance pending suit

7   **Child support**   76

8   **Matrimonial property and the family home**   83
     Property rights • Trusts and the family home • Matrimonial home
     rights

9   **Financial relief on termination of marriage**   94
     Financial provision orders • Property adjustment orders • The
     new provisions of the Family Law Act 1996 • The guidelines for
     determining ancillary relief • Variation and consent orders •
     Financial provision on death

Part Three
CHILDREN

10   **Introduction to the Children Act 1989**   123

11   **Children and parents**   126
     Legitimacy • Children born by human-assisted reproduction •
     Surrogacy • Parental responsibility • The Gillick case and Gillick
     competence • Obtaining parental responsibility

12   **Resolution of disputes**   136
     Fundamental principles • The Welfare checklist • Section 8
     orders • Child abduction

13   **Local authorities and the family**   147
     Scope of local authority duties • Care and supervision orders •
     Other orders and measures

14   **Adoption**   159
     The effects of adoption • Conditions of adoption • Freeing for
     adoption • Who may adopt?

Appendix Family Law Act 1996   169

Index   203

Preface

Family Law is exciting and dynamic and the aim of this book is to try to convey some of that excitement to the reader.

The Family Law Act 1996 tried to address the failings of the existing divorce law, but its stormy passage through Parliament has only resulted in the postponement of its implementation. At the time of writing, it is probable that Part II, which introduces the new divorce process, will not be in effect until the early part of 1999, but it is included in Chapter 4.

The law relating to children remains a fertile area for statutory interpretation of the Children Act 1989. I have tried to ensure that relevant cases are incorporated into the text but, bearing in mind the nature of the subject, there may still be decisions taking place which will have a bearing on some of the issues contained in this book.

It is hoped that this book will be useful for undergraduates on LLB programmes but especially for those undertaking the subject on the modular programmes increasingly being introduced by universities.

My thanks to John Cushion, not only for the welcome invitation to produce this work, but also for his help and guidance through to publication.

As befits an edition of Family Law, I could not conclude without a mention of my wife Catherine and my daughters, Cassie and Antonia, without whose loving and undying support I could not have completed this work.

The law is stated as at 15 December1997, subject to my comments on the Family Law Act 1996.

TW

Table of Cases

Re A and Others (Minors) (Residence Order: Leave to Apply) [1992] 2 FLR 154   *142*

A *v* A [1974] 1 All ER 755   *66*

Ash *v* Ash [1972] 1 All ER 582   *29*

Ashley *v* Blackman [1988] 3 WLR 222   *105*

Attar *v* Attar [1985] FLR 649   *101, 102*

Attwood *v* Attwood [1968] 3 All ER 385   *100*

Re B (Care or Supervision Order)[1996] 2 FLR 693   *151*

Re B (Minors: Access) [1992] 1 FLR 142   *141*

Re B (Termination of Contact) [1993] Fam 301   *152*

B *v* B [1993] 1 FCR 211   *123*

B *v* B [1990] FCR 967   *106*

B *v* B (A Minor) (Residence Order) [1992] 2 FLR 327   *139*

B *v* B (Custody) [1985] FLR 166   *138*

Banik *v* Banik [1973] 3 All ER 455   *34*

Bannister *v* Bannister [1980] 10 Fam Law 240   *29*

Barclays Bank *v* O'Brien [1994] 1 AC 180   *89*

Barder *v* Barder (Caluori Intervening) [1987] 2 All ER 440   *112*

Bateman *v* Bateman [1979] 2 WLR 377   *108*

Baxter *v* Baxter [1947] 2 All ER 886; [1948] AC 274   *16, 18*

Re Beaumont [1980] Ch 444   *116, 118*

Re Besterman [1984] Ch 458   *118*

Birmingham City Council and Others *v* H (A Minor) [1994] Fam Law 114   *153*

Re Bishop (dec'd) [1965] 1 All ER 249   *84*

Bishop *v* Plumley [1991] 1 FLR 121   *116*

Blackwell *v* Blackwell [1943] 2 All ER 579   *84*

Blackstock *v* Blackstock [1991] 2 FLR 308   *50*

Bradley *v* Bradley [1973] 3 All ER 750   *30*

Brickell *v* Brickell [1973] 3 All ER 750   *34*

Brixey *v* Lynas [1996] 2 FLR 499   *138*

Brooks *v* Brooks [1995] 2 FLR 13   *97, 103*

Buckland *v* Buckland [1967] 2 All ER 3003   *18*

Burns *v* Burns [1984] 1 All ER 244   *91*

Re C (Minors) (Parental Responsibility) [1992] FLR 1   *133*

C *v* C (Custody Appeal) [1991] 1 FLR 223   *137*

C *v* C (Child Abuse: Access) [1988] 1 FLR 462   *141*

Re Callaghan [1985] Fam 1   *118*

Cheni *v* Cheni [1962] 3 All ER 87   *11*

Chipchase *v* Chipchase [1941] 2 All ER 560   *10*

Clarkson *v* Clarkson [1930] 143 LT 775   *27*

Cleary *v* Cleary & Hutton [1974] 1 WLR 735   *28*

Re Cole [1963] 3 All ER 433   *85*

Coleman *v* Coleman [1972] 3 All ER 886   *95*

Conran *v* Conran [1997] *The Times*, 15 July   *102, 107*

Cooke *v* Head [1972] 2 All ER 388   *91*

Corbett *v* Corbett [1970] 2 All ER 332   *7, 15*

Re Coventry [1980] 1 Ch 461   *116, 118*

Re D (Consent to Adoption) [1977] AC 602   *137, 163*

Re D (A Minor) [1976] 1 All ER 326; Fam 185   *144*

Re D (Minor)(Care or Supervision Order) [1993] 2 FLR 423   *153*

Re D and H (Care: Termination of Contact) [1997] 1 FLR 841   *152*

D *v* A [1845] 1 Rob Eccl 279   *16*

D *v* D (Child of the Family) [1980] 2 FLR 939   *66*

D *v* D (Nullity: Statutory Bar) [1979] 3 WLR 185   *21*

D *v* M (Custody Appeal) [1983] Fam 83   *138*

Dancer *v* Dancer [1948] 2 All ER 147   *10*

Daubney *v* Daubney [1976] 2 All ER 453   *100*

Davis *v* Vale [1971] 2 All ER 1021   *88*

Delaney *v* Delaney [1990] 2FLR 457   *100*

Re Dennis [1981] 2 All ER 140   *117*

Dennis *v* McDonald [1982] 1 All ER 590   *88*

Duxbury *v* Duxbury [1987] 1 FLR 71   *106*

Re E (A Minor)(Wardship) [1993]1 FLR 386   *132*

E *v* E (Financial Provision) [1990] 2 FLR 233   *97*

Edgar *v* Edgar [1980] 3 All ER 887   *64*

Evans *v* Evans [1989] 1 FLR 351   *103*

Eves *v* Eves [1975] 3 All ER 768   *86*

F *v* F (Ancillary Relief: Substantial Assets) [1995] 2 FLR 45   *106*

Falconer *v* Falconer [1970] 3 All ER 449   *86*

Re Figgis (dec'd) [1969] 1 Ch 123   *84*

Ford *v* Ford [1987] Fam Law 232   *17*

Re Fullard [1981] Fam 42   *115, 118*

Fuller *v* Fuller [1973] 2 All ER 650   *32*

Furniss *v* Furniss (1982) 12 Fam Law 30   *106*

Re G (Adoption: Freeing Order) [1997] 2 FLR 202   *165*

George *v* George [1986] 2 FLR 347; Fam Law 294   *54*

Gillick *v* West Norfolk and Wisbech Area Health Authority and the DHSS [1986] AC 112   *3, 131*

Gissing *v* Gissing [1971] AC 886; [1970] 2 All ER 780   *2, 84, 85, 86*

Gojkovic *v* Gojkovic [1990] 2 All ER 84, CA   *101, 102*

Goodman *v* Gallant [1986] 1 All ER 311; 1 FLR 513   *85*

Goshawk *v* Goshawk [1965] 109 SJ 290   *27*

Grant *v* Edwards [1986] 2 All ER 426, CA   *86*

Re H (A Minor) (Parental Responsibility) [1993] 1 FLR 484   *133, 140*

Re H (Shared Residence; Parental Responsibility) [1994] 1 FLR 717   *143*

Re H (Minors)(Sexual Abuse: Standard of Proof) [1996] AC 563; 1 All ER 1   *151*

Re H (Prohibited Steps Order) [1995] 1 FLR 638   *141*

H *v* H [1954] P.258   *19*

Hammond *v* Mitchell [1992] 2 All ER 109   *92*

Hardy *v* Hardy [1981] 2 FLR 321; 11 Fam Law 153, CA   *100*

Hedges *v* Hedges [1991] 1 FLR 196   *104*

Heseltine *v* Heseltine [1971] 1 All ER 952; 1 WLR 342   *84*

Hirani *v* Hirani [1982] 4 FLR 232, CA   *18*

Horner *v* Horner [1982] 2 All ER 495; Fam 90   *54*

Horton *v* Horton [1947] 2 All ER 871, HL   *17*

Hyde *v* Hyde [1866] LP 1 P & D 1302   *7*

J *v* C [1970] AC 668   *136, 138*

Jenkins *v* Livesey (formerly Jenkins) [1985] 1 All ER 106   *111, 113*

Jelley *v* Iliffe [1981] Fam 128   *119*
Re Jennings [1994] cH 286   *118*
Jessel *v* Jessel [1979] 1 WLR 1148   *111*
Johnson *v* Walton [1990] 1 FLR 350   *54*
Jones *v* Maynard [1951] 1 All ER 802
84

Re K (Care or Supervision Order) [1995]
1 FLR 675   *153*
Kashmir Kaur *v* Gill [1988] 3 WLR 39
91
Kaur *v* Singh [1972] 1 All ER 292   *17*
Re KD (A Minor) (Ward: Termination of
Access) [1988] 2 FLR 139   *137*
Re K,W & H (Minors)(Medical
Treatment)[1993] 1 FLR 854   *132*
Katz *v* Katz [1972] 3 All ER 219   *29*
Kingsnorth Trust Ltd *v* Tizard [1986] 1
WLR 783   *89*
Knibb *v* Knibb [1987] 2 FLR 396   *107*
Kokosinski *v* Kokosinski [1980] 1 All ER
1106   *103*
Kyte *v* Kyte [1987] 3 All ER 1041   *103*

Le Brocq *v* Le Brocq [1964] 3 All ER 464
30
Leadbeater *v* Leadbeater [1985] FLR 789
100, 101, 103
Livingstone-Stallard *v* Livingstone-
Stallard [1974] 2 All ER 776   *29*
Lloyds Bank plc *v* Rosset [1990] 1 All ER
1111   *87*

Re M (A Minor) (Care Order: Threshold
Conditions) [1994] 2AC 424   *150*
Re MW (Adoption: Surrogacy) [1995] 2
FLR 759   *129*
M *v* M (Financial Provision) [1987] 2
FLR 110   *100, 101, 102, 105*
M *v* M (Transfer of Custody) [1987] 2
FLR 146   *137*
Malone *v* Harrison [1979] 1 WLR 1353
116
Martin (BH) *v* Martin (BW) [1977] 3 All
ER 762   *108*
Mehta *v* Mehta [1945] 2 All ER 690   *19*
Mesher *v* Mesher [1980] 1 All ER 126
96, 107

Messina *v* Smith [1971] 2 All ER 1046
19
Midland Bank plc *v* Cooke and Another
[1995] 2 FLR 915   *87, 88*
Midland Bank plc *v* Dobson and
Dobson [1986] 1 FLR 171   *87*
Minton *v* Minton [1979] 1 All ER 79
104
Mohamed *v* Knot [1969] 1 QB1   *12*
Mouncer *v* Mouncer [1972] 1 All ER 289
32

Re N (A Minor: Access) [1992] 1 FLR 134
141
National Provincial Bank *v* Ainsworth
[1965] 2 All ER 472   *89*

Re O (A Minor) (Care Order: Education
Procedure) [1992] Fam Law 487
151
Re O (Minor) (Imposition of Conditions)
[1995] 2 FLR 124   *140*
Oxfordshire CC *v* P [1995] 1 FLR 552
157

Re P (Minors) (Wardship Surrogacy)
(1987) *The Times*, 1 August   *129*
Park, In the Estate of [1953] 2 All ER
408; 2 All ER 1411; 3 WLR 307   *19*
Parker *v* Parker [1972] 1 All ER 410   *34*
Patel *v* Patel [1988] 2 FLR 179   *56*
Peacock *v* Peacock [1984] 1 All ER 1069
74
Pettit *v* Pettit [1970] AC 777   *2, 84, 85,*
86, 88
Preston *v* Preston [1982] Fam Law 17
101
Preston-Jones *v* Preston-Jones [1951] 1
All ER 1245   *27, 127*
Pugh *v* Pugh [1951] 2 All ER 680   *15*
Pulford *v* Pulford [1923] P.185   *30*

Quoraishi *v* Quoraishi [1985] FLR 780
31

Re R (Adoption) [1967] 1 WLR 34   *162*
Re R (Custody (Minors)) [1986] 1 FLR 6;
Fam Law 15   *136*

Re R (A Minor) (Wardship: Consent to Treatment) [1992] Fam 11   *131*

Richards *v* Richards [1984] AC 174   *47, 50*

Richardson *v* Richardson [1994] 1 FLR 826   *104*

Riley *v* Riley [1986] 2 FLR 429   *140*

Re Roberts (dec'd) [1978] 3 All ER 225   *22*

Re Rogers Question [1948] 1 All ER 328   *88*

Rukat *v* Rukat [1975] 1 All ER 343   *34*

Re S (Minor: Custody) [1991] 2 FLR 388   *138, 140*

Re S (A Minor) (Parental Responsibility) [1995] 2 FLR 648   *133*

S *v* S [1961] 3 All ER 133   *27*

Samson *v* Samson [1960] 1 All ER 653   *85*

Schuller *v* Schuller [1990] 2 FLR 193; Fam Law 299   *100*

Seaton *v* Seaton [1986] 2 FLR 398; Fam Law 267   *105*

Shallow *v* Shallow [1978] 2 All ER 483   *106*

Singh *v* Singh [1971] 2 All ER 828   *17, 18*

Slater *v* Slater [1982] 3 FLR 364   *101*

Spencer *v* Camacho [1983] 13 Fam Law 114   *54*

Summers *v* Summers [1986] 1 FLR 343   *50*

Suter *v* Suter and Jones [1987] 2 All ER 336; 2 FLR 232   *99*

Stockford *v* Stockford (1982) 12 Fam Law 30   *106*

Szechter *v* Szechter [1971] 2 WLR 1703   *19*

Re T (A Minor) (Care or Supervision Order) [1994] 1 FLR 103   *151*

Re T (Divorce: Interim maintenance: Discovery) [1989] Fam Law 438; [1990] 1 FLR 1   *74*

T *v* T (Ouster Order) [1987] 1 FLR 181   *50*

Tanner *v* Tanner [1975] 3 All ER 776   *92*

Thomas *v* Fuller-Brown [1988] 1 FLR 237   *91*

Thwaite *v* Thwaite [1981] 2 All ER 789   *110*

Turton *v* Turton (1988) Ch 542   *88*

Twiname *v* Twiname [1992] 1 FCR 185 CA   *95*

Vaughan *v* Vaughan [1973] 3 All ER 449   *54*

Re W (Adoption; Homosexual) [1997] 2 FLR 406   *166*

Re W (An Infant) [1971] AC 682   *163*

Re W (A Minor) (Medical Treatment) [1992] 4 All ER 627   *132*

Re W (A Minor) (Non-patrial) [1986] Fam 54   *160*

Re W (A Minor) (Residence Order) [1992] 2 FLR 322   *140*

W(RJ) *v* W(SJ) [1971] 3 All ER 303   *66*

Wachtel *v* Wachtel [1973] 1 All ER 829   *102, 106*

Walker *v* Walker and Hanson [1981] NZ Recent Law 257   *138*

Waterman *v* Waterman [1989] 1 FLR 380   *104*

Re Wilkinson [1978] Fam 22   *116*

Williams and Glyn's Bank Ltd *v* Boland [1981] AC 487   *89*

Williams (LA) *v* Williams (EM) [1974] 3 All ER 377   *100*

Table of statutes

Administration of Estates
Act 1925 *114*
Administration of Justice
Act 1970
s. 1(2) *143*
Adoption Act 1976 *48,*
159
s. 6 *160, 161, 163*
s. 7 *162*
s. 12 *133, 159*
s. 12(6) *159, 162*
s. 13(1) *161*
s. 13(2) *161*
s. 13(3) *166*
s. 14(1)(b) *166*
s. 14(2) *166*
s. 15(1) *166*
s. 15(3) *166*
s. 16 *161*
s. 16(1)(b) *162*
s. 16(2) *162*
s. 17 *167*
s. 18 *161, 164*
s. 18(2) *164*
s. 18(7) *164*
s. 20 *164, 165*
s. 20(1) *165*
s. 20(3)(a) *165*
S. 20(3)(b) *165*
s. 39 *159*
s. 39(4) *159*
s. 47(1) *160*
s. 51(1) *160*
s. 51A *160*
s. 72 *162*
s. 72(1) *161, 167*
Child Abduction Act
1984
s. 1 *144*
s. 2 *144*

Child Abduction and
Custody Act 1985
Part I *145*
Part II *145*
Child Support Acts
1991–1995 *39, 61, 62,*
68, 74, 76, 106, 109,
130
s. 1(1) *76*
s. 1(3) *77*
s. 2 *79*
s. 3(2) *77*
s. 6 *79*
s. 6(9) *79*
s. 9(4) *79*
s. 27 *78*
s. 46 *79*
Schedule 4 *80*
Children Act 1989 *1, 3,*
9, 35, 43, 48, 52, 123–5,
129, 136, 159, 161
s. 1(1) *123, 136, 142*
s. 1(2) *123, 139*
s. 1(3) *137, 151*
s. 1(5) *123, 139, 151*
s. 2(1) *132*
s. 2(4) *124*
s. 2(5) *133*
s. 2(6) *134*
s. 2(7) *133*
s. 2(8) *134*
s. 2(9) *134*
s. 3 *124*
s. 3(1) *129*
s. 3(5) *134*
s. 4 *124, 134, 143, 165*
s. 4(1) *132*
s. 4(1)(2) *132*
s. 4(3) *133*
s. 5(6) *133*

s. 8 *124, 125, 132,*
133, 134, 137, 139,
140, 141, 142, 143,
144, 151, 159, 162
s. 8(3) *125*
s. 8(4) *125*
s. 9(5)(a) *141*
ss. 9(6)(10)(11) *143*
s. 9(7) *140*
s. 9(14) *143*
s. 10(1) *141*
s. 10(1)(a) *141*
s. 10(1)(b) *141*
s. 10(4) *142*
s. 10(5) *142*
s. 10(8) *142*
s. 10(9) *142*
s. 11 *139*
s. 11(4) *140*
s. 11(7) *140*
s. 12(2) *133*
s. 12(2)(3) *143*
s. 12(3)(a) *159*
s. 17(1) *147*
s. 17(10) *147*
s. 17(11) *148*
s. 18(1) *148*
s. 18(5) *148*
s. 20 *141, 149*
s. 20(1) *148*
s. 20(3) *149*
s. 20(4) *149*
s. 20(6) *149*
s. 20(7) *150*
s. 20(8) *149*
s. 22(3) *149*
s. 22(4)(5) *152*
s. 22(5) *130, 138, 149*
s. 23(6) *149*
s. 23(7) *149*

s. 23(8)   149
s. 31   124, 150
s. 31(9)   150
s. 33(3)(a)   152
s. 33(3)(b)   152
s. 33(3)   133
s. 33(4)   152
s. 34   156
s. 34(1)   152, 153
s. 34(11)   152
s. 34(4)   152, 153
s. 36(1)   154
s. 36(4)   154
s. 37   157
s. 39(1)   153
s. 39(2)   153
s. 41(1)   156
s. 43(i)   154
s. 43(6)   154
s. 43(8)   154
s. 44   155
s. 44(1)(a)   155
s. 44(1)(b)   155
s. 44(1)(c)   155
s. 44(4)   133, 155
s. 44(5)   155
s. 44(6)(a)   156
s. 44(10)   156
s. 44(13)   156
s. 45   155
s. 46(1)   156
s. 47(1)   155
s. 48(1)   156
s. 48(3)   156
s. 48(9)   156
s. 100   124, 144
Schedule 2, Part I   148
Children and Young
  Persons Act 1933,
  s. 1   130
County Courts Act 1984
  s. 38   55
Divorce Reform Act 1969
  2, 36, 37
Domestic Proceedings
  and Magistrates
  Courts Act 1978   4,
  39, 65, 98, 108, 125

s. 1   65, 66, 68, 69
s. 2   66, 67, 69, 70
s. 3   65, 69, 70, 72
s. 3(1)   67
s. 3(3)   66
s. 3(4)   68
s. 4(1)   69
s. 5   72
s. 5(1)   70
s. 5(3)   70
s. 6   68, 69, 70
s. 6(9)   68
s. 7   68, 69, 70
s. 19   69
s. 19(5)   69
s. 20(1)   70
s. 20(6)   70
s. 20(7)   70
s. 20(11)   70, 71
s. 20(12)   70
s. 25(2)   70
s. 27   69
s. 29   69
s. 88   66
Domestic Violence and
  Matrimonial
  Proceedings Act 1976
  47, 49
Domicile and Matri-
  monial Proceedings
  Act 1973   72
s. 1   8
s. 3   8
s. 5(2)   44
s. 5(3)   23
Domestic Proceedings
  and Magistrates
  Courts Act 1978   47,
  71, 98
Education Act 1944   130
Family Law Act 1986
  45, 145
s. 13   45
s. 33   144
s. 34   144
s. 37   144
s. 44(2)   45
s. 46   24, 45

s. 46(1)   23, 24
s. 46(2)   24
s. 51   24
Family Law Act 1996   2,
  4, 36–8, 61, 65, 74, 92,
  97, 102, 112
Part I   37
Part IV   3, 39, 47, 48,
  125
s. 3   40
s. 7   39, 40
s. 7(4)   40
s. 7(12)   40
s. 8   37, 40
s. 8(4)   37
s. 8(9)   37
s. 9   41, 42, 98
s. 9(2)   41
s. 10   41, 44
s. 11   42
s. 11(1)   43
s. 11(4)   43
s. 13   38
s. 23   38
s. 30   48, 90
s. 30(2)   90
s. 30(4)   91
s. 33   49, 51, 52, 90
s. 33(1)   49
s. 33(5)   90
s. 33 (7)   50
s. 35   51, 52
s. 36   52
s. 37   52, 55
s. 38   52
s. 39(2)   54
s. 40   53
s. 42   53
s. 42(2)(a)   54
s. 42(2)(b)   54
s. 46(1)   55
s. 47(6)   55
s. 47(8)   55
s. 57   54
s. 58   55
Schedule 1   42, 98
Schedule 2   97
Schedule 4   89

Family Law Reform Act
1969
s. 20(1)   28, 127
s. 23(1)   127
s. 26   127
Family Law Reform Act
1987   126
s. 1   126
s. 27   128
s. 28   22
Human Fertilisation and
Embryology Act 1990
128, 166
s. 27   128
s. 28   128
s. 30   129
Inheritance (Provision
for Family and
Dependants) Act 1975
22, 114, 115
s. 1(1)   115
s. 1(3)   116
s. 1(2)(a)   117
s. 1(2)(b)   117
s. 3(1)   117
Intestates Estates Act
1952
Schedule 2   115
Law of Property Act 1925
s. 30   92
s. 53(2)   85
s. 70(1)(g)   88
Law Reform (Mis-
cellaneous Provisions)
Act 1970   92
s. 2(1)   92
s. 2(2)   84
s. 3(1)   92
Law Reform (Succession)
Act 1995   113, 116
s. 3(a)   113
s. 3(b)   114
s. 4   114
Legal Aid Act 1988   44
Legitimacy Act 1969,
s. 2   127
Legitimacy Act 1976,
s. 1   22, 128

Magistrates Courts Act
1980, s. 127   66
Marriage Act 1836   9
Marriage Acts 1949–1994
8–11, 14
Marriage Act 1949
s. 5   9
s. 24   15
s. 25   15
s. 48   15
s. 49   15
Marriage Act 1994   10
Marriage (Prohibited
Degrees of Relation-
ship) Act 1986   14
Married Womens
Property Act 1882
s. 17   83, 84, 91
Married Womens
Property Act 1964,
s. 1   84
Matrimonial and Family
Proceedings Act 1984
99
Part III   45
s. 39   3
Matrimonial Causes Act
1857   2
Matrimonial Causes Act
1973   2, 3, 4, 13, 26, 28,
44, 85, 97, 103, 116,
125
s. 1(1)   26
s. 1(2)   26
s. 1(2)(a)   26, 28
s. 1(2)(b)   26, 29, 65
s. 1(2)(c)   26, 30, 65
s. 1(2)(d)   32, 44
s. 1(2)(e)   27, 34, 44
s. 1(2)(f)   27, 32
s. 1(4)   34
s. 2   28
s. 2(3)   29
s. 2(5)   31, 32, 33
s. 2(6)   32
s. 3(1)   26
s. 5   33
s. 5(2)   34

s. 5(3)   33
s. 6(1)   34
s. 10   35
s. 10(1)   33
s. 10(3)   35
s. 11   14
s. 12   16, 18
s. 13   20
s. 13(1)   21
s. 13(2)   21
s. 13(3)   21
ss. 23A or 24   52
s. 22   73, 74
s. 23(1)   94
s. 23(1)(b)   95
s. 23(1)(d)(e)   109
s. 23(1)(c)   95
s. 23(1)(f)   109
s. 23(2)(a)   108
s. 23(3)   96
s. 23(3)(c)   95
s. 23(4)   108
s. 23(5)   94
ss. 23 and 24   22
s. 24(1)(a)   96
s. 24(1)(a)(b)   109
s. 24(1)(b)   96, 111
s. 24(1)(c)   96, 109
s. 24(1)(c)(d)   111
s. 24A   97
s. 24A(1)   111
s. 24A(3)   97
s. 25   65, 68, 99, 106,
107
s. 25(1)   99, 109
s. 25(1)(f)   103
s. 25(1)(g)   103
s. 25(2)   72, 99, 109
s. 25(3)   73
s. 25(4)   73, 109
s. 25A   95, 99
s. 25A(1)   104
s. 25A(2)   95, 104
s. 25A(3)   104
s. 27   71, 72, 73
s. 27(6B)   73
s. 27(7)(a)   72
s. 28(1)   95

s. 28(1)(b) *72*
s. 28(1A) *104, 111*
s. 28(2) *72*
s. 29 *72*
s. 29(2) *110*
s. 29(3) *110*
s. 29(4) *110*
s. 31 *73*
s. 31(1) *111*
s. 31(4) *112*
s. 31(5) *73*
s. 31(6) *112*
s. 31(7) *113*
s. 31(7)(b) *113*
s. 31(8) *112*
s. 31(10) *111*
s. 33A *110*
s. 34 *63, 64*
s. 34(1) *64*
s. 34(2) *63*
s. 34(4) *64*
s. 35(1) *64*
s. 36 *63, 64*

s. 37(1)(a) *113*
s. 37(1)(b) *113*
s. 41 *35, 36*
s. 47 *11*
s. 52(1) *36, 108*
Matrimonial Homes Act
  1967 *89*
Matrimonial Homes Act
  1983 *47, 48, 49, 50, 89,*
  90
Matrimonial Proceedings
  and Property Act
  1970 *62, 88*
s. 37 *88, 91, 92*
s. 39 *83*
Mental Health Act
  1983 *16*
s. 1 *20, 21*
s. 13(3) *21*
Nullity of Marriage Act
  1971 *13, 20*
Pensions Act 1995,
  s. 166 *33, 103*

Protection from
  Harassment Act 1997
  56
s. 1 *56*
s. 2 *56*
s. 3 *56*
s. 3(3) *56*
s. 3(6) *56*
s. 3(9) *56*
s. 4 *56*
Social Security Act 1986
s. 24 *62*
s. 26(3) *62*
Social Security
  Administration Act
  1992, s. 107 *62,*
  105
Supreme Court Act 1981,
  s. 37 *55*
Surrogacy Arrangements
  Act 1985, s. 1A *129*
Wills Act 1837 *113*
s. 18A *22*

Abbreviations

AA1976	Adoption Act
CA 1989	Children Act
CSA 1991	Child Support Act
DMPA 1973	Domicile and Matrimonial Proceedings Act
DPMCA 1978	Domestic Proceedings and Magistrates Courts Act
DRA 1969	Divorce Reform Act
FLA 1996	Family Law Act
LPA 1925	Law of Property Act
MCA 1973	Matrimonial Causes Act
MFPA 1984	Matrimonial and Family Proceedings Act
MHA 1983	Matrimonial Homes Act

1

Introduction

1. Scope of family law

To many people, 'family' means husband, wife and 2.4 children. To a certain extent, English law reflects that view in so far as it regulates the formation of marriage, its dissolution and the property and proprietary rights which arise from that relationship.

However, modern society is not entirely like that. More and more couples chose to cohabit and approximately 22% of children born each year are born out of wedlock but to parents who either share the same address or, at least, register the birth jointly. The fact that such couples enjoy certain property rights and personal protection from their partner arises from no consistent or discernable public policy.

Much of the controversy surrounding parliamentary bills presented late in the life of the Major government arose because of the traditional 'family values' upheld by some members of Parliament who advocated that legislation should be seen to support the sanctity of marriage.

The interests of children have also come to the fore, particularly since the implementation of the Children Act 1989. Their relationship with their parents or those who have parental responsibility for them (the so-called 'private law') and the circumstances when local authority intervention becomes necessary (the 'public law') are issues which will be addressed later.

To be able to understand the modern law, it is helpful to understand and appreciate the factors which have contributed to and developed the modern law.

2. The development of divorce law

Prior to the Reformation, the ecclesiastical courts exercised jurisdiction and it was not possible to obtain a decree which would terminate marriage and enable remarriage (a divorce *a vinculo matrimonii*). It was possible to obtain a decree of nullity, to say that there never had been a marriage, and a divorce *a mensa et thoro* which was the equivalent of the modern judicial separation. Even when the Crown took over jurisdiction after the Reformation, it was still only possible to dissolve a marriage by a private Act of Parliament, a process only available to a privileged and wealthy few.

The Matrimonial Causes Act 1857 transferred jurisdiction to a new divorce court which was allowed to grant divorce decrees, initially only on the grounds of adultery. Further legislation led to the transfer of business to the Family Division of the High Court, where it resides today, and by 1937 the grounds for divorce were adultery, cruelty (mental as well as physical) and desertion. These were all 'fault-based' grounds and only the 'innocent' party could file a petition.

Pressure for reform mounted during the 1960s. The Archbishop of Canterbury formed a working party whose report was entitled *Putting Asunder* which favoured the retention of 'fault-based divorce'. The Law Commission, *The Reform of the Grounds for Divorce, the Field of Choice*, Cmnd 3123, proposed that irretrievable breakdown should be the basis of a decree and the ensuing Divorce Reform Act 1969, which became the Matrimonial Causes Act 1973 (MCA 1973) was an uneasy compromise between the two. Irretrievable breakdown has to be evidenced by one of the five facts, three of which are the fault grounds from the pre-existing law. The failure of the 1969 Act to achieve the objectives set out by the Law Commission and the increasing divorce rates led to further pressure for reform, and amidst controversy the Family Law Act 1996 (FLA 1996) was passed and the concept of 'fault-based divorce' was finally abandoned.

Much of the Act is subject to regulations yet to be passed and pilot schemes still to be implemented, and for the unfortunate law student it means that until at least the summer of 1999 it will be necessary to have an understanding of both the MCA 1973 and the FLA 1996.

3. The development of property law in family matters

Blackstone wrote that 'man and woman become one ... but she is suspended [to him] ... he is her Lord and Baron'. In other words, all property rights vested in the husband. The Married Women's Property Acts from 1883 onwards fortunately brought the law into twentieth century thinking but some aspects of Blackstone still haunt us today.

In relation to the matrimonial home, for many couples their major asset, it was only in the 1970s that equity addressed questions of ownership and beneficial interests in *Pettit* v *Pettit* and *Gissing* v *Gissing* and Lord Diplock recognised that we now lived not just in a property-owning society but 'a property-owning mortgaged to a building society democracy'. The principles which evolved will be discussed later.

Perhaps of more significance to married couples are the powers given to the court by the MCA 1973 in matrimonial proceedings to award lump sums or 'property adjustment orders' which enable the court to rearrange and adjust property ownership between spouses in accordance with matters to be taken into account as set out in s. 25(2).

When Part IV of the FLA 1996 is implemented, it will be possible for spouses (and others) to apply for Occupation Orders regulating who and who may not reside in the family home and upon what terms.

4. Development of child law

If the husband was 'Lord and Baron' to his wife, then the Father was also Lord and Master of his children, having almost proprietary rights over them. It was late in the nineteenth century that the courts were given power to award custody of the child to anyone other than the father and well into this century before mother was given an equal recognition in respect of her own children. In 1948, Local Authorities were given responsibility to take into care children who were 'beyond parental control'. During the 1980s there were a number of public enquiries into the deaths of children under the supervision of Local Authorities, most notably Jasmine Beckford, Tyra Henry and Kimberly Carlisle. If they highlighted the problems of negligence, the Cleveland affair emphasised the problems of an over-zealous authority. Around the same time, the House of Lords had issued their landmark decision in *Gillick* v *West Norfolk and Wisbech Area Health Authority* (1986) to the effect that parents had responsibilities to their children, rather than rights over them.

These matters triggered the law reform process which was already ongoing and led to the passing of the Children Act 1989 (CA 1989), 'the greatest reform of child law in living memory' (per Lord Mackay).

5. Jurisdiction

The Family Division of the High Court can hear defended divorces under the MCA 1973 and all matters in relation to children's proceedings.

The County Courts are the courts in which all matrimonial causes begin and under the Matrimonial and Family Proceedings Act 1984, s. 39 there is discretionary power to transfer proceedings to the High Court at any stage during the action. The court also has sole power to administer the 'special procedure' whereby divorce is granted by the District Judge without the necessity for either party to attend court. The County Court also has jurisdiction to deal with ancillary relief under the MCA 1973.

The Magistrates Court is the court in which all public law matters relating to children begin. The Domestic Proceedings and Magistrates Courts Act 1978 gave them power, *inter alia*, to award periodical payments to a spouse where their partner had wilfully neglected to maintain them. In view of the delay in the commencement of proceedings under the FLA 1996, this option is likely to become of increasing importance and will be dealt with in more depth later.

Progress test 1

1. Explain what is meant by the expression 'family law'.

2. Outline the development of divorce to the present day.

3. Explain the difference in property matters in relation to married couples who are not divorcing, cohabitants and married couples who take matrimonial proceedings.

4. Outline some of the important issues which led to the introduction of the Children Act 1989.

5. Summarise the jurisdiction of the High Court and the County Court in matrimonial proceedings.

6. What is the jurisdiction of the family proceedings courts in relation to family matters?

Marriage and its breakdown

PART ONE

Marriage and its breakdown

2

Marriage

1. Definition

The definition of marriage in English law was propounded by Lord Penzance in *Hyde* v *Hyde* (1866): 'I conceive that marriage, as understood in Christendom, may be defined as the voluntary union for life of one man and one woman to the exclusion of all others.'

This definition contains four elements:

(a) *Voluntary*. The absence of consent makes the marriage voidable (see Chapter 3).

(b) *For life*. This appears to mean no more than that the parties intend it to be for life at the time of the wedding.

(c) *Parties of the opposite sex*. Although the law still refuses marriage between same-sex partners, this part of the definition is not without its problems.

> *Corbett* v *Corbett* (1970). April Ashley had been born male but had undergone a complete sex change. She was treated as female by social security and by the passport authorities but the House of Lords held that gender is determined at birth and cannot be changed.

(d) *Monogamous*. Bigamy is a crime under English law and such marriages are void. However, in certain circumstances, we do recognise polygamous marriages celebrated in other countries.

STATUTORY FORMALITIES UNDER THE MARRIAGE ACTS 1949–1994

2. Legal requirements

The parties to a marriage must:

(a) possess the capacity to marry *and*

(b) comply with specified formalities.

3. Capacity

Capacity to marry is determined by a person's premarital place of domicile. The formalities which govern the marriage itself are determined by the law of the place where it is celebrated.

Domicile is a legal concept which links a person with a particular legal system. A person's domicile is the place where he has his permanent home. It must be a place which has its own legal system, e.g. England/Wales or Scotland but not Britain or the United Kingdom. Domicile is not the same as nationality. A person may have more than one nationality or be stateless, but he cannot have more than one domicile at any one time.

There are three ways in which domicile is acquired:

(a) Every child acquires a domicile of origin at birth. For a child of married parents this will be the father's domicile but a child of unmarried parents will take the domicile of its mother, as will a child born posthumously.

(b) A child then has dependant domicile until it reaches the age of 16 which means that its domicile will change with that of the parent on whom it depends under the Domicile and Matrimonial Proceedings Act 1973, s. 3.

(c) A person over the age of 16 may acquire a domicile of choice by moving to another country with a settled intention of living there permanently (DMPA 1973, s. 1).

A person can never be left without a domicile. If a person abandons a domicile of choice, the domicile of origin will revive unless or until he or she acquires a new domicile of choice.

The requirements of English law regarding capacity to marry apply to anyone domiciled in England and Wales, whether they marry in this country or abroad, and any marriage in breach of these requirements will be void (see Chapter 3).

To have capacity, the following have to be satisfied:

(a) One party must be male and the other female.

(b) Neither party must be already lawfully married.

(c) Both parties must be aged 16 or over.

(d) The parties must not be related within the prohibited degrees of consanguinity or affinity as set out in the Marriage Acts 1949–1986.

4. Formalities of marriage

Until 1753 little formality was required beyond the freely given consent of the parties. Lord Hardwicke's Act in 1753 abolished the informal common law marriage and replaced it with a public church ceremony. The Marriage Act 1836 introduced the additional options of a civil ceremony in a register office or a religious ceremony celebrated in a non-Anglican place of worship.

Today the position is governed by the Marriage Acts 1949–1994 as amended by the Children Act 1989. All marriages which take place in England and Wales must comply with the statutory formalities, irrespective of the domicile of the parties.

Children aged between 16 and 18 can only marry with the consent of their parents, the Local Authority (if in care) or anyone who has a residence order under the CA 1989.

5. Marriage in the Church of England

By s. 5 of the Marriage Act 1949, marriages in the Anglican Church can only be solemnised:

(a) after the publication of banns (see **6** below)

(b) by common licence (see **7** below)

(c) by special licence (see **8** below) or

(d) by superintendent registrar's certificate (see **9** below).

Anglican marriages must be celebrated by a clergyman in the presence of two or more witnesses and must follow the authorised form of service. The ceremony must take place in the church in which banns were read or as specified in the licence.

6. Banns

A bann is a proclamation in church, in the form of a public notice, of an intended marriage. Banns must be read on the three successive Sundays preceding the marriage in the respective parish churches of the parties. They should be published in the names by which the parties are most commonly known.

> *Dancer* v *Dancer* (1948). Born as the legitimate daughter of Mr & Mrs Knight, the wife went with mother to live with a Mr Roberts whose name she adopted from the age of three. HELD Publication in her assumed name was proper.

> *Chipchase* v *Chipchase* (1941). She used her adoptive name to conceal a previous marriage. HELD Not proper publication.

7. Common licence

This is issued by the diocesan Registrar in substitution of banns. It can authorise marriage in the church of the parish where the parties have resided for at least 15 days, or at the church which is the usual place of worship of either of the parties.

8. Archbishop's special licence

The licence is entirely at the discretion of the Archbishop of Canterbury but, if granted, permits the ceremony to take place anywhere, any time.

9. Non-Anglican marriages

Prior notice must be given by Registrar's Certificate, giving 21 days notice, or by Superintendent Registrar's Certificate and Licence, giving 24 hours notice. Under the Marriage Act 1994, the Registrar can issue certificates to marry outside his district and outside the district of either parties' residence.

A civil marriage will normally take place in a register office open to the public, but since the Marriage Act 1994 it is possible to marry in premises approved by the local authority for the solemnisation of marriage, subject to any conditions imposed by the Secretary of State 'so as to secure that members of the public are permitted to attend.' It is assumed, in the absence of interpretation, that premises means a building of some kind and it will not be possible to marry in the open air, for example in one's garden.

The ceremony must be conducted in the presence of two witnesses *and* the Registrar of the district in which the premises are situated.

A non-Anglican religious ceremony must take place in a building which is a meeting place for religious worship specifically registered for the purpose, e.g. a mosque or a Hindu temple.

The ceremony must take place 'with open doors' and in the presence of two or more witnesses and an authorised person, who will usually be the relevant minister of religion. Jews and Quakers may conduct marriage ceremonies in accordance with their own rules although they must comply with the normal civil preliminaries.

RECOGNITION OF FOREIGN MARRIAGES

10. Recognition of foreign marriages

As a general rule a marriage celebrated abroad will be recognised here if the parties have complied with the formal requirements of that country and have the capacity to marry according to the law of their pre-marriage domicile. Foreign marriages may be entirely valid in accordance with these criteria but still offend against moral principles which are the basis of our law, such as polygamy. Simon P in *Cheni* v *Cheni* (1962) suggested that such marriages might still be recognised:

> 'What I believe to be the true test [is] whether the marriage is so offensive to the conscience of the English court that it should refuse to recognise and give effect to the proper foreign law.'

11. Polygamous or potentially polygamous marriages

An English marriage is a monogamous union so that no person domiciled in England and Wales may contract a polygamous marriage abroad and no polygamous marriages may be celebrated in this country whatever the domicile of the parties.

English law will, however, recognise as valid a polygamous or a potentially polygamous marriage contracted abroad under a law which permits polygamy if both parties were also domiciled abroad at the time. The MCA 1973, s. 47 gives the parties to such a marriage the right to claim matrimonial relief, including divorce and nullity, provided they comply with the law regarding jurisdiction.

A potentially polygamous marriage is one in which one of the parties is allowed to take further spouses during the currency of the marriage but has not yet done so.

Mohamed v *Knot* (1969). The parties had married in Nigeria in accordance with Muslim law which permits polygamy and the wife was only 13 years old. HELD The marriage was recognised as valid as it was permitted by the pre-marriage law of domicile of the parties.

Progress test 2

1. To what extent do you consider Lord Penzance's definition of marriage is relevant to marriage today?

2. What are the requirements for a valid marriage under English law?

3. Who has capacity to marry?

4. Advise the parties in the following circumstances:

(*i*) A and B are devoted followers of their local football team and wish to be married on the pitch at the stadium. They are willing to pay the cost of obtaining a licence.

(*ii*) C and D are going on a Mediterranean cruise on a British ship and want to know if the captain can marry them.

(*iii*) E was born a man but has recently undergone a complete physical sex change. She wishes to know if she can lawfully marry her female lesbian partner.

5. In what circumstances will a foreign marriage be recognised as valid in English law?

3

Void and voidable marriages

1. Introduction

Before English law recognised divorce, nullity was the only way to terminate marriage during the lives of the spouses. A decree of nullity meant that a marriage was null and void. In other words, the marriage had never existed at all.

Jurisdiction was initially with the ecclesiastical courts but after the Reformation in the sixteenth century, the common law began to limit the grounds on which the ecclesiastical courts could pronounce a decree after the death of either party. This led to the distinction between void and voidable marriage which underpins modern statute law. The void marriage is invalid from the outset and may be declared so after the death of the parties. The voidable marriage is valid unless and until it is declared null and void by the courts and it can only be challenged while the parties are alive.

The present law was codified in the Nullity of Marriage Act 1971 now consolidated in the MCA 1973. Although the Acts only applied to marriages taking place after 31 July 1971, the only difference today is that lack of consent before that date made the marriage void, and after that date they are voidable.

2. Distinction between void and voidable marriages

A void marriage is void *ab initio*. This means that it has never existed in law and therefore needs no formal decree to annul it. However, a party to such a marriage may still wish to obtain a decree, as he or she will then be entitled to seek financial and property orders under the MCA 1973 as on marital breakdown (see Chapter 9). Any interested party may challenge the validity of a void marriage.

Avoidable marriage is valid in all respects until a decree of nullity is obtained and only the parties themselves may seek a decree to annul the marriage.

VOID MARRIAGES

3. Void marriages under MCA 1973

MCA 1973, s. 11 provides that a marriage is void on the following grounds only:

(a) That it is not a valid marriage under the provisions of the Marriage Acts 1949–1994, because

(i) the parties are within the prohibited degrees of relationship *or*

(ii) either party is under the age of 16 *or*

(iii) the parties have intermarried in disregard of certain requirements as to the formation of marriage.

(b) That at the time of marriage either party was already lawfully married.

(c) That the parties are not respectively male and female.

(d) In the case of a polygamous marriage entered into outside England and Wales, that either party at the time of the marriage was domiciled in England and Wales.

4. Prohibited degrees

The prohibitions are based on Consanguinity (related by blood) or Affinity (related by marriage). In the former category, a man may not marry his mother, daughter, grandmother, granddaughter, sister, aunt or niece. In the second category, a spouse can marry into his former spouse's family, e.g. his sister-in-law, however his first marriage was terminated. Under the Marriage (Prohibited Degrees of Relationship) Act 1986 a spouse may marry step-daughter or granddaughter, step-mother or step-grandmother provided that both are over 21 and the younger was never a child of the family. Spouses may also marry their daughter-in-law or mother-in-law provided that both are over 21 and both their spouses are dead.

5. Either party under sixteen

English law will not permit the marriage of any under-age person domiciled in England.

Pugh v Pugh (1951). He was domiciled in England and married a 15-year-old Hungarian girl in Austria. Both those countries permitted marriage under 16 but it was HELD void under English law.

6. Formal defects

The Marriage Acts 1949–1986 are complicated with regard to the requirements for a valid ceremony. Some defects may make the marriage void and some have no effect on validity at all. By virtue of s. 25 (Church of England marriages) and s. 49 (other marriages) a marriage will be void if both parties 'knowingly and wilfully' disregard any of the following:

(a) Marriage celebrated in church or chapel which may not publish banns.

(b) Failure to carry out proper preliminaries.

(c) Marriage after parental objection.

(d) After banns or certificate have expired.

(e) Married by person not in Holy Orders or in the absence of the Registrar.

Sections 24 and 48 make specific reference to reasons which will *not* invalidate the marriage, namely:

(a) Failure to comply with residence requirements.

(b) Absence of consents for minors.

(c) Building not certified as a place of worship or not the usual place of worship of either.

(d) Incorrect declaration to obtain permission to marry in a district where neither resides because there is nowhere in their districts to marry according to the rites of their religious beliefs.

7. Bigamy

Bigamy is committed if either party is validly married to another at the time of the ceremony.

8. Parties must be male and female

See Chapter 2 (*see* 2:3) and *Corbett* v *Corbett* (1970).

9. Polygamous marriages

This topic has also been addressed in Chapter 2 (*see* 2:11).

VOIDABLE MARRIAGES

10. Voidable marriages under MCA 1973

The MCA 1973, s. 12 provides that a marriage is voidable on the following grounds only:

(a) That the marriage has not been consummated owing to the incapacity of either party to consummate it.

(b) That the marriage has not been consummated owing to the wilful refusal of the respondent to consummate it.

(c) That either party to the marriage did not validly consent to it, whether in consequence of duress, mistake, unsoundness of mind or otherwise.

(d) That at the time of the marriage either party, though capable of giving a valid consent, was suffering (whether continuously or intermittently) from a mental disorder within the meaning of the Mental Health Act 1983 of such a kind or to such an extent as to be unfitted for marriage.

(e) That at the time of the marriage the respondent was suffering from venereal disease in a communicable form.

(f) That at the time of the marriage the respondent was pregnant by some person other than the petitioner.

11. Non-consummation

Consummation takes place as soon as the parties have sexual intercourse after the marriage has been solemnised. Intercourse must be 'ordinary and complete' and not 'incipient, imperfect and unnatural' *per* Dr Lushington in *D* v *A* (1845). The combined decisions of relevant cases requires erection and penetration for a reasonable time but not necessarily ejaculation or orgasm. A single act of intercourse is sufficient to consummate a marriage provided it complies with these requirements.

> *Baxter* v *Baxter* (1947) HL. HELD The use of contraception such as a condom will not prevent consummation if intercourse is otherwise complete.

For a marriage to be voidable, the failure to consummate must result from the incapacity of either party or the wilful refusal of the respondent.

12. Incapacity

This may be based on a physical abnormality or on psychological causes and it is irrelevant that the respondent is capable of having intercourse with other partners. An 'invincible repugnance' to the act of intercourse with a spouse may suffice, but in *Singh* v *Singh* (1971) a rational decision not to permit intercourse, although understandable, did not.

The incapacity must be permanent and incurable. It will be deemed incurable if remedial surgery is dangerous or the respondent refuses to undergo an operation which may cure the defect.

Either of the parties may petition on the ground of incapacity, which means that a party may rely on his or her own incapacity in contrast to wilful refusal where the party refusing cannot petition.

13. Wilful refusal

The majority of nullity petitions based on non-consummation rely on the respondent's wilful refusal to consummate the marriage. This must be 'a settled and definite decision come to without just excuse': *Horton* v *Horton* (1947).

> *Ford* v *Ford* (1987). The parties married while the husband was in prison. Whilst prison rules prohibited the parties from having sexual intercourse during visits there was clearly the opportunity to do so and many prisoners took advantage of this. Mr Ford did not. When granted a home visit, he did not go to his wife's home. HELD He showed a clear intention not to pursue a married life with his wife and the marriage was annulled.

However, a petition will fail if the respondent can show just excuse for his or her behaviour. The parties may, for example, have gone through a civil ceremony of marriage on the understanding that they would not live together until a religious ceremony had taken place.

> *Kaur* v *Singh* (1972). In such a case, one party's refusal to go through the second ceremony amounted to a wilful refusal to consummate.

A refusal to undergo treatment for a physical defect which prevents intercourse will amount to wilful refusal to consummate provided the treatment is not dangerous. A refusal to have intercourse without the use of contra-

17

ception is not a refusal to consummate. It is viewed as a sort of conditional consent.

> *Baxter* v *Baxter* (1948). Both were Roman Catholics but she was advised that a pregnancy could be dangerous so she insisted on contraception. He insisted that they should continue to observe their faith and not use contraception. HELD This was not wilful refusal.

14. Lack of consent

Parties must give their express consent to marriage but s. 12 makes specific reference to the lack of real consent where it has been given under duress, as a result of a mistake or by a person of unsound mind.

15. Duress

For duress to operate, there must be fear sufficiently grave to vitiate true consent. In the absence of fear the marriage will be valid.

> *Singh* v *Singh* (1971). An arranged marriage between two young Sikhs, against the girl's wishes, was held to be valid because it was entered into out of a sense of obligation to the family and religious tradition. There was no evidence of fear.

> *Hirani* v *Hirani* (1982). A young petitioner had been threatened by her parents to turn her out of the home unless she married the man of their choice. HELD by the Court of Appeal: The question was whether the threats were sufficient to overbear the will of the individual and destroy the reality of the consent. The test is subjective, so that if the petitioner gave consent because she was genuinely in fear, it is irrelevant that others of ordinary courage might not have done so.

It is not necessary for the fear to arise from the behaviour of the other party to the marriage. The threats or conduct giving rise to fear may emanate from a third party, especially parents.

> *Buckland* v *Buckland* (1967). The husband was falsely accused of corrupting a girl aged 15 and was told by her father that he would be convicted and imprisoned for years unless he married her, which he did. HELD The marriage was annulled.

The courts have also been willing to consider the conduct of totalitarian regimes as a valid source of fear, and hasty marriages contracted for the purpose of escape have been annulled for lack of consent.

H v *H* (1954). A young Hungarian girl feared what might happen to her at the hands of a victorious Russian army and married to avoid this.

Szechter v *Szechter* (1971). In similar circumstances, a young Jewish girl feared brutality from the Polish security services.

In both cases the fears were held to be sufficient to amount to duress, and the marriages were annulled.

16. Mistake

A mistake will invalidate a marriage only if it relates to the nature of the ceremony or the identity of the other party.

Mehta v *Mehta* (1945). The wife believed that she was participating in a ceremony of conversion to the Hindu faith. HELD The marriage was void.

A mistake as to the effect of the ceremony rather than its nature will not invalidate a marriage.

Messina v *Smith* (1971). She was a foreign national facing deportation for prostitution and only married to obtain British nationality from her husband. HELD The marriage was valid despite the parties' intention never to cohabit. They clearly understood that they had gone through a ceremony of marriage.

17. Unsoundness of mind

Under this head, the party must be so affected as not to understand the nature of marriage nor the duties so imposed. The test was laid down by Singleton LJ *In the Estate of Park* (1953):

'To ascertain the nature of the contract of marriage a man must be mentally capable of appreciating that it involves the responsibilities normally attaching to marriage. Without that degree of mentality it cannot be said that he understands the nature of the contract'.

There is a presumption of sanity and the burden of proof is on the person impeaching the validity of the marriage. If a party is found to be generally insane, the burden shifts to any person seeking to uphold the validity of the marriage to show that it took place during a lucid interval.

This ground is now rarely used because the following ground (*see* **18** below) is easier to prove.

18. Mental disorder

This ground, introduced by statute in 1937, recognised that a person might be mentally unfit for marriage but still capable of giving valid consent.

Lack of fitness must arise from a mental disorder suffered at the time of the marriage, although it may be intermittent rather than continuous. Mental disorder is defined in the Mental Health Act 1983, s. 1 to mean:

> 'Mental illness, arrested or incomplete development of mind, psychopathic disorder and any other disorder or disability of mind'.

19. Venereal disease and pregnancy by another

These two remaining grounds were introduced in 1937 to cover specific circumstances which did not otherwise give grounds for annulment. A petition based on either of these grounds will fail unless the court is satisfied that the petitioner was ignorant of the facts at the time of the marriage.

BARS TO A DECREE

20. Bars to a decree

The Nullity of Marriage Act 1971 specified certain circumstances in which a decree of nullity could not be granted even if the relevant ground was satisfied. These are the statutory bars and they are now contained in the MCA 1973, s. 13.

The bars only apply to marriages which are voidable. There are no longer any bars to the granting of a decree in the case of a void marriage; if one of the grounds is made out a decree must be granted.

The three statutory bars are

- Approbation
- Time
- Knowledge.

21. Approbation

To allow a petitioner to challenge the validity of a marriage if his or her behaviour has clearly implied an acceptance of it was considered unjust to the respondent and also contrary to public policy. The statutory bar of approbation contained in s. 13(1) of the MCA 1973 sets out the circumstances in which this bar will apply today.

It prevents a court from granting a decree if satisfied by the respondent:

(a) That the petitioner, with knowledge that it was open to him to have the marriage avoided, so conducted himself in relation to the respondent as to lead the respondent reasonably to believe that he would not seek to do so *and*

(b) That it would be unjust to the respondent to grant the decree (MCA 1973, s. 13(1)).

Public policy is no longer a relevant consideration. The court must concern itself with the question of justice to the respondent and not with any wider considerations or moral judgments.

D v D *(Nullity; Statutory Bar)*(1979). The fact that the parties had adopted a child was held to be irrelevant even though it might be considered contrary to public policy for a marriage to be annulled in these circumstances.

22. Time

By virtue of MCA 1973, s. 13(2), a decree may not be granted on the ground of lack of consent, mental unfitness, venereal disease or pregnancy by another unless the proceedings were instituted within three years of the date of the marriage. This bar is absolute with one very limited exception. A judge may grant leave for proceedings to be commenced outside the three-year period if the petitioner has at some time during that period suffered from a mental disorder (as defined by the Mental Health Act 1983, s. 1 (*see* **18** above)) and the judge considers it just in all the circumstances to do so.

The time limit bar does not apply to the non-consummation grounds.

23. Knowledge

By virtue of MCA 1973, s. 13(3) the court cannot grant a decree on the ground of the respondent's venereal disease or pregnancy by another unless it is satisfied that the petitioner was ignorant of this when the marriage took place. The bar will not apply if the husband knew about the pregnancy but only discovered subsequently that he was not the father.

24. Effects of a decree

The distinctions between the void and voidable marriage become relevant again when considering the effects of a decree.

A void marriage is void *ab initio*. This means that it has never had any legal existence although it may still have legal consequences. When granting a decree of nullity, for example, the court has the same power to make financial and property orders under MCA 1973, ss. 23 and 24 as it does on divorce. The children of void marriages will be treated as legitimate if both or either of the parties reasonably believed that the marriage was valid at the time of conception (or insemination if fertilisation takes place *in vitro*) or the date of marriage if later. This is the effect of the Legitimacy Act 1976, s. 1 as amended by the Family Law Reform Act 1987, s. 28.

A person who has obtained a decree of nullity on the basis of a void marriage may still be treated as a former wife or husband under the Inheritance (Provision for Family and Dependants) Act 1975 and apply for financial relief from the estate of a former spouse. The same applies to a person who has in good faith entered into a void marriage but not sought a decree.

A decree granted after 31 July 1971 will only operate to annul a voidable marriage after it has been made absolute. The marriage will be treated as existing for all purposes up to that date. Thus any children born to the parties will be legitimate and a will made prior to the date of marriage will be revoked by the marriage (*Re Roberts (Dec'd.)* (1978)).

After decree absolute, neither spouse will be able to claim on the intestacy of the other although they may make a claim under the Inheritance Acts (see above). Under the Wills Act 1837, s. 18A, if a will has been made during the marriage, any provision by one spouse for the other will lapse.

Financial relief under MCA 1973, ss. 23 and 24 is available as with a void marriage.

MARRIAGES WITH A FOREIGN ELEMENT

25. Juridiction in marriages with a foreign element

Problems of jurisdiction and recognition may arise where a marriage has a foreign element. The parties may have married abroad but now seek to have that marriage annulled in this country. They may seek recognition of a decree of nullity obtained abroad in order to remarry here or seek some form of matrimonial relief in our courts.

Under the Domicile and Matrimonial Proceedings Act 1973, s. 5(3) provides that a court in England and Wales will only have jurisdiction in nullity proceedings if either of the parties to the marriage was

(a) Domiciled in England and Wales on the date when the proceedings are begun *or*

(b) Habitually resident there throughout the period of one year ending with that date *or*

(c) (in the case of a void marriage only) Died before that date and was either domiciled there at death or had been habitually resident there throughout the year before death.

Habitual residence is a different concept from domicile and describes the place where a person voluntarily resides with a degree of settled purpose. Temporary or occasional brief absences will not detract from this. Neither will more prolonged stays at a holiday home, provided that there can still be said to be ordinary residence in this country.

The court has a discretion to stay proceedings where they are simultaneously brought in another jurisdiction. This discretion will be exercised on the balance of fairness between the parties, taking into account relevant factors such as delay, expense and the convenience of witnesses.

Once jurisdiction is established, the rules which govern which law will apply are relatively straightforward. The formalities which govern marriage are determined by the law of the place where it is celebrated. If the parties comply with these requirements, the marriage will be valid. If they fail to do so, it will be invalid.

It seems unlikely that the English courts would enforce a prohibition under foreign law which would be unconscionable or repugnant to English law, such as one based on colour or caste.

26. Recognition of foreign decrees

A foreign decree of nullity will be recognised as valid by the English courts if it fulfills the requirements of the Family Law Act 1986, s. 46(1):

(a) The decree must have been obtained 'by means of proceedings.' This requires a degree of formality or at least the involvement of some state agency, if only to register the decree.

(b) The decree must be effective under the law of the country where it was obtained.

23

(c) Either party to the marriage must have been habitually resident in that country or domiciled there or one of its nationals at the time the decree was granted.

There are countries which permit marriages to be annulled or dissolved with no formality whatsoever. Such decrees fall outside the ambit of s. 46(1) but may nevertheless be recognised provided that the parties fulfil certain requirements set out in s. 46(2). Each party must be domiciled in that country or one party must be domiciled there and the other in another country which would also recognise the validity of the decree. Neither party must have been habitually resident in the United Kingdom throughout the year preceding the decree.

Even when the requirements of s. 46 are fulfilled, there are circumstances in which a foreign decree of nullity will not be recognised. These are set out in the FLA 1986, s. 51. To summarise, recognition will be withheld where:

(a) The decree is irreconcilable with a previous judicial decision made or recognised by a UK court *or*

(b) The decree was made at a time when there was no valid marriage under UK law *or*

(c) In the case of a decree obtained by means of proceedings, the respondent was not given proper notice or reasonable opportunity to take part in the proceedings *or*

(d) In the case of a decree obtained otherwise, there is no official document certifying that the decree is effective in the country where it is granted and/or recognised as valid in the country where one of the parties was domiciled at the time *or*

(e) In either case, recognition of the decree would be manifestly contrary to public policy.

Progress test 3

1. What are the differences between a void and voidable marriage, and what are the consequences of those differences?

2. List the grounds which render a marriage void.

3. List the grounds which render a marriage voidable.

4. H and W married after a brief courtship. On honeymoon, H was unable to have an erection which meant they could not have intercourse. W thought this was due to an excess of champagne. However, the problem continued

on their return and W persuaded H to have a medical examination. The doctor advised H to abstain from alcohol for a time but H refused and indulged in even heavier drinking. Advise W.

How, if at all, would your answer differ if their inability was due to W's physical problems which could only be rectified by a painful operation?

5. In what circumstances may lack of consent affect the validity of a marriage?

6. What are the statutory bars to a decree of nullity?

7. When, and on what grounds, will the court recognise a foreign decree of nullity?

4

Divorce

Because of the delay in implementing the FLA 1996, it is necessary to be familiar with both the existing and the new law. (See Appendix for the text of the FLA 1996.)

DIVORCE UNDER THE MATRIMONIAL CAUSES ACT 1973

1. The time qualification for divorce

By virtue of MCA 1973, s. 3(1) a divorce petition cannot be presented within one year of marriage. This bar is absolute but, once the year has elapsed, any matters which occurred during that first year of marriage may be used as the basis for a petition for divorce.

2. Irretrievable breakdown

The sole ground for divorce is that the marriage has broken down irretrievably: MCA 1973, s. 1(1). The only way a petitioner may establish this is by proving one of the following five facts set out in s. 1(2) of the MCA 1973, namely:

(a) That the respondent has committed adultery and the petitioner finds it intolerable to live with the respondent: s. 1(2)(a).

(b) That the respondent has behaved in such a way that the petitioner cannot reasonably be expected to live with the respondent: s. 1(2)(b).

(c) That the respondent has deserted the petitioner for a continuous period of at least two years immediately preceding the presentation of the petition: s. 1(2)(c).

(d) That the parties to the marriage have lived apart for a continuous period of at least two years immediately preceding the presentation of the petition and the respondent consents to a decree being granted: s. 1(2)(e).

(e) That the parties to the marriage have lived apart for a continuous period of at least five years immediately preceding the presentation of the petition: s. 1(2)(f).

The 'special procedure' applies to undefended divorce proceedings whereby the judge grants a decree on the basis of an affidavit submitted by the petitioner, supporting the allegations made in the petition. Neither party is required in court unless the petition is opposed. However, divorce is rarely defended. The Legal Aid Board normally will not support applications because eventually the divorce becomes inevitable. The number of cases in each year is in single figures. Nevertheless, it is still necessary to have a sound knowledge of the substantive law.

ADULTERY AND INTOLERABILITY

3. Definition of adultery

Adultery involves voluntary or consensual sexual intercourse between a married person and a person of the opposite sex to whom he or she is not married.

A victim of rape does not commit adultery because it is not voluntary (*Clarkson* v *Clarkson* (1930)) and neither does a person who is mentally incapable of giving consent (*S* v *S* (1961)). Drunkenness is only a defence if it is involuntary, i.e. that non-alcoholic drinks had been 'spiked' (*Goshawk* v *Goshawk* (1965)).

Adultery requires penetration of the female by the male; unlike consummation, it does not require the act of intercourse to be complete.

4. Proof of adultery

Adultery can be difficult to prove. In many cases, the respondent will admit to the adultery and has made a written admission. If adultery is not admitted, it must be proved in other ways, for example:

(a) Where there is evidence of opportunity and inclination, such as a couple sharing a bedroom overnight.

(b) Where the wife has given birth to a child after a long period apart from her husband: *Preston-Jones* v *Preston-Jones* (1951).

(c) Where the respondent is suffering from venereal disease which he has not caught from the petitioner.

(d) Where blood tests or DNA sampling proves that the husband is not the father of his wife's child. Section 20(1) of the Family Law Reform Act 1969 allows the court discretion to order bodily samples to be taken to determine paternity and, if a party refuses, the court will draw such inferences as it deems proper.

5. Intolerability

Proof of adultery will not of itself establish irretrievable breakdown. The petitioner must also show that he or she finds it intolerable to live with the respondent. The test is subjective: does this petitioner find it intolerable to live with this respondent?

Usually the adultery will be the cause of intolerability, but it need not be. The petitioner may be unable to tolerate the respondent for a totally different reason. This is the interpretation of the MCA 1973 by the Court of Appeal in *Cleary* v *Cleary & Hutton* (1974). Thus the petitioner may not care about her spouse's adultery but 'blowing his nose more than [she] liked' would satisfy the requirements of s. 1(2)(a).

6. Living together after adultery

The MCA 1973, s. 2 contains provisions designed to encourage attempts at reconciliation by precluding a spouse from relying on their partner's adultery if they have lived together for one or more periods exceeding in total six months after the adultery became known to the spouse. This bar is absolute and will even apply to cohabitation after decree nisi, in which case a decree absolute will be denied. In a sense, this is a negative provision in that there is no encouragement in the provisions for the parties to seek help by way of marriage guidance or counselling during the period. The Law Commission saw this as one of the major failings of the MCA 1973.

RESPONDENT'S BEHAVIOUR

7. Behaviour

The petitioner must satisfy the court that the respondent has behaved in a particular way and the petitioner cannot reasonably be expected to live with the respondent because of this. These are two separate requirements and are mutually dependent.

Behaviour is more than a mere state of affairs or a state of mind. It may take the form of an act or omission or it may be a course of conduct: *Katz* v *Katz* (1972). It can include violence by an alcoholic husband (*Ash* v *Ash* (1972)), constant criticism (*Livingstone-Stallard* v *Livingstone-Stallard* (1974)), all forms of obsessive behaviour, sexual activities which do not constitute adultery, nagging, threats and insults. It may be a number of complaints, trivial in themselves, which taken together become unreasonable (*Livingstone-Stallard*). There must be some disparity between the spouses: a heavy drinker cannot complain of the other's drunkenness (*Ash*).

8. Reasonableness

Petitions brought under s. 1(2)(b) of the MCA 1973 are often mistakenly referred to as 'unreasonable behaviour' petitions but the question is not whether the respondent has behaved unreasonably but whether the petitioner can reasonably be expected to live with the respondent.

> *Bannister* v *Bannister* (1980). The trial judge took the view that the husband's actions did not constitute unreasonable behaviour. He was overruled on appeal because the question was 'was it unreasonable to expect the wife to live with him?'

Dunn J in *Livingstone-Stallard* v *Livingstone-Stallard* said the test is:

> 'Would any right-thinking person come to the conclusion that this husband has behaved in such a way that this wife cannot reasonably be expected to live with him, taking into account the whole of the circumstances and the character and personalities of the parties?'

The test is partly objective and partly subjective. The court must be objective in assessing the effect of the respondent's behaviour on the petitioner but subjective in taking into account the circumstances of the parties.

9. Living together

Under MCA 1973, s. 2(3) the fact that the parties have lived together for a period or periods not exceeding six months in total after the final incident relied on by the petitioner must be disregarded by the court in determining whether the petitioner can reasonably be expected to live with the respondent.

This is a similar provision to that relating to adultery, designed to give the parties an opportunity to reconcile. Unlike adultery, it is not an absolute bar. A petition will not necessarily fail if there has been cohabitation for more than six months after the conduct complained of. There may be good reasons why the petitioner has continued to live with the respondent and it may still be unreasonable to expect them to live together in the future. Examples were given in *Bradley* v *Bradley* (1973). The petitioner may have stayed out of concern for the welfare of the children. She may have had nowhere else to go. She may have feared that the respondent would damage the property or its contents in her absence.

DESERTION

10. Simple and constructive desertion

Desertion is rarely relied on to prove irretrievable breakdown. This is because a divorce can be obtained after two years' separation, with the respondent's consent, without the necessity of complying with the conditions which s. 1(2)(c) imposes.

The petitioner must prove that desertion has occurred and that it has lasted for a continuous period of two years immediately preceding the petition. The deserter is the spouse who intends to bring cohabitation to an end. So, the spouse who leaves with such intent is in *simple desertion*. However, a spouse who drives out the other by their conduct is said to be in *constructive desertion* because he or she has brought about the separation.

11. Essentials of desertion

Desertion has four essential elements:

(a) *Separation*
This is normally brought about by one spouse leaving the matrimonial home, but this does not have to be the case. 'Desertion is not the withdrawal from a place, but from a state of affairs' *per* Lord Merrivale in *Pulford* v *Pulford* (1923). A state of separation can exist even though the parties continue to live under the same roof provided that there has been a rejection of all the obligations of marriage. The abandonment of some but not all marital duties will not suffice. In *LeBrocq* v *LeBrocq* (1964) the petition failed because the wife continued to cook the husband's meals and he paid her a housekeeping allowance.

(b) *Intention to desert*
Even where there is separation there is no desertion unless the deserting party intends to remain permanently separated. Temporary separation,

such as holiday or business, or involuntary, such as imprisonment, will not constitute desertion unless intention is communicated to the other party.

(c) *Absence of consent*
There can be no desertion if the petitioner has consented to the separation. Thus, a separation agreement entered into freely and voluntarily is evidence of consent.

(d) *Absence of good cause*
The respondent may be justified in leaving the petitioner because of misconduct or a reasonable belief that there are grounds for separation. The misconduct must be 'grave and weighty' and more than the ordinary wear and tear of married life.

> *Quoraishi* v *Quoraishi* (1985). The wife was justified in leaving her husband when he took a second wife even though he was legally entitled to do so.

12. Termination of desertion

(a) *Resumption of cohabitation*
Although resumption obviously terminates desertion, s. 2(5) specifies that the court must disregard any period or periods not exceeding six months in which the parties have lived together in the same household. A petitioner may therefore attempt reconciliation for a period or periods of up to six months in total after the desertion has commenced and still not prejudice the right to rely on it should the attempt fail. Any reconciliation period must be excluded, however, in computing the period of desertion.

(b) *A decree of judicial separation*
Desertion is terminated by such a decree because it relieves the parties of the duty to cohabit.

(c) *Loss of intention*
If a spouse makes a genuine offer to return, and the other rejects it without justification, the latter will be in desertion.

SEPARATION

13. Two years' separation

There are two elements to be satisfied when relying on this fact. First, it is necessary to show that the parties have lived apart for a continuous period of two years immediately preceding the presentation of the petition. Secondly, the respondent must consent to the decree.

14. Living apart

The MCA 1973, s. 1(2)(d) provides for divorce by consent, but, whatever the wishes of the parties, a decree cannot be granted unless they have lived apart for the two-year period.

Section 2(6) provides that a husband and wife shall be treated as living apart unless they are living with each other in the same household. This is the same test as for desertion.

As with desertion, problems may arise when the parties claim to have lived separate and apart but under the same roof. The court must then consider the domestic arrangements to decide whether there are, in fact, one or two households.

> *Mouncer* v *Mouncer* (1972). Although the parties had slept in separate rooms, they ate their meals together and the wife did most of the housework for them both. HELD They were not living apart.

> *Fuller* v *Fuller* (1973). The husband moved in with the wife and her boyfriend when his health failed. Although she provided him with meals and care, he occupied his own room and paid for his keep. She shared a bedroom with her boyfriend. HELD He had the status of a lodger rather than a husband and the wife's petition under s. 1(2)(f) succeeded.

15. For a continuous period of two years

The separation must be for a continuous period of two years. As with desertion, s. 2(5) of the MCA 1973 applies. The parties may therefore live together for a period or periods of up to six months without breaking the continuity of a period of separation. The periods when they live together must, however, be excluded from any calculation of the two-year period required by s. 1(2)(d). Although the Act is not specific, it is clearly intended that any period or periods of cohabitation exceeding six months in total will end the separation which must then start anew.

16. Consent

The onus of proving consent lies on the petitioner. In practice this is satisfied by the respondent confirming agreement in writing having completed the acknowledgment of service of the petition.

A respondent may give consent conditionally, for example that the petitioner will not seek an order for costs against the respondent.

Consent may be withdrawn at any time up to decree nisi and for any reason whatsoever. The proceedings will then be stayed. After decree nisi a respondent may withdraw consent if he or she has been misled (whether intentionally or otherwise) by the petitioner about any matter which he or she took into account in deciding to consent and this rescinds the decree: MCA 1973, s. 10(1).

17. Five years' separation

There is only one requirement to be satisfied when relying on this fact. The parties must have lived apart for a continuous period of five years immediately preceding the presentation of the petition. Living apart has the same meaning as it does in two-year separation cases. Section 2(5) applies so that a period or periods of cohabitation not exceeding six months in total may be disregarded when calculating the five-year period. No consent is required.

18. Defence of grave hardship

When the law was introduced in 1971, it was feared that the provision allowing divorce without consent after five years' separation would be a 'Casanova's Charter' permitting unscrupulous husbands to divorce their innocent wives with impunity. It was therefore felt necessary to include in the legislation some measure of protection for spouses divorced against their will.

MCA 1973, s. 5 provides that a respondent to a petition based on five years' separation may oppose the grant of a decree on the ground that the dissolution of the marriage will result in grave financial or other hardship and that it would be wrong in all the circumstances to dissolve the marriage. The hardship must be caused by the *dissolution* of the marriage.

Hardship is specifically defined in s. 5(3) to include the loss of the chance of acquiring any benefit which the respondent might acquire if the marriage were not dissolved. Not surprisingly, the few reported financial hardship cases turn almost entirely on the loss of pension rights, and these cases have been made largely irrelevant by the Pensions Act 1995, s. 166 (see Chapter 9).

Other hardship has been alleged in several cases but never successfully pleaded. With one exception the reported cases turn on religious or social hardship.

Rukat v *Rukat* (1975) The wife had lived in Sicily away from her husband for 25 years. Defending the petition, she maintained that she would not be accepted in the community if divorced. HELD She had not shown that the divorce would make any difference to her social status as she had been living as a separated wife for so long.

Banik v *Banik* (1973) Both parties were Hindu. The wife claimed that divorce would make her a social outcast and also deny her the spiritual benefit of dying as a married woman. HELD The wife failed to establish that she would suffer in the manner alleged.

Even if the respondent can prove that the decree will cause hardship the court must still grant it unless it would be wrong in all the circumstances to do so. The court must have regard to all the circumstances including, specifically, the conduct of the parties, their interests and the interests of any children or other parties concerned: MCA 1973, s. 5(2).

Brickell v *Brickell* (1973) The court considered that the respondent had contributed to the marital breakdown by her conduct. HELD The defence failed even though the wife was able to establish grave financial hardship.

Parker v *Parker* (1972) The petitioner's wish to remarry was taken into account because his continued cohabitation with his girlfriend was alleged to impede his chance of promotion in the police force.

BARS TO A DECREE

19. Bars to a decree nisi

There are circumstances in which the court may not grant a decree nisi even though one of the five facts has been proved. In addition to the grave hardship defence, which only applies to petitions under s. 1(2)(e), there is one other defence applicable to all cases. The court may refuse a decree if it is not satisfied that the marriage has irretrievably broken down: MCA 1973, s. 1(4).

The question of irretrievable breakdown will depend upon the prospects of reconciliation. Rules of Court made under s. 6(1) require solicitors to certify that they have discussed with the petitioner the possibility of reconciliation and given to the petitioner names and addresses of persons qualified to help. This requirement is limited in effect as it applies only to petitioners who are represented in the proceedings.

20. Bars to decree absolute

A marriage is only fully terminated when decree nisi is made absolute, usually six weeks after the grant of decree nisi although there is power to expedite decree absolute in certain situations.

There are two situations where the court can refuse to make the decree absolute:

(a) Where the respondent has applied to the court for consideration of his or her financial position after divorce.

(b) Where the court is not satisfied that proper arrangements have been made for the children of the family.

21. Financial position after divorce

A respondent may apply to the court to consider his or her financial position after divorce if a decree has been granted on the basis of two or five years' separation but not otherwise: MCA 1973, s. 10. If the respondent does so the court cannot make the decree absolute unless it is satisfied either that the petitioner should not be required to make financial provision for the respondent or that the financial provision made is reasonable and fair or the best that can be made in the circumstances.

In considering what financial provision, if any, should be made the court must consider all the circumstances including the age, health, conduct, earning capacity, financial resources and financial obligations of each party and the likely position of the respondent if the petitioner dies first: MCA 1973, s. 10(3).

22. The children's interests

The court also has power to defer decree absolute in the interests of any child of the family. Under s. 41 of the MCA 1973 (as amended by the CA 1989) it has a duty to consider whether it should exercise any of its powers under the CA 1989 in respect of any children of the family (see 12.5 for a discussion of these powers). When doing so it will have to take into account arrangements which have been made or are proposed to be made for their upbringing and welfare. In exceptional circumstances it may direct that the decree shall not be made absolute until further order, but this power may only be exercised where:

(a) The circumstances require, or are likely to require, the court to make an order under the CA 1989 *but*

35

(b) It cannot do so without further consideration *and*

(c) There are exceptional circumstances which make it desirable in the interests of the child for decree absolute to be deferred.

A child of the family is defined by s. 52(1) of the MCA 1973 as:

(a) A child of both parties *and*

(b) Any other child, not being a child who is placed with those parties as foster parents by a local authority or voluntary organisation, who has been treated by both those parties as a child of the family.

Section 41 applies to a child of the family below the age of 16 years or below the age of 18 if receiving education or training. It may also apply to an adult child if the court so directs.

DIVORCE UNDER THE FAMILY LAW ACT 1996

23. Introduction

The Law Commission in *Facing the Future* (Law Com No 170 (1988)) found that the Divorce Reform Act 1969 (DRA 1969) had failed to remove bitterness, distress and humiliation from divorce; and that the law was often confusing and incomprehensible and did nothing to encourage saving the marriage. The Law Commission found 'overwhelming support' for irretrievable breakdown as the basis of divorce but not by establishing fault. It recommended divorce over a period of time (i.e. one year) to allow for consideration of future arrangements and for reflection.

The then government accepted the proposals in principle but insisted that arrangements for finance and the upbringing of children should be dealt with before the marriage was dissolved. However, the Bill endured a stormy and difficult passage through Parliament and many concessions and amendments were made, particularly through the government's own backbenchers.

The Lord Chancellor is required to introduce numerous regulations under the Act, there are pilot schemes to be undertaken and the result is that the FLA 1996 will not be implemented until the year 1999 at the earliest.

References to sections in this part of the chapter are to the FLA 1996 unless otherwise stated.

24. General principles

The DRA 1969 contained no reference to the Law Commission's proposals on which it was based whereas the FLA 1996 sets them out as General Principles in Part I. They are:

(a) That the institution of marriage should be supported. Where a marriage has broken down, the married couple should be encouraged to take all practical steps to save the marriage, whether by marriage counselling or otherwise.

(b) Where marriages are being brought to an end, this should be done with minimum distress to the parties and their children, so as to encourage the best possible relationships between them and without incurring unreasonable costs.

(c) Any risk of violence to a party to the marriage or to any children, on account of the other party, should, as far as reasonably practicable, be removed or diminished.

25. The information meeting

Section 8 provides that before divorce proceedings can commence, a party must have attended an information meeting not less than three months before making a statement of marital breakdown (which is the start of proceedings). By s. 8(4), if both parties make the statement they have the option of attending a meeting together, or of attending separate meetings.

Where one party has made a statement, the other party must attend an information meeting before making any application to the court to contest the application, or make applications in respect of any child or children and/or property and financial matters.

The purpose of the meeting is to provide the party or parties with information about matters which may arise during the divorce process. Full details are to be set out in regulations as provided by s. 8(9). Such regulations must, in particular, deal with the giving of information about

(a) Marriage counselling and other marriage support services.

(b) The importance to be attached to the welfare, wishes and feelings of children.

(c) How the parties may acquire a better understanding of the ways in which children can be helped to cope with the breakdown of a marriage.

(d) The nature of the financial questions that may arise on divorce or separation, and services which are available to help the parties.

(e) Protection available against violence and how to obtain support and assistance.

(f) Mediation.

(g) The availability of independent legal advice and representation.

(h) The principles of legal aid and where the parties can get advice about obtaining it.

The meeting must be conducted by a person who is qualified and appointed in accordance with provisions also to be introduced by the Lord Chancellor. Such person will have no financial or other interest in any marital proceedings between the parties.

In at least one pilot scheme, the meetings will be group meetings.

The meeting must take place *not less than three months before* making the statement but it is not clear how long before the statement it must be. For example, if a party attends the meeting, then, say, goes abroad to work for a year, would he or she have to attend another meeting before filing a statement of marital breakdown? Will it be possible to attend a meeting early in the marriage and keep it 'in the bank' in case the marriage fails in the future?

There is also a provision for a party not to attend a meeting in 'prescribed circumstances' but as yet there appears to be no indication as to what those circumstances might be.

26. Counselling and mediation

Section 23 allows for the Lord Chancellor to make regulations which will enable eligible couples to obtain marriage counselling funded by the State during the period for reflection and consideration (*see* **29** below).

Section 13 encourages the use of mediation by enabling the court, after filing of the statement of marital breakdown, to direct the parties to attend a meeting with a mediator to give the opportunity for them to agree to make use of mediation.

Mediation and counselling are significantly different. The former enables couples to meet face to face with the object of resolving their differences over finance, property and children. Counsellors try to assist in saving the marriage and a mediator must refer couples to a counsellor if such a prospect appears possible.

THE STATEMENT OF MARITAL BREAKDOWN

27. The statement

The statement can be filed by either or both of the parties but in either case it must state that he or she (or both) is aware of the purpose of the period for reflection and consideration and wishes to make arrangements for the future.

Once again, the Lord Chancellor may make rules as to the form in which a statement is to be made, the information which must accompany it and the way in which it is to be given to the court and served on the other party. The person making the statement must also state whether or not he or she has made any attempt at reconciliation since the information meeting.

28. Commencement of proceedings

The statement is actually the commencement of the proceedings and it is only from this date forward that applications can be made in respect of the children and financial and property matters. This could cause problems in practice, because of the three-month wait following the information meeting. Spouses requiring financial support will be able to make applications under the Domestic Proceedings and Magistrates Courts Act 1978 (DPMCA 1978) and the Child Support Act 1991 (CSA 1991). However, there is no obvious provision to deal with disputes concerning the matrimonial home. It is possible to obtain occupation orders under Part IV (*see* Chapter 5) but the factors which the court must take into account will not always be present.

The statement also marks the commencement of the period of reflection and consideration.

29. The period of reflection and consideration

After a statement has been made, there must be a period for the parties to reflect on whether the marriage can be saved, to have an opportunity to effect a reconciliation, and to consider what arrangements should be made for the future.

Section 7 provides that, until this period expires, there can be no application for a divorce order or for a separation order.

The period for reflection and consideration is *nine months* beginning with the fourteenth day after the day on which the statement is received by the court. This period, added to the three months wait between the information meeting and the filing of the statement, ensures that no divorce order can be made in less than one year.

Even during the passage of the Bill, MPs were questioning how this provision would work, e.g. when and where would the reflection take place? And in cases where the marriage was beyond saving, because one partner was in a new relationship or the spouse had been the victim of violence, would not this period more likely lead to recrimination rather than reflection?

There are a number of occasions allowing for an extension of the period but none allowing it to be shortened.

30. Extensions to the period

Section 7(4) allows for an extension where there has been inordinate delay on the court's part in serving a copy of the statement on the other party. The period is extended until service is effected.

It is also possible to grant an extension where the parties are attempting reconciliation. The extension is for the period from the request by the parties until the date the attempt breaks down. If that period exceeds 18 months, a new statement of marital breakdown must be filed.

A six-month extension can be granted in the following circumstances:

(a) Under s. 7 if an application for a divorce order is made by one party and the other party applies to the court, within a prescribed period, for time for further reflection.

(b) If there is a child of the family who is under the age of 16 when the application for a divorce order is made, but that extension ceases when the child attains 16.

However, by virtue of s. 7(12), no extension of the period can be made if, at the time when the application for a divorce order is made, there is an occupation order or a non-molestation order in force in favour of the applicant, or of a child of the family, or the court is satisfied that delaying the making of a divorce order would be significantly detrimental to the welfare of any child of the family.

31. Entitlement to a divorce or separation order

A person is entitled to such orders under s. 3 if (but only if)

(a) The marriage has broken down irretrievably.

(b) The requirements of s. 8 about information meetings (*see* **25** above) are satisfied.

(c) The requirements of s. 9 about the parties' arrangements for the future (*see* **33** below) are satisfied *and*

(d) The application has not been withdrawn.

A divorce order may not be made if an order preventing divorce is in force under s. 10 (*see* **40** below).

32. Irretrievable breakdown of marriage

A marriage is to be taken to have broken down irretrievably if a statement has been made by one (or both) of the parties that the maker of the statement (or each of them) believes that the marriage has broken down after the period for reflection and consideration has ended. The application must be accompanied by a declaration by the party making the application that having reflected on the breakdown, and having considered the parties' arrangements for the future, the marriage cannot be saved.

The statement of marital breakdown and the application for a divorce order or for a separation order do not have to be made by the same party.

An application for an order cannot be made if a period of one year has passed since the end of the period for reflection and consideration.

33. Arrangements for the future

A divorce order or a separation order will not be made unless the requirements about the parties' arrangements for the future are satisfied. By virtue of s. 9(2) one of the following must be produced to the court:

(a) A court order (made by consent or otherwise) dealing with their financial arrangements.

(b) A negotiated agreement as to their financial arrangements.

(c) A declaration by both parties that they have made their financial arrangements.

(d) A declaration by one of the parties (to which no objection has been notified to the court by the other party) that
(*i*) he has no significant assets and does not intend to make an application for financial provision
(*ii*) he believes that the other party has no significant assets and does not intend to make an application for financial provision *and*
(*iii*) there are therefore no financial arrangements to be made.

34. Exemptions

Schedule 1 provides for four circumstances where an applicant may be exempt from complying with s. 9. In all four, the court must be satisfied that the requirements of s. 11 concerning the welfare of children have been met and that the applicant has, during the period for reflection and consideration, taken such steps as are reasonably practicable to try to reach agreement about the parties' arrangements.

35. The first exemption

The applicant has made an application to the court for financial relief and has complied with all requirements of the court in relation to proceedings for financial relief but

(a) *The other party has delayed* in complying with the requirements of the court or *has otherwise been obstructive or*

(b) For reasons which are beyond the control of the applicant, or of the other party, *the court has been prevented from obtaining the information* which it requires to determine the financial position of the parties.

36. The second exemption

Because of the *ill health or disability* of or injury to the applicant, the other party or a child of the family, the applicant has not been able to reach agreement with the other party about those arrangements and is unlikely to be able to do so in the foreseeable future and a delay in making the order would be significantly detrimental to the welfare of any child of the family or would be seriously prejudicial to the applicant.

37. The third exemption

The applicant has found it *impossible to contact the other party* and as a result it has been impossible for the applicant to reach agreement with the other party about their financial arrangements.

38. The fourth exemption

An occupation order or a non-molestation order is in force in favour of the applicant or a child of the family, made against the other party and the applicant has, during the period for reflection and consideration, *taken such steps as are reasonably practicable to try to reach agreement* about the parties' financial arrangements but has been unable to do so and a delay in making the order would be significantly detrimental to the welfare of any child of the family or would be seriously prejudicial to the applicant.

39. Welfare of the children

Section 11(1) provides that, in any proceedings for divorce or separation, the court shall consider, where there are children, whether it should exercise any of its powers under the CA 1989 in the light of the arrangements which have been, or are proposed to be, made for their upbringing and welfare. If it appears likely that it will need to exercise those powers but further consideration needs to be given to the case because there are exceptional circumstances, it may direct that the divorce order or separation order is not to be made until the court orders otherwise.

In deciding whether to exercise its powers, the court shall treat the welfare of the child as paramount.

The section applies to any child of the family who has not reached the age of 16 at the date when the court considers the case.

In making the decision as to whether to postpone the divorce order or separation order, s. 11(4) provides that the court shall also have particular regard, on the evidence before it, to

(a) The wishes and feelings of the child considered in the light of his or her age and understanding and the circumstances in which those wishes were expressed.

(b) The conduct of the parties in relation to the upbringing of the child.

(c) The general principle that, in the absence of evidence to the contrary, the welfare of the child will be best served by
(*i*) having regular contact with those who have parental responsibility for it and with other members of its family *and*
(*ii*) the maintenance of as good a continuing relationship with its parents as is possible.

(d) Any risk to the child attributable to
(*i*) the place where the person with whom the child will reside is living or proposes to live
(*ii*) any person with whom that person is living or is proposing to live *or*
(*iii*) any other arrangements for the child's care and upbringing.

In effect, the Act reinforces the court's general principle that normally the welfare of the child will be best served by having regular contact with both parents and other members of the family.

ORDERS PREVENTING DIVORCE

40. The hardship bar

Section 10 replaces the hardship bar in cases of divorce under ss. 1(2)(d) and (e) of the MCA 1973 (see **18** above). It applies to all divorces where an application for a divorce order has been made by one of the parties to the marriage but not where there has been a joint application. The other party may ask the court for an order that the marriage is not to be dissolved. Such an order (an 'order preventing divorce') may be made only if the court is satisfied

(a) That dissolution of the marriage would result in substantial financial or other hardship to the other party or to a child of the family *and*

(b) That it would be wrong, in all the circumstances (including the conduct of the parties and the interests of any child of the family), for the marriage to be dissolved.

The word 'grave' in the MCA 1973 has been replaced with 'substantial.' During the passage of the Bill, the Lord Chancellor stated that the effect of the change would be to reduce the statutory criterion to 'as low a standard as it can go.'

41. Legal aid

Part III amends the Legal Aid Act 1988 to allow the Legal Aid Board to cover the cost of mediation for those eligible for legal aid. The government are monitoring how mediation works before deciding how to implement the provisions. Anyone seeking legal representation must attend a meeting with a mediator to explore whether mediation might not be the most suitable in all the circumstances, without either party being influenced by fear of violence or other harm. However, where the case is complex, urgent or mediation is not appropriate, legally aided representation will be available to eligible parties.

42. Jurisdiction

This is governed by the Domicile and Matrimonial Proceedings Act 1973. Section 5(2) provides that a court in England and Wales will only have jurisdiction in divorce proceedings if either of the parties to the marriage:

(a) Is domiciled in England and Wales on the date when the proceedings are begun *or*

(b) Was habitually resident here throughout the period of one year ending with that date.

Once a petition has been filed, the court will have jurisdiction in other proceedings concerning the marriage.

As with nullity, the court has a discretion to stay proceedings where they are brought simultaneously in another jurisdiction. If proceedings for divorce (or nullity) are brought simultaneously in Scotland, Northern Ireland, the Channel Islands or the Isle of Man the court is bound to order a stay on the application of either party provided that the following three conditions are satisfied:

(a) The parties must have resided together since the celebration of the marriage.

(b) The place where they last resided together must have been in the other jurisdiction.

(c) One of the parties must have been an habitual resident in that jurisdiction throughout the last year they lived together.

The purpose of these conditions is to ensure that proceedings are continued in the appropriate jurisdiction.

43. Recognition of foreign decrees

The Family Law Act 1986 governs the circumstances in which a divorce obtained outside England and Wales will be recognised here. There are different criteria for decrees granted in the British Isles and those granted elsewhere.

Under s. 44(2) any divorce, annulment or judicial separation granted by a court of civil jurisdiction in any part of the British Isles is recognised throughout the United Kingdom.

A foreign divorce will be recognised by the English courts if it fulfills the requirements of the FLA 1986, s. 46. Recognition of a foreign divorce is important if either of the parties wishes to remarry in this country or seeks ancillary relief under Part III of the Matrimonial and Family Proceedings Act 1984.

Where there been an overseas divorce or decree of nullity, recognised in England and Wales, either party may apply for financial provision or property adjustment in an English court, subject to leave. Leave will be granted under s. 13 if

(a) either party is domiciled in England or Wales *or*

(b) either party has been habitually resident in England or Wales for the preceding 12 months *or*

(c) either had a beneficial interest in a dwelling house in England or Wales which had been their matrimonial home.

Progress test 4

1. Under the MCA 1973, what is the ground for divorce and how may it be proved?

2. H and W have been married for two years. H is a practising catholic who does not believe in divorce. He is very unhappy, however, because he believes W devotes far too much time to her church, which is an obscure American-based evangelical sect. She ignores his constant entreaties to spend more time with him. In a rage, H confessed that he had had sexual intercourse with a married woman three years ago. This admission deeply offends W.

    Advise W who wishes to terminate the marriage.

3. H and W have been married for 18 months. W is very keen on cookery and attends evening classes on international cuisine. According to her tutors, she is very accomplished but H refuses to try any of her dishes, insisting on traditional English fare. He also spends most of his leisure time at the Rugby club, either training, playing or drinking. W seeks advice about the possibility of divorcing H. Would your answer differ, and if so why, if instead of cookery, W was a hockey player of county standard?

4. Explain the difference between desertion and living apart.

5. On what grounds may a decree of divorce be refused?

6. List the general principles contained in Part 1 of the FLA 1996.

7. Outline the new divorce process under the FLA 1996.

8. Explain the significance of s. 9 of the FLA 1996 and consider what changes it makes to the MCA 1973 provisions.

9. How far, if at all, do you consider the new divorce law will succeed in its objectives?

10. In what circumstances will an English court recognise the validity of a divorce granted elsewhere?

5

Domestic violence

1. Introduction

This chapter is concerned with the court orders available to protect individuals from violence and molestation and court orders which require a violent partner to leave the family home.

Violence is a criminal offence, and the fact that it is committed in the home is no defence. However, the object of the criminal law is punishment and, with the exception of custodial sentences, does little to protect the victim. It is more appropriate to concentrate on the injunctive remedies.

Before the FLA 1996 Part IV came into force on 1 October 1997 the law was in an unsatisfactory state. In *Richards* v *Richards* [1984] in the House of Lords, Lord Scarman described the legal remedies available for domestic violence as: 'a hotchpotch of enactments of limited scope passed into law to meet specific situations or to strengthen the powers of specified courts.'

Briefly, the Matrimonial Homes Act 1983 (MHA 1983) was the jurisdiction for spouses to obtain 'Ouster Orders' of the matrimonial home, requiring a spouse to leave or not return to the home. The Domestic Violence and Matrimonial Proceedings Act 1976 afforded similar rights to cohabitant-habitants in respect of their family home and also provided for 'Non-molestation Orders' for both spouses and cohabitants. The Domestic Proceedings and Magistrates Courts Act 1978 gave the magistrates power to grant 'Exclusion Orders' similar to ouster orders and personal protection orders but only to spouses in circumstances of actual or threatened violence.

As well as complexity, there were persons such as ex-spouses who were afforded no protection by the Acts at all. The Law Commission made recommendations which were accepted by the former government and introduced initially as the Family Homes and Domestic Violence Bill. This was withdrawn at a very late stage but now the same proposals appear as Part 4 of the FLA 1996 (see Appendix).

THE FAMILY LAW ACT 1996 PART IV

2. Associated persons

It should be appreciated that the FLA 1996 provides protection to a much wider class of persons than the legislation it replaced. Basically, anyone can apply for orders if they are associated with another.

A person is associated with another person if

(a) They are or have been married to each other.

(b) They are cohabitant-habitants or former cohabitants.

(c) They live or have lived in the same household, otherwise merely by reason of one of them being the other's employee, tenant, lodger or boarder. This will probably include those in a same-sex relationship.

(d) They are relatives.

(e) They have agreed to marry one another (whether or not that agreement has been terminated). Evidence of the agreement to marry is required, e.g. writing, gift of a ring or 'a ceremony'.

(f) In relation to any child they are the parent of the child or a person who has or has had parental responsibility for the child.

(g) They are parties to the same family proceedings.

Protection is also afforded to 'relevant children'. A relevant child means

(a) Any child who is living with or might reasonably be expected to live with either party to the proceedings.

(b) Any child in relation to whom an order under the Adoption Act 1976 or the Children Act 1989 is in question in the proceedings.

(c) Any other child whose interests the court considers relevant.

3. Right to occupy matrimonial home

'Matrimonial home rights' (s. 30) is the new terminology for 'statutory rights of occupation' under the re-enacted MHA 1983.

The MHA 1983 was concerned with a spouse's right to occupy the matrimonial home and how this may be protected and enforced; a fuller discussion can be found in Chapter 6. The previous jurisdiction for ouster orders is replaced by the FLA 1996 and the new 'Occupation Orders'.

OCCUPATION ORDERS

4. Occupation orders

This new order replaces Ouster Orders and Exclusion Orders. The duration of the orders and matters taken into consideration by the courts vary according to the parties' relationship and their entitlement or otherwise to occupy the property.

5. Applicant entitled to occupy the home

Section 33 of the FLA 1996 in effect merges the Matrimonial Homes Act 1983 and the Domestic Violence and Matrimonial Proceedings Act 1976 and the key test is: *Is it their property?*

Section 33(1) applies if a person ('a person entitled') is entitled to occupy a dwelling house by virtue of a beneficial estate or interest or contract or by virtue of any enactment giving that person the right to remain in occupation or has matrimonial home rights in relation to that dwelling house.

The dwelling house must be, or at any time has been, the home of the person entitled and of another person with whom that person is associated. The FLA 1996 extends the definition to include a dwelling house which was at any time intended by the person entitled and any such other person to be their home. This would deal with a situation where the house had been bought but never occupied, for example because it was being repaired or redecorated, or even being built.

The person entitled may apply to the court for an order under s. 33 which may

(a) Enforce the applicant's entitlement to remain in occupation as against the other person.

(b) Require the respondent to permit the applicant to enter and remain in the dwelling house or even part of it.

(c) Regulate the occupation of the dwelling house by either or both parties.

(d) Prohibit, suspend or restrict the exercise by the respondent of any right to occupy the dwelling house.

(e) If the respondent has matrimonial home rights in relation to the dwelling house and the applicant is the other spouse, restrict or terminate those rights.

(f) Require the respondent to leave the dwelling house or any part of it.

(g) Exclude the respondent from a defined area in which the dwelling house is included.

In deciding whether to exercise its powers under this section, the court shall have regard to all the circumstances including

(a) The housing needs and housing resources of each of the parties and of any relevant child.

(b) The financial resources of each of the parties.

(c) The likely effect of any order, or of any decision not to make an order, on the health, safety or well being of the parties and of any relevant child.

(d) The conduct of the parties in relation to each other and otherwise.

The court has complete discretion as to whether or not it will make an order.

These provisions are similar to the MHA 1983 (though wider in scope) and it might be useful to look at some of the existing case law to see how the courts have approached these matters.

Richards v *Richards* (1984). The conduct of the parties need not be violent but there must be something more than trivial complaints.

Blackstock v *Blackstock* (1991). Wife started a fight in which she suffered a broken arm and the husband had a smashed cheekbone. It would be wrong to expel the husband in circumstances where she was equally to blame.

Summers v *Summers* (1986). There were violent quarrels during which husband raged and smashed things but the court stated that an ouster order was a 'draconian' order and would not be made lightly.

T v *T* *(Ouster Order)* (1987). Although children's needs are not first and paramount they are still extremely important. Thus, in this case it was considered right for the court to decide a custody application first and decide the ouster application in light of that decision.

Balance of harm test

By virtue of s. 33(7), if it appears to the court that the applicant or any relevant child is likely to suffer significant harm attributable to the conduct of the respondent if an order is not made, the court shall make the order [i.e. *is under duty to do so*] unless it appears to it that

(a) The respondent or any relevant child is likely to suffer significant harm if the order is made, *and*

(b) The harm likely to be suffered by the respondent or child in that event is as great as, or greater than, the harm which is likely to be suffered by the applicant or child if the order is not made.

An order under this section may, in so far as it has continuing effect, be made for a specified period, until the occurrence of a specified event or until further order.

6. Applicant is former spouse with no existing right to occupy the home

This is an entirely new provision which may not be used very often in practice. Property matters are usually resolved in ancillary proceedings and *have to be resolved* to obtain a decree under the FLA 1996. In any event, it will be a most unusual circumstance that a former spouse would want to return to the former matrimonial home and, not only that, satisfy the criteria for making an order. Nevertheless, s. 35 applies if one former spouse is entitled to occupy a dwelling house by virtue of a beneficial estate, etc. as in s. 33 and the other former spouse is not so entitled. Again, the dwelling house must have been at any time their matrimonial home or was at any time intended by them to be their matrimonial home.

The former spouse not so entitled may apply to the court for an order. If the applicant is in occupation, an order under this section must contain provision:

(a) giving the applicant the right not to be evicted or excluded from the dwelling house or any part of it by the respondent for the period specified in the order *and*

(b) prohibiting the respondent from evicting or excluding the applicant during that period.

(c) If the applicant is not in occupation, the order must contain provisions the same as those in s. 33.

In deciding whether to make an order, the court shall have regard to all the circumstances including not only the matters set out in **5** above but also

(a) The length of time that has elapsed since the parties ceased to live together

(b) The length of time that has elapsed since the marriage was dissolved or annulled *and*

(c) The existence of any pending proceedings between the parties for

51

property adjustment orders under s. 23A or 24 of the MCA 1973, or orders for financial relief under the CA 1989 or relating to the ownership of the dwelling house.

Section 35 also contains a 'balance of harm' provision similar to that in s. 33.

An order under this section may not be made after the death of either of the former spouses and ceases to have effect on the death of either of them. It must be limited so as to have effect for a specified period not exceeding six months, but may be extended on one or more occasions for a further specified period not exceeding six months.

7. Applicant is cohabitant or former cohabitant with no existing right to occupy the home

Section 36 contains identical provisions to s. 35 (*see* **6** above) with the following variations. The circumstances to be taken into account in addition to those listed in above are

(a) The nature of the relationship.

(b) The length of time during which they have lived together as husband and wife.

(c) Whether there are or have been any children who are children of both parties or for whom both parties have or have had parental responsibility.

(d) The length of time that has elapsed since the parties ceased to live together.

There is a 'balance of harm' provision but the courts have a discretion to apply it rather than a duty. The order may only be extended on one occasion (not one or more as in s. 35).

8. Other circumstances

There are provisions in the FLA 1996 identical to s. 35 dealing with an applicant who is a spouse or former spouse and neither applicant nor respondent has right to occupy the dwelling house (s. 37) and with an applicant who is a cohabitant or former cohabitant and neither applicant nor respondent has right to occupy (s. 38).

If application for an occupation order is made under s. 33, 35, 36, 37 or 38 and the court considers that it has no power to make the order under the section concerned, but that it has power to make an order under one of the other sections, the court may make an order under that other section.

9. Additional powers

By virtue of s. 40 the court may on, or at any time after, making an occupation order:

(a) Impose on either party obligations as to repair and maintenance of the dwelling house or the discharge of rent, mortgage or other outgoings.

(b) Order a party occupying the dwelling house or any part of it to make periodical payments to the other in respect of the accommodation.

(c) Grant either party possession or use of furniture or other contents.

(d) Order either party to take reasonable care of same.

(e) Order either party to take reasonable steps to keep the dwelling house and any furniture or other contents secure.

In deciding whether and, if so, how to exercise its power the court shall have regard to all the circumstances of the case including the financial needs and resources of the parties and the financial obligations which they have or are likely to have including financial obligations to each other and to any relevant child.

Children under 16 can apply for an order with leave and if of sufficient understanding. Under Children Act amendments a parent may be removed from the home. Previously, the child had to be removed, usually into local authority care.

NON-MOLESTATION ORDERS

10. Non-molestation orders

Under s. 42 a Non-molestation Order means an order containing either or both of the following provisions:

(a) Prohibiting a person ('the respondent') from molesting another person, who is associated with the respondent.

(b) Prohibiting the respondent from molesting a relevant child.

In deciding whether to exercise its powers under this section and, if so, in what manner the court shall have regard to all the circumstances including the need to secure the health, safety and well being of the applicant or of any relevant child.

There is no definition of molestation so one must turn to existing case law for guidance as to its meaning. Molestation includes a wide variety of behaviour, but the underlying question is: 'Does it cause distress or harm'? The following have been held by the courts to amount to molestation:

Vaughan v *Vaughan* (1973). Visiting the wife's home in the early hours of the morning and late at night and calling at her place of work.

Horner v *Horner* (1982). Repeatedly telephoning the school where the wife worked as a teacher and hanging insulting posters about her on the school railings.

George v *George* (1986). Screaming abuse at the wife when she came to collect the children after access visits.

Spencer v *Camacho* (1983). Searching through a partner's handbag without her consent.

Johnson v *Walton* (1990). Sending semi-nude photographs of a partner to the newspapers with the intention of causing distress or harm.

The order may refer to molestation in general or particular acts of molestation or both and may be made for a specified period or until further order.

INJUNCTION PROCEEDINGS

11. Issue of injunction proceedings

Applications for non-molestation orders or occupation orders can be made ancillary to other family proceedings (s. 42(2)(a) and s. 39(2)) or without the need to issue other proceedings (s. 42(2)(a) and s. 39(2)). The court also has power to make a non-molestation order 'if in any family proceedings to which the respondent is a party the court considers that the order should be made for the benefit of any other party to the proceeding or any relevant child even though no such application has been made' (s. 42(2)(b)).

Proceedings under the Act are started by originating application but the court may grant an injunction *ex parte* (without notice to the respondent and in his absence) if there is a real and immediate danger of serious injury or irreparable damage.

The court means the High Court, the County Court or the Magistrates Court (s. 57), but the latter is not competent to deal with any disputed question as to entitlement to occupy.

12. Enforcement

By virtue of s. 37, where the court makes either an occupation order or a non-molestation order, and it appears that the respondent 'has used or threatened violence against the applicant or relevant child', the court *shall* attach a power of arrest to the order unless the court is satisfied that in all the circumstances of the case the applicant or child will be adequately protected without it.

If the order is made *ex parte,* the court *may* attach a power of arrest if there is violence or a threat thereof, and there is a risk of significant harm to the applicant or child from the respondent if such power is not attached immediately.

If a power is attached, a constable may arrest without warrant a person whom he has reasonable cause for suspecting to be in breach of any such order: s. 47(6). A person so arrested must be brought before the 'relevant judicial authority' within 24 hours, no account being taken of Sundays, Christmas day or Good Friday. The matter may be dealt with immediately, or the person may be bailed or remanded in custody for up to eight days.

Section 58 provides that the 'relevant judicial authority' is:

(a) For breach of a High Court order, a High Court Judge.

(b) For breach of a County Court order, a Judge or District Judge of that or any other County Court.

(c) For breach of a magistrates order, any Magistrates Court.

Where the order does not contain a power of arrest, the applicant can apply to the relevant judicial authority for the issue of a warrant of arrest (s. 47(8)), but it must be substantiated on oath that the respondent has failed to comply with the order.

In any case where the court has power to make an occupation or non-molestation order, the court may accept an undertaking from the respondent but cannot attach a power of arrest: s. 46(1).

If the court thinks a power of arrest is appropriate, it cannot accept an undertaking.

13. The inherent jurisdiction

There may be cases where persons are not associated but one still needs protection from the other. In such circumstances application may be made to the court which has power to grant injunctions from s. 37 of the Supreme Court Act 1981 which also applies to the county court by virtue of s. 38

County Courts Act 1984. It is often said that such orders are made under the inherent jurisdiction of the court but, in fact, that jurisdiction is now codified and consolidated in the Supreme Court Act which provides that a court may grant an interlocutory or final injunction in all cases in which it appears just and convenient to do so.

However, an injunction can be granted only if it is ancillary and incidental to a legal right which the applicant is pursuing in legal proceedings and, in addition, there must be a sufficient link between the main action and the injunction.

> *Patel* v *Patel* (1988). Nephews in a family feud threatened violence to their uncle at his home. HELD An injunction would be granted because they were trespassers.

HARASSMENT

14. The Protection from Harassment Act 1997

This Act came into force on 18 June 1997 as a remedy for 'stalking.' However, it is so drafted that it can include domestic situations as well and could be used as an alternative to both the FLA 1996 and the inherent jurisdiction.

Section 1 of the Act provides that a person must not pursue a course of conduct which amounts to harassment of another and which the person knows or ought to know amounts to harassment. The test is: would a reasonable person possessing the same information think the conduct amounted to harassment. Conduct means that there must be more than one act of harassment.

Sections 2 and 4 create criminal offences but the courts are given power to issue restraining orders forbidding the offender from doing anything specified by the order for the protection of the victim. This is in addition to any other penalty, such as a fine, which the court chooses to impose.

Section 3 creates a statutory tort of harassment and the victim may claim damages for any anxiety caused by or financial loss resulting from the harassment. Section 3(3), which is not yet in force, empowers the High Court or county court to grant an injunction restraining the defendant from pursuing any conduct which amounts to harassment. There will be no power to attach a power of arrest but the applicant will be able to apply for the issue of a warrant. Sections 3(6) and 3(9), also not yet in force, make it an offence to do anything prohibited by an injunction, punishable by up to five years imprisonment on indictment.

It seems possible that, even for associated persons, this will be an alternative and possibly more effective remedy to a non-molestation order but whether the court will allow the FLA 1996 to be 'bypassed' remains to be seen.

Progress test 5

1. Who are associated persons for the purposes of the FLA 1996?

2. Distinguish between an occupation order and a non-molestation order.

3. Outline the differences between orders under ss. 33, 35 and 36 respectively.

4. How might one obtain relief under the Supreme Court Act 1981?

5. What advantages, if any, are there in taking proceedings under the Protection from Harassment Act 1997?

6. H and W live in a house owned by H. After being made redundant, H began drinking heavily and assaulted W on two occasions, causing bruising to her face and arms. H refuses to move out, W has nowhere to go. Advise W.

7. G lived with B in a council flat with their daughter, age 3. The flat is in B's sole name. After B threatened them with violence, G and her daughter went to a women's refuge. What remedies are available to allow her to return to the family home?

PART TWO

Family property and financial provision on divorce

6

Financial obligations during marriage

1. Introduction

During the subsistence of the marriage, there are various ways in which a spouse may obtain financial provision from the other for themselves and for the children of the family. There are two significant points of note concerning these provisions and how these may be enforced:

(a) When the FLA 1996 is fully implemented these remedies will be increasingly important given the compulsory waiting time in the new divorce proceedings between the information meeting and the granting of the decree, especially where no agreement can be reached between the parties.

(b) The Child Support Acts 1991–1995 will be the most likely to provide the basis of maintenance for the natural children of the family, bearing in mind that the Child Support Agency will raise an assessment without resort to the courts. It is probable that spouses will only apply to the courts in cases where they seek a lump sum order or the children are not 'qualifying children'. More detailed consideration of the Acts can be found in Chapter 7.

DUTY TO MAINTAIN

2. The common law duty to maintain

The husband's common law duty to maintain extended to providing his wife with the necessities of life: a home, food and clothing. He could do this by purchasing the necessary items for her or by giving her an allowance to cover their cost. In addition, at common law, wives were presumed to have authority to pledge their husband's credit for necessities while the parties were cohabiting. This was known as the wife's 'agency of necessity'. It was abolished by the Matrimonial Proceedings and Property Act 1970.

In common law a wife had no right to be maintained if the parties were living apart by agreement, or for any reason other than the husband's misconduct. The right to maintenance was co-extensive with the right to consortium. If a wife lost the right to consortium because of her own misconduct, her husband was released from his duty to maintain her.

The common law duty to maintain still exists but is largely unimportant today because of the numerous statutes which enable spouses to enforce maintenance through various courts.

3. Public law duty to maintain

The common law duty to maintain is concerned with the private rights of spouses. Since the introduction of the Poor Law in Elizabethan times there has existed a public law or statutory duty to maintain which is still reflected in our welfare benefits system today.

The Benefits Agency (formerly the Department of Social Security) may seek reimbursement from a liable relative under ss. 24 and 26(3) of the Social Security Act 1986 where income support is paid to a claimant. Income support is the benefit available to anyone over the age of 18 years whose income falls short of a specified level, provided that neither they nor their partner works more than 16 hours per week.

For the purpose of the Act spouses are under a duty to maintain each other and any children they may have. As a result of the Social Security Act 1992, s. 107, that duty is extended to ex-spouses, probably because of the large number of divorce settlements where the husband gave up his interest in the house in return for the wife, or more likely social security, taking on the mortgage repayments. If income support is paid to an unsupported wife, therefore, the state may claim reimbursement, in part or full, from the husband.

Further, under the CSA 1991 each parent has an obligation to maintain a qualifying child and the absent parent may be required to provide financial support for such a child as determined by a maintenance assessment carried out by the Child Support Agency (see Chapter 7).

Payments may be collected from a liable relative by agreement but, if not, may be enforced by a direct order in favour of the Benefits Agency or by diversion of payments due to the claimant under a maintenance order in the claimant's favour.

If a spouse has obtained a maintenance order herself, the court may be authorised to divert any payments made under the order to the Benefits

Agency. The wife will then be able to collect benefit regularly irrespective of whether or not her husband keeps up the maintenance payments.

MAINTENANCE AND SEPARATION AGREEMENTS

4. Scope of the agreements

Spouses may make enforceable agreements regulating their own financial affairs, but the law is concerned to ensure that spouses fulfil their obligations to each other and their children and do not enter agreements in ignorance or under duress. So, spouses are not entirely free to reach an agreement on their own terms and there is a statutory right to apply to the court to vary the terms of an agreement where circumstances have changed.

A *separation agreement* is an agreement between spouses to live apart. It may include other terms regulating their financial affairs, including provision for payment of maintenance. A *maintenance agreement* is a private agreement between spouses which provides for the payment of maintenance. It may also include other financial arrangements but it will not deal with separation. Maintenance and separation agreements are binding and enforceable in accordance with the usual principles of contract law.

Agreements which undermine the institution of marriage will be void on the ground that they are contrary to public policy. Thus a separation agreement which provides for the immediate separation of the parties will be valid. An agreement which regulates their legal rights in the event of a possible separation in the future will not. The only exception to this rule is a reconciliation agreement which may contain provisions governing a future separation should the reconciliation fail.

As with any other contract, a maintenance or separation agreement may be invalid if there is evidence of fraud, duress, undue influence or mistake.

Sections 34 and 36 of the MCA 1973 contain special rules which apply to any maintenance agreement as defined by the Act.

Section 34(2) defines maintenance agreements broadly as agreements making financial arrangements between spouses when living separately, including rights and liabilities with respect to the maintenance or education of any child, whether or not a child of the family.

It is clear from the statutory definition that the Act will apply to a wide range of agreements between spouses (or ex-spouses) in addition to agreements for the payment of maintenance. Separation agreements that make no express financial provision may be included. Agreements relating to the occupation of the matrimonial home or the use of the family car may be maintenance agreements since they contain financial arrangements.

Where ss. 34 and 36 apply there are two principal effects:

(a) A term restricting the right to apply to a court for financial provision will be void: s. 34(1). This provision does not preclude a court from taking into account the terms of any agreement (and the circumstances in which it was made) when considering a subsequent application for financial relief.

> *Edgar* v *Edgar* (1980). The wife accepted property worth £100,000 and agreed not to apply to the court for ancillary relief in divorce proceedings. When she later petitioned for divorce, the restriction was held to be void but the Court of Appeal refused to make a lump sum order. The wife had accepted the original settlement after receiving professional advice which she had chosen to disregard.

(b) Either party may apply to a court to vary the terms of the agreement: s. 35(1). Applications may be made to a divorce county court during the lifetime of the parties, provided that at least one of them is for the time being domiciled or resident in England and Wales. A family proceedings court also has power to vary an agreement, provided that both parties are resident in England and Wales and at least one party resides in the commission area for the court.

The court must be satisfied that by reason of a change in the circumstances in the light of which any financial arrangements were made or omitted from the agreement (including a change foreseen by the parties when making the agreement) the agreement should be altered or that the agreement does not contain proper financial arrangements with respect to any child of the family.

In either case, any maintenance provision made or varied by the court will last for whatever period the court may specify but this may not exceed the joint lives of the parties (where the payments are unsecured) or the life of the payee (where the payments are secured): s. 34(4). In either case, payments must cease on the remarriage of the recipient. Where maintenance payments for children are made, they must comply with the usual age limits.

Section 36 enables applications for variation to be made after the death of one party where the agreement provides for payment to continue, provided that the paying party was domiciled in England and Wales at the date of death. Application can be made by the surviving party or the personal representatives of the deceased, but must be made within six months of the date when representation was taken out except with leave of the court. Only the High Court or the county court may hear applications under s. 36.

FINANCIAL PROVISION IN MAGISTRATES' COURTS

5. Domestic Proceedings and Magistrates Courts Act 1978

Where spouses do not reach an agreement, it may be necessary to seek a financial order in the courts. The family proceedings court has had power to make financial orders in domestic cases since 1878. The modern jurisdiction arises from the DPMCA 1978 which extended to the family proceedings court a system very similar to that in operation in the divorce courts. It is possible for a family proceedings court to make maintenance and lump sum orders in favour of a spouse or a child of the family under three separate provisions depending on the circumstances.

6. The Section 1 grounds

The family proceedings court may make a financial order where an applicant satisfies one of the grounds contained in s. 1 of the Act. It is important to note that the behaviour and desertion grounds which were identical to s. 1(2)(b) and s. 1(2)(c) of the MCA 1973 are repealed by the FLA 1996. The remaining grounds are as follows:

(a) *Failure to provide reasonable maintenance for the applicant.*
This is simply a question of fact whether the provision made by the respondent is reasonable. It is not necessary to show that the respondent's failure is deliberate or the result of negligence. The respondent may not even be aware that the payments are insufficient.

In practice, the courts will almost always need to consider the means and needs of the parties in order to determine whether any provision made by the respondent is reasonable.

An application may be made on this ground in the High Court or county court and it may be helpful to consider the way in which the matter is approached in the higher courts. First the court is to have regard to all the circumstances in deciding whether the ground is made out. Then it is expressly required to consider the matters set out in s. 25, MCA 1973 (*see* 9:11) which include (*inter alia*) the income, earning capacity and resources of the parties and their conduct where it would be inequitable to disregard it. In the family proceedings court the justices are also required under s. 3 to consider such matters when deciding whether to exercise their powers to make an order but not, strictly speaking, when deciding whether the initial ground is proved.

(b) *Failure to provide, or make proper contribution towards, reasonable maintenance for any child of the family.*

Child of the family as defined in s. 88 means

(*i*) A child of both parties *and*

(*ii*) Any other child who has been treated by both parties as a child of the family, excluding any child placed with the parties as foster parents by a local authority or voluntary organisation.

What constitutes behaviour towards a child to make him or her a child of the family will depend on the facts of each individual case (*D* v *D* *(Child of the Family)* (1980)) but must be judged objectively: how would the reasonable person interpret such behaviour? It is immaterial, therefore, that a wife has deceived her husband as to the child's paternity [*W(RJ)* v *W(SJ)* (1971)], although this may affect the way in which the court decides to exercise its discretion to make an order.

An unborn child cannot be treated as a child of the family, as treatment involves behaviour and it is only possible to behave towards a child who is living and 'capable of being perceived by one or more of the senses': Bagnall J in *A* v *A* (1974).

Once the ground is established, s. 3(3) specifies the matters which the court must take into account when deciding what order, if any, to make. In this context, first consideration must be given to the welfare of any child of the family under the age of 18 years.

There are no bars, as such, to the making of an order under the Act, except for the general rule contained in s. 127 Magistrates' Courts Act 1980 which requires an application to be made within six months of the date when the ground for making the application arose.

The family proceedings court may properly refuse to hear an application where the financial issues are complex or where the High Court is already dealing with substantially the same matter and there is a possibility of conflicting orders.

If the ground in s. 1 is proved, the court may make periodical payment orders and lump sum orders in favour of the applicant and any child of the family, under s. 2. Periodical payment orders will provide for maintenance to be paid at such intervals as the court thinks appropriate and may be ordered for a specified period. Where an order is made in favour of a child of the family, the court may order payment direct to the child or to the applicant for the child's benefit.

Lump sum orders may be made in favour of the applicant and any child of the family, but the award cannot exceed £1,000 on any one occasion.

When making an order under s. 2, the court is required to take into account the following matters:

(a) When deciding whether and how to exercise such powers, it has a duty to have regard to all the circumstances of the case but to give first consideration to the welfare of any minor child of the family who is not yet eighteen; s. 3(1).

(b) When making a periodical payments or lump sum order by virtue of s. 3(1) it must have particular regard to the following matters:

(i) The income, earning capacity, property and other financial resources which each of the parties has or is likely to have in the foreseeable future, including in the case of earning capacity any increase in that capacity which it would in the opinion of the court be reasonable to expect a party to take steps to acquire.

(ii) The financial needs, obligations and responsibilities which each party has or is likely to have in the foreseeable future.

(iii) The standard of living enjoyed by the parties before the occurrence of the conduct which is alleged as the ground of the application.

(iv) The age of the parties and the duration of the marriage.

(v) Any physical or mental disability of either party.

(vi) The contributions which each party has made or is likely in the foreseeable future to make to the welfare of the family, including any contribution by looking after the home or caring for the family.

(vii) The conduct of each party, where in the court's opinion it would be inequitable to disregard it.

Where the order is in favour of a child, the court must also have regard to:

(a) The financial needs of the child.

(b) The child's income, earning capacity (if any), property and other financial resources.

(c) Any physical or mental disability.

(d) The standard of living enjoyed by the family before the occurrence of the conduct which is alleged as the ground of the application.

(e) The manner in which the child was being, and in which the parties expected him to be, educated or trained.

Where a child of the family is not the child of the respondent, s. 3(4) requires the court to have regard to:

(a) Whether the respondent has assumed any responsibility for the child's maintenance and if so, to what extent, for how long and on what basis.

(b) Whether the respondent did so knowing that the child was not his.

(c) The liability of any other person to maintain the child.

Because of the provisions of the CSA 1991–1995, the court is most likely now to be considering applications for orders for periodical payments against a party to the marriage who is not the natural parent of the child in question, and the factors laid down in s. 3(4) will be of particular relevance.

These guidelines are substantially the same as those which apply under s. 25 MCA 1973 when a court is considering an application for financial relief in divorce proceedings; much of the case law relating to s. 25 is also relevant to applications in the family proceedings court (see Chapter 9).

7. Agreed orders

Section 6 contains a special procedure for making orders by agreement. Either party may apply on the ground that either he or his spouse has agreed to make financial provision as set out in the application.

The court may then make an order in the agreed terms if it is satisfied that:

(a) The respondent has agreed *and*

(b) It would not be contrary to the interests of justice to make the order.

Section 6(9) provides that where a respondent is not present or legally represented at the hearing of an agreed application, the court cannot make an order unless it has evidence of the respondent's consent and details of financial resources.

The powers of the court when making an agreed order are no wider than usual except that there is no upper limit for lump sum orders. The agreement will determine the duration of the order, otherwise the courts' usual powers apply.

8. Section 7: voluntary separation orders

Where spouses have been living apart for a continuous period of three months or longer, neither party has deserted the other, and the other party has during the three months preceding the application been making periodical payments for the benefit of the applicant or a child of the family, the other spouse may make an application under s. 7 notwithstanding that no grounds exist under s. 5, 1 or 6.

The court may make a periodical payments order in favour of the applicant and any child of the family (provided that the CSA 1991 does not apply) but not a lump sum order. Quantum is determined by reference to voluntary payments made by the respondent prior to the application, and the applicant has to specify the aggregate amount of payments made during the three months before the application. Any order made by the court must not then exceed this, or any amount it may have ordered under s. 1.

If the application is for the benefit of a child of the family who is not the respondent's child, the court must not make an order unless it would have done so under s. 1.

When considering these matters, the court must be guided by the factors listed in s. 3 (*see* 6 above). When considering the previous standard of living enjoyed by the parties, the court must look at the period before they separated.

9. Interim orders

A considerable period may sometimes elapse between the making of an application and the final hearing. To avoid hardship during this period, the court is given power under s. 19 to make an interim order for periodical payments for a spouse and any child of the family, where appropriate. Interim orders may also be made by the High Court if it orders the magistrates to rehear an application following an appeal under s. 29 or an earlier refusal to hear the case by the magistrates under s. 27.

An interim order may be backdated to the date of application. It may last a maximum of three months (s. 19(5)) but may be extended by a further order or orders not exceeding in total a period of three months (s. 19). An interim order will automatically cease to have effect when the court makes a final order or dismisses the application.

10. Duration of orders

An order for the benefit of a spouse may not commence before the date of application or extend beyond the death of either party: s. 4(1).

The order may continue beyond divorce, unless the divorce court otherwise orders, and the remarriage of the payee will also terminate the order, even if that marriage is subsequently found to be void or voidable.

An order obtained under s. 7 will cease to have effect if the parties resume cohabitation and an order under s. 2 or s. 6 may be made while the parties are actually living together but will terminate if they continue to live together or resume cohabitation for a continuous period exceeding six months.

A maintenance order which provides for payment direct to a child (and not to the applicant for the child's benefit) will not be affected if the parties resume cohabitation unless the court so directs (s. 25(2)), but such orders are subject to the usual age limits. These provide for orders to cease on the child's 17th birthday in the first instance although they may be extended to 18 years and beyond if the child's welfare requires it and

(a) The child is, or will be, or if an order were made would be, receiving instruction at an educational establishment, or undergoing training for a trade, profession or vocation, whether or not the child is also, or will also be, in gainful employment, *or*

(b) There are special circumstances which justify this course.

Section 5(3) applies to the making of orders as well as their duration. Under s. 5(1) no order for periodical payments or a lump sum may be made in favour of a child who has attained the age of 18 years unless the criteria in s. 5(3) apply.

11. Variation of orders

The court may vary or revoke a periodical payments order (including an interim order) whether made under s. 2, 6 or 7. It may suspend or revive a provision of the order (s. 20(6)), usually where a respondent loses his job. The order can then be revived as soon as he obtains employment again.

In certain situations, a lump sum order may be made on an application for variation: s. 20(1). Where, for example, the original order was made under s. 2, the court may make an order, subject to the maximum limit of £1,000, even if there has already been an earlier lump sum order: s. 20(7). It is not unusual for this power to be used where payments have been irregular and arrears have accrued.

If the original order was made by agreement under s. 6, a lump sum order can be made on variation and may exceed the limit of £1,000 if the respondent agrees.

There is no power to order a lump sum payment on an application to vary a periodical payments order made under s. 7 because the court had no power to order a lump sum on the original application.

Either party may apply for variation. Where an order is made in favour of a child, the child may also seek variation if over the age of 16: s. 20(12).

When considering an application, s. 20(11) requires the court to give effect to any agreement reached between the parties where it is just to do so. If there is no agreement or the court refuses to implement one, it must have regard to all the circumstances of the case but give first consideration to the welfare of any child of the family who is under 18 years. Section 20(11) specifies that the circumstances of the case shall include any change in the matters which the court was obliged to consider when making the original order, i.e. the factors set out in s. 3.

There is no power to vary a lump sum payment but where the original order provides for payment by instalment the court may vary the number or amount of the instalments and the date on which they fall due.

FAILURE TO PROVIDE REASONABLE MAINTENANCE

12. Financial orders in the High Court and county court

Most applications for financial orders in the High Court or county court are made in the course of divorce proceedings, but a spouse may also seek a financial order in the higher courts on the grounds of failure to provide reasonable maintenance: s. 27 MCA 1973.

There is one single ground for an application under s. 27. Either party to a marriage may apply if the other has

(a) failed to provide reasonable maintenance for the applicant *or*

(b) failed to provide, or to make proper contribution towards, reasonable maintenance for any child of the family.

The jurisdiction is similar in many ways to that of the family proceedings court under the DPMCA 1978 but there are marked differences which may make one procedure more appropriate than the other in particular circumstances.

Under s. 27:

(a) The court has power to make a secured periodical payments order. It may also secure instalments of a lump sum payment.

(b) There is no upper limit to the lump sums which may be ordered.

(c) Interim orders may be made without time limit.

(d) An order may still be enforced even if the parties continue or resume cohabitation after the order is made. In the family proceedings court the order will automatically cease if cohabitation continues for six months.

However, the procedure is seldom used, probably because the divorce jurisdiction offers a wider range of orders for capital provision and an applica-

71

tion under s. 27 will be more expensive than a similar application under the DPMCA 1978.

Application should be made to the county court but the case may be transferred to the High Court if it is defended or this is considered desirable for some other reason. Under the Domicile and Matrimonial Proceedings Act 1973 the court will have jurisdiction if:

(a) Either party is domiciled in England and Wales when the application is made *or*

(b) The applicant has been habitually resident here throughout the period of one year ending with that date *or*

(c) The respondent is resident here on that date.

13. Orders under s. 27 MCA

The court may order secured or unsecured periodical payments and unlimited lump sum payments for the applicant and any child of the family.

No restriction is placed on the use of lump sum orders but s. 27(7)(a) specifically provides that they are available to meet any liability or expenses reasonably incurred in maintaining the applicant and any child of the family prior to the order. The court may direct that a lump sum be paid by instalments which may be secured.

Periodical payments orders may be backdated to the date of application. An unsecured order in favour of a spouse will last for the joint lives of the parties unless the court specifies a shorter period or it terminates for other reasons: s. 28(1)(b). A secured order can last for the life of the payee. Both types of order may continue even if the marriage is dissolved or annulled, but will terminate on remarriage of the payee: s. 28(2).

The duration of orders in favour of children is governed by s. 29 which contains the same provisions as s. 5 DPMCA 1978 (*see* **10** above).

14. Factors to be taken into account

The court is given guidance on the factors to be taken into account in deciding whether the respondent has failed to provide reasonable maintenance and what order, if any, to make.

These are continued in s. 25(2) of the MCA and are substantially the same as applied under s. 3 DPMCA 1978 (*see* **6** above), and also when the court is considering an application for financial provision in divorce proceedings subject to the following minor differences:

(a) The court is not required to give first consideration to the welfare of any child of the family under the age of 18 unless financial provision is sought for that child. In the family proceedings court, and also in divorce proceedings, the welfare of any minor child of the family must always be first consideration.

(b) In s. 27 applications the court is required instead to consider the family's standard of living as it was before the failure to maintain, as opposed to before the breakdown of the marriage.

(c) A s. 27 application does not terminate a marriage and there is no requirement to consider loss of benefits such as pension rights.

Where an application is made for failure to maintain a child of the family, the court must have regard to all the circumstances of the case including the matters listed in s. 25(3) and must give first consideration to the child's welfare.

In addition, if the respondent is not the natural father of the child, the court must take into account the matters referred to in s. 25(4) (see Chapter 9).

15. Variation

The court has power to vary, discharge, suspend or revive a periodical payments order (including an interim order) under s. 31. There is also a separate power under s. 27(6B) to revive a maintenance order in favour of a child of the family.

The court cannot vary the amount of a lump sum order but it may vary the amount or date of any instalments and, where these are secured, it may vary the security.

A lump sum order can be made on variation of a periodical payments order in favour of a child but not a spouse: s. 31(5).

MAINTENANCE PENDING SUIT

16. Maintenance pending suit

Under existing divorce law, a periodical payments order in favour of a spouse can only take effect from decree absolute (or final decree in the case of judicial separation). Since the need for financial support will often arise before that time, the court can order one party to make periodical payments to the other in the form of a maintenance pending suit: s. 22 MCA 1973. However, since the introduction of the 'special procedure' in divorce, the decree absolute may be made before a determination of an order pending suit. When the FLA 1996 comes fully into force, property matters will have to be resolved *before* the decree of divorce or judicial separation. As a result, maintenance pending suit will disappear.

Either spouse may apply for maintenance pending suit and it is immaterial whether they are petitioner or respondent in the proceedings. There is no power to order maintenance pending suit for children, as the court has power to make a periodical payments order for their benefit at any time in the proceedings.

In the case of the children, it is most likely that their maintenance will be dealt with under the CSA 1991 (see Chapter 7).

The court may order maintenance pending suit at any time between the filing of the petition and final decree, and must end on determination of the suit, whether by final decree or dismissal.

Section 22 contains no guidance on the matters to be taken into account by the courts when considering an application for maintenance pending suit. The court must make whatever order it thinks 'reasonable'. It will have to consider the financial needs of the applicant and the respondent's ability to pay: *Peacock* v *Peacock* (1984). The previous standard of living enjoyed by the parties will also be relevant.

> *Re T (Divorce: interim maintenance and discovery)* (1990). The parties' standard of living was held to justify an order of £25,000 per annum, although the court was also influenced by a previous agreement made between the parties.

The availability of welfare benefits may also be relevant.

Progress test 6

1. How may a spouse obtain maintenance from another during the subsistence of the marriage?

2. What powers do the family proceedings court have to order maintenance, and in what circumstances?

3. What matters will be taken into account when making such orders?

4. Explain the powers of the High Court to make orders for financial provision when no divorce proceedings are pending.

5. How may parties reach agreement as to maintenance, and what powers exist to vary such agreements?

6. What do you understand by the expression 'maintenance pending suit'?

7. H went to work abroad on a two-year contract, but told his wife W that he would probably not return because he could not stand her cooking or domestic habits. They entered into a written agreement that he would pay her a notional sum of £25 per week, on the basis that she was in full time employment at that time.

H has returned to the UK with a new cohabitant partner and child but W has been out of work for several months. There is little prospect of full time employment in the region where she lives. Advise W, who is religiously opposed to divorce.

7

Child support

1. Introduction

The then Conservative government in 1990 issued a White Paper entitled *Children Come First* and proposed legislation requiring an 'absent parent' to make a significant contribution to the support of (normally) the child or children.

To achieve this ambition, the Child Support Act 1991, which came into force in April 1993, established a Child Support Agency ('the Agency') to investigate, assess and enforce such payments. The agency ousted the jurisdiction of the court. There was no discretion and no appeal.

The controversy surrounding the implementation of the Act is well documented. Its failings were exposed within a relatively short period of time and the Chief Executive of the Agency resigned amidst constant allegations that it was the Treasury, not children, who came first.

The outcome was that the government produced another White Paper, *Improving Child Support*, which implemented changes by the Child Support Act 1995, supplemented by regulations which implement many of the changes with effect from April 1995.

For the purposes of this chapter, and indeed the book, references to the CSA are references to the 1991 Act as amended by the regulations and the 1995 Act.

2. The purpose of the Act

The basic principle of the CSA is set out in s. 1(1) by stating that each parent of a qualifying child is responsible for maintaining the child.

The aim of the CSA is to try to ensure that *absent parents* (whether married or not) make a more significant contribution to the support of their natural children but not of their step-children. The obligation placed on the absent parent is to make payments for a *qualifying child* as determined by a maintenance assessment: s. 1(3). The definition extends to adopted children, and applies to children under 16 or under 19 if still in full time education.

An absent parent is defined in s. 3(2) of the CSA as the parent who is not living in the same household with the child where the child has its home with a person who is, in relation to it, *a person with care.* In deciding who is absent and who has care, the ultimate criteria is that the person with whom the child spends less than 187 nights in a year is 'absent!'

3. Calculating child maintenance

A formula will be applied to determine the appropriate level of child maintenance in each case. The formula is extremely complicated but is designed to be applied in every assessment so that consistency in determining the level of child maintenance is achieved. Whilst this is a laudable aim, the rigidity of the formula does not always achieve those objectives. In a recent case, decided on other grounds, a millionaire was assessed by the Agency as having no income!

(a) The first step in calculating the level of child maintenance is to establish the *maintenance requirement.* This is basically the amount equivalent to the level of income support which would be payable in respect of the child in question, subject to the deduction of child benefit. The result is that there is an element of financial support for the caring parent.

(b) It is then necessary to calculate the *assessable income* of each parent. This is the balance of net income after deducting exempt income, which is the amount designed to cover basic living expenses. However, the parties' actual living expenses are irrelevant because living expenses are based on income support rates relevant to each party's domestic circumstances. Since April 1995, reasonable housing cost is allowed in full.

However, hire purchase, loan and credit card payments made by the absent parent, even if for the benefit of the caring parent, will not be taken into account.

(c) Once assessable income is calculated, the next step is to apply the *basic deduction rate* of 50% to the couple's combined assessable income. If the resulting figure is equal to or less than the maintenance requirement, each parent is liable for half their assessable income.

For example, where the family has a maintenance requirement of £70, the absent father has an assessable income of £140, and the mother has no income of her own, the father would be required to pay one-half of his assessable income, i.e. £70 per week.

Even if the absent parent is in receipt of income support, that parent will still be required to make a minimum contribution of £4.80 per week, unless living with other children.

(d) Where the basic deduction rate exceeds the maintenance requirement, the additional element method must be used instead. Having satisfied the maintenance requirement using the basic deduction rate, *an additional deduction rate* of between 15% and 25% (depending on the number of qualifying children) is applied to the balance of the assessable income. But, since April 1995, the absent parent will not be assessed to pay maintenance of more than 30% of net income under the formula, subject to the minimum amount of £4.80 per week.

(e) So that the absent parent does not fall below subsistence level a *protected income level* may be applied. This means that the maintenance assessment would be adjusted to ensure that the absent parent and his or her new family do not fall below subsistence level.

(f) Where both parents have an assessable income, their liability to pay maintenance is directly proportionate to their share of the combined assessable income.

4. Position of the putative father

Where the alleged father denies paternity for the purposes of child maintenance, s. 27 of the CSA provides that the Secretary of State or the carer of the child may apply to the court for a declaration of parentage. The court can then direct DNA testing to be carried out.

Where the child support officer makes a finding of paternity on the evidence and proceeds to make a maintenance assessment, the putative father may appeal to the family proceedings court.

This apart, a court has no jurisdiction to make orders for child maintenance except in the following circumstances:

(a) In respect of step-children.

(b) In respect of children aged 16 years or over who are in receipt of advanced education or training for a trade profession or vocation.

(c) In respect of children of wealthy parents where 'top-up' provision would be appropriate because there is a ceiling on the level of maintenance payable under CSA.

(d) In respect of school fees for children.

(e) In respect of the additional needs of disabled children.

The jurisdiction of the court is unaffected in respect of lump sum or property adjustment orders.

5. Benefit cases

Where the carer parent is in receipt of income support, family credit, or disability working allowance, that parent is required to authorise the Secretary of State to take action to recover child support maintenance from the absent parent: s. 6.

The carer parent is required to complete and return a maintenance application form and to give information to enable the absent parent to be traced, the amount of child support maintenance payable by the absent parent to be assessed, and that amount to be recovered from the absent parent: s. 6(9).

Where the carer parent refuses to authorise the Child Support Agency to seek maintenance or to provide them with information to assess the maintenance liability of the absent parent, that parent's benefit may be reduced: s. 46.

The carer parent is offered an opportunity to explain the failure to co-operate, and if the officer of the Agency considers that there are reasonable grounds for believing that the claimant or child would suffer harm or undue distress, no further action will be taken. In exercising any discretion, the officer is required to have regard to the welfare of any child likely to be affected by the decision: s. 2. However, where no reasonable grounds are established, the benefit will be reduced for a period of 12 months by 50% and then 25% for a further six months.

6. Non-benefit cases

Where the carer parent is not in receipt of family credit or income support, there is a choice so far as claiming maintenance for the child is concerned:

(a) to apply to the Agency for a maintenance assessment *or*

(b) to enter into a maintenance agreement with the absent parent *or*

(c) to rely on Child Maintenance (Written Agreements) Order 1993.

However, any attempt to restrict the right to apply a maintenance assessment is void: s. 9(4).

7. The effect on clean break orders

In view of the foregoing provisions, clean break orders whereby one spouse pays a lump sum to the other with no periodical payments will become less common, because the absent parent is going to be required to provide a greater level of support than previously. The fact that the absent parent has given up an interest in a substantial asset, i.e. the home, will not affect the assessments under the formula.

In respect of pre-CSA agreements the 1995 changes provide that where the absent parent transferred capital, usually in the form of the matrimonial home, to the parent with care, a further allowance calculated according to the value of the property transferred will be given.

No additional allowance is given if the value of the transfer was less than £5,000. Where the value is between £5,000 and £9,999 the additional allowance to be added to exempt income is £20 per week. Between £10,000 and £24,999 the allowance is £40 per week and where the value exceeds £25,000 the allowance is £60 per week.

8. Departure directions

The 1995 Act seeks to incorporate greater flexibility into the scheme by a series of *departure directions* which the Secretary of State may implement if two conditions are fulfilled:

(a) The case falls within one or more of the cases set out in Part 1 of Schedule 4 *and*

(b) It is his opinion that it would be just and equitable to give the departure direction.

The overall effect of a departure direction will be to permit the Agency to take account of additional expenses borne by the absent parent, the fact that the absent parent has transferred property to the parent with care or that the parent with care is not utilising an asset to maximise its income-producing potential so as to reduce the maintenance assessment which would otherwise be payable.

The additional or *'special expenses'* include:

(a) Costs incurred in long-distance travelling to work. With the exception of self-employed parents travelling in excess of 150 miles per week will be allowed.

(b) Costs incurred by an absent parent in maintaining contact with the child such as travel expenses.

(c) Debts incurred before the parent became an absent parent in relation to the child. Debts are not defined, but certain debts such as gambling debts, trade or business debts and use of credit cards are excluded.

(d) Pre-1993 commitments which it is impossible or would be unreasonable to expect the parent concerned to withdraw from.

(e) Costs incurred by a parent in supporting a child who is not his but is part of his family.

Each is subject to rigorous conditions before it can qualify for consideration and, even then, the Secretary of State must form the opinion that it would be just and equitable to grant a departure direction. In making a decision he must take into account:

(a) The financial circumstances of the absent parent.

(b) The financial circumstances of the parent with care.

(c) The welfare of the child.

(d) Whether a direction would result in a relevant person ceasing paid employment

There are also matters he cannot take into account, including

(a) Who was responsible for the breakdown.

(b) The existence of a new relationship.

The procedure for an application is to be made by regulation, but it must be made in respect of an existing maintenance assessment, state the grounds for departure and state whether it is based on

(a) The effect of the current assessment *or*

(b) A change in the circumstances of the case since the assessment was made.

Progress test 7

1. What are the purposes and underlying principles of the Child Support Act 1991?

2. Outline the principles for the calculation of child maintenance.

3. Explain the residual role of the court in respect of child maintenance.

4. To what extent has the Child Support Acts affected clean break orders under the MCA?

5. Give a brief description of the matters which come within the Departure directions of Part 1 Schedule 4 of the CSA 1995.

8

Matrimonial property and the family home

1. Introduction

Spouses do not always agree on the ownership of property and it may be necessary to resolve disputes in the courts. When seeking a divorce, judicial separation or a decree of nullity, the courts have wide powers to redistribute family assets and property whatever arrangements they may have made previously (*see* Chapter 9). But there are circumstances where it is important to determine property rights during the subsistence of the marriage, because the parties do not seek a divorce or because third parties, such as a building society, claim an interest.

However, spouses do not always formalise property matters but, nevertheless, the principles of property and trust law apply to determine ownership and beneficial interests just the same as with everyone else.

Cohabitants obviously have no recourse to the divorce courts and their only remedies lie in these areas. There are a number of procedures available.

PROPERTY RIGHTS

2. The Married Womens Property Act 1882 s. 17

The MWPA 1882 provides a summary procedure for the determination of property rights. It is available to

(a) Spouses

(b) Former spouses, within three years of decree absolute with leave of the court under s. 39 Matrimonial Proceedings and Property Act 1970

(c) Couples who were formerly engaged to marry, within three years of termination of the engagement by virtue of s. 2(2) Law Reform (Miscellaneous Provisions) Act 1970.

There is no power to adjust or alter property rights on a s. 17 application. The court may make such order with respect to the property as it thinks fit, usually a declaration as to the respective interests of the parties and, where appropriate, an order for sale.

Section 17 applies to all property, real or personal, and even property no longer in the possession or control of the parties.

3. General principles as to common funds

Difficulties arise where spouses pool their incomes into a common fund, such as a joint bank account. In such cases they will each have a joint interest in the whole fund: *Jones* v *Maynard* (1951). If one dies, the survivor will normally take all. If one party purchases an item with funds withdrawn from the joint account that item will belong to that person unless there is evidence to the contrary.

> *Re Bishop [deceased]* (1965). Shares purchased by a wife in her own name from funds withdrawn from the joint account were her absolute property.

Where the fund is fed by the husband alone, the presumption of advancement will operate to give the wife a joint interest: *Re Figgis [deceased]* (1969).

Where the wife alone feeds the fund, prima facie the husband will hold the fund on resulting trust for his wife in the absence of evidence to the contrary: *Heseltine* v *Heseltine* (1971).

However, in the important cases of *Pettit* v *Pettit* (1970) and *Gissing* v *Gissing* (1971) the House of Lords cast some doubt upon the modern relevance of the presumptions of advancement and resulting trust.

4. Married Womens Property Act 1964 s. 1

By virtue of s. 1 a wife is given an equal share in any money she is able to save from a housekeeping allowance provided by her husband, unless there is evidence of contrary intention.

The Act only applies post-implementation of the Act on 25 March 1964. The old common law rules apply to payments made before that date and to housekeeping allowances made by wives to husbands, which is basically that the money and any property purchased with it will belong to the spouse making the allowance: *Blackwell* v *Blackwell* (1943).

The Act is not particularly important because of the construction of the phrase 'housekeeping allowance'.

5. Ownership of gifts

Wedding gifts will belong to the parties jointly if that was the intention of the donor. In the absence of evidence to substantiate this, they will belong to the spouse whose relative or friend donated them: *Samson v Samson* (1960). This will also apply to other gifts such as anniversary presents given to the parties jointly during the marriage but not to individual gifts such as birthday and Christmas presents.

When it comes to gifts between spouses, it is not always apparent what were the parties intentions. Where the property is clearly for personal use, e.g. jewellery, intention will be obvious and the physical handing over of the gift will amount to delivery and perfect the gift. Where the property will continue to be used by both parties, such as furniture, there is no apparent change of possession and the court is reluctant to infer delivery: *Re Cole* (1963).

TRUSTS AND THE FAMILY HOME

6. The matrimonial or family home

The matrimonial home is often a family's major asset and disputes concerning its ownership have given rise to much litigation. It is important to remember that on divorce the courts have wide powers under the MCA 1973 to redistribute family property. However, those who can't divorce (because they have never married) or those who won't divorce (because of religious objection) must rely on the following principles.

A beneficial interest in land can only be created or transferred by a signed written document, unless it comes into being as a result of an implied, resulting or constructive trust: Law of Property Act 1925, s. 53(2). This section has been utilised extensively by the courts to determine property rights in the matrimonial home.

Where a conveyance or transfer expressly names the parties in whom the legal title and any beneficial interests are to vest, this will be conclusive in the absence of fraud or mistake: *Goodman v Gallant* (1986).

7. Resulting, implied or constructive trusts

If the property was conveyed into the sole name of one spouse, the other will have no interest unless the existence of a trust can be established: *Pettit v Pettit* (1970) and *Gissing v Gissing* (1971). The House of Lords also dismissed any concept of family or community property, as recognised in a number of jurisdictions in the United States. Their Lordships stated that only Parliament had authority to so do, and in the subsequent three decades since their judgment Parliament has shown no inclination to implement such a concept.

To establish a trust, a non-owning party must first satisfy the court that there was a common intention that the property should be jointly owned though not necessarily in equal shares. The court will then look at the conduct of the parties to ascertain whether there was common intent.

The joint decisions of *Pettit* and *Gissing* make it clear that a trust cannot be created simply because it seems fair to do so.

Where a non-owning spouse makes a direct contribution towards the cost of purchasing the property there is a (rebuttable) presumption that the parties intend to create a resulting trust: *Falconer* v *Falconer* (1970).

The contribution may take a variety of forms, but to establish an interest the partner must have paid all or part of the purchase price, or the deposit, or may have made a direct contribution towards the mortgage repayments.

Where a husband pays for a property but places it in his wife's name the presumption of resulting trust may sometimes be rebutted by the presumption of advancement, that is that it was an outright gift. *Pettit* appears to have made it clear that advancement between spouses is an outdated concept.

If a spouse makes an indirect contribution towards the cost of purchase or improvement of the property, the court may imply a trust if there is evidence of common intention and it is clear that the non-owning spouse has acted to his or her detriment in relying on that intention.

In *Eves* v *Eves* (1975) Lord Denning referred to this as 'a constructive trust of a new model' and was prepared to recognise a general contribution to the home, including looking after the children, as giving rise to a proprietary interest. It is in conflict with *Gissing*, even though purportedly following it, and no more has been heard of the new model constructive trust since Lord Denning's retirement. However, Ms Eves succeeded in her claim because the two other judges, whilst refusing to follow Lord Denning, found that there was evidence of common intention because the male partner had told her that the house had to be in his name because she was under 21 (the then age of majority). Why else should he make an excuse?

Similarly, in the case of *Grant* v *Edwards* (1986) the court was prepared to infer a common intention because it was clear from the evidence that the parties had shared everything and had always treated the house as if it belonged to them both. The male partner had also made the excuse that the house should be in his sole name 'because otherwise it might cause difficulties with her divorce'.

Midland Bank v *Dobson and Dobson* (1986). There was a common intention to share a beneficial interest in the property but the wife's claim failed as she had suffered no detriment. She had made neither direct contribution towards the deposit nor the mortgage and her only indirect contribution was to purchase some household equipment and redecorate the property.

In *Lloyds Bank* v *Rosset* (1990) the House of Lords took the opportunity to review the case law through the speech of Lord Bridge, the other Law Lords concurring. He saw two situations:

(i) Where there was common intention, evidenced by agreement, even if based on 'ill remembered conversations, however imprecise the terms,' and acted upon to the other party's detriment

(ii) In the absence of agreement, conduct which would lead to the presumption of a trust.

In the instant case, Mrs Rosset spent seven weeks decorating and supervising workmen so that a derelict house would become habitable for the family in time for Christmas. Nevertheless, their Lordships thought her contribution was 'trifling,' 'no more than any wife would do' and insufficient to infer a common intention that she should have a beneficial interest in the property. Indeed, Lord Bridge went so far as to say that only direct contributions to the deposit or the mortgage instalments would satisfy the common intention.

This decision, in particular, disadvantages women, especially those who stay at home to look after children and have no income of their own to contribute towards the mortgage. However, the Court of Appeal in the case of *Midland Bank* v *Cooke and Another* (1995) seem to have reverted to the notion adopted by Lord Denning in *Eves* v *Eves*. The Court found that there was a direct contribution to the purchase price by the wife in the form of a joint gift from the husband's parents of the deposit on their first house. Once an interest is established, the court is permitted to 'undertake a survey of the whole course of dealings between the parties relevant to their occupation and ownership of the house and their sharing of its burdens and advantages'. The Court then went on to say that (*inter alia*) the rearing of three children and the provision of a home for the family were relevant factors and the wife was awarded a half share. 'One could hardly have a clearer example of a couple who had agreed to share everything equally.'

These factors were disregarded in *Pettit, Gissing* and *Rosset*, but if the decision in *Cooke* allows a partner to be rewarded by a proprietary interest, it is to be welcomed.

87

8. The Matrimonial Proceedings and Property Act 1970

Section 37 of this Act gives to a spouse a share or increased share in the beneficial interest of property, real or personal, where they have made a *substantial contribution to its improvement*.

A contribution may be in money or money's worth. A party could therefore pay for an improvement to the property or actually carry out the improvement himself or herself. But the improvement must be substantial.

The Act applies only to improvements and not to the routine maintenance work although the difference can sometimes be difficult to define.

> *Pettit* v *Pettit* (1970). Lord Reid suggested that the work should be of a capital or non-recurring nature, not simply D.I.Y.

> *Davis* v *Vale* (1971). The payment for the connection of mains electricity and the provision of a water heater, sink unit and fireplaces were considered to be substantial.

9. Quantification of the beneficial interest

Where a beneficial interest has been established by operation of a resulting, implied or constructive trust it will be necessary to quantify that interest. Again the court will look at the intention of the parties. Where it is not easy to ascertain, it is usual to apportion the share in proportion to the contribution made by the claimant over the whole period of ownership: *Re Rogers Question* (1948).

Where the contribution has been erratic, the court may fall back on the equitable maxim that 'equality is equity'. Unless there is evidence to the contrary, the parties' share will be calculated from the date of sale, not from the date the relationship broke down: *Turton* v *Turton* (1988). Where the departure is entirely voluntary, it may be necessary to give credit for a proportion of both capital and interest elements: *Dennis* v *Macdonald* (1982).

The decision in *Midland Bank* v *Cooke* (1995) should not be overlooked because that was an example of the court taking into account the whole history of the relationship.

10. Protecting a beneficial interest against third parties

Having established a beneficial interest in a property, it is important to protect that interest in the event of a sale or mortgage to a third party.

If the title is registered, the equitable interest of a spouse in actual occupation of the property may be an overriding interest under s. 70(1)(g) of the

Law of Property Act 1925 (LPA 1925). In *Williams and Glyn's Bank Ltd* v *Boland* (1981) two husbands had mortgaged their homes to the bank to secure their business overdraft but their wives, who had contributed to the acquisition and were in occupation, knew nothing of the arrangement. The bank had made no enquiry and their interest was overridden by that of the wives.

If the title is unregistered, a prospective purchaser or mortgagee will only be bound by a spouse's equitable interest where he has actual or constructive notice of it; *Williams and Glyn's Bank Ltd* v *Boland* (1981) held that the courts will expect third parties to make reasonable and thorough enquiries to ascertain who is in occupation of a property and what interest they may have.

> *Kingsnorth Trust Ltd* v *Tizard* (1986). The home was in his name. After separation, W stayed when H was away and cared for the children. H applied for a mortgage and arranged a survey at a time when W was staying away. HELD W was still in occupation.

> *Barclays Bank* v *O'Brien and Another* (1994). Wife claimed husband had misrepresented the nature of the mortgage. She thought it was only on the house, in fact it extended to his company's overdraft and she had acted under his undue influence. HELD by the House of Lords: The bank were put upon enquiry, fixed with husband's notice and the mortgage was set aside.

A spouse with an equitable interest in the matrimonial home will also have a right of occupation which can be protected by registration (*see* 12 below).

MATRIMONIAL HOME RIGHTS

11. Matrimonial Homes Act – right to occupy the matrimonial home

Statutory rights were created by the Matrimonial Homes Act 1967 (amended by the Matrimonial Homes Act 1983 and now contained in Schedule 4 of the Family Law Act 1996) following the decision in *National Provincial Bank* v *Ainsworth* (1965) that a personal right of occupation did not bind third parties. The legislation not only gives a non-owning spouse a right of occupation but also creates machinery for registering that right so as to bind third parties such as purchasers and mortgagees.

12. Matrimonial home rights

Matrimonial home rights (formerly called the statutory rights of occupation under the MHA 1983) arise where one spouse has a proprietary right of occupation and the other does not.

Section 30 of the FLA 1996 extends matrimonial home rights to a spouse who has only an equitable interest in the property. This would include a wife who claims to be entitled to a beneficial interest under a resulting, implied or constructive trust as discussed above.

Section 30(2) defines matrimonial home rights as follows:

(a) If in occupation, a right not to be evicted or excluded from the dwelling house or any part thereof by the other spouse except with the leave of the court.

(b) If not in occupation, a right with the leave of the court so given to enter into and occupy the dwelling house.

These rights will only arise if a property is occupied or has at one time been occupied as the matrimonial home.

They will not apply, for example, to a cottage owned by one spouse and used only for holidays. They may, on the other hand, exist in relation to several properties where a couple has more than one home.

The right will cease to exist if the marriage is terminated by death or divorce. In the event of a matrimonial dispute or estrangement, however, the court has power to extend a spouse's right of occupation which would otherwise be terminated, provided that an application is made during the marriage: s. 33(5).

13. Enforcing matrimonial home rights

One spouse may wish to enforce his or her rights against the other or limit the partner's right to occupy. He, or more usually she, may also wish to protect and enforce those rights against third parties.

Under s. 33 the court has power to make a variety of orders relating to the occupation of the matrimonial home, on the application of either party, provided that one spouse has matrimonial home rights under the Act.

The need to protect matrimonial home rights against third parties is of vital importance if a non-owning spouse is to avoid having the home sold or mortgaged over his or her head. Where a spouse has matrimonial home rights, these may be protected by registration, either as a Class F Land Charge where the title is unregistered, or by entry on the register where the title is registered.

Once registered, the matrimonial home rights will be a charge upon the property and no sale or mortgage may take place unless the spouse with rights consents or the registration is discharged by the court. When considering an application to discharge a registration the court has a wide discretion and may consider not only the circumstances of the spouse whose matrimonial home rights are in issue but also the circumstances of the person applying for discharge. Usually this will be the other spouse but occasionally it may be a purchaser who has bought the property in ignorance of the charge: *Kashmir Kaur* v *Gill* (1988).

Where a matrimonial home is rented, a tenant's spouse will have matrimonial home rights under s. 30(4) and cannot be evicted by the tenant. The spouse may seek a court order declaring or regulating those rights in the usual way.

A tenant's spouse may pay the rent in lieu of the tenant and will then be protected from eviction by the landlord. The spouse's occupation will be treated as possession by the tenant for the purposes of the housing legislation and the spouse may therefore be entitled to security of tenure until the marriage comes to an end.

14. Cohabitants

The principles of trust law which enable a non owning spouse to claim an interest in the matrimonial home by contribution also apply to a cohabitant. However, the courts have been less willing to infer a common intention to create a beneficial interest where the contribution has been indirect.

> *Burns* v *Burns* (1984). A cohabitant's contribution to the housekeeping expenses and purchase of certain household equipment during the course of a nineteen-year relationship was held to be insufficient and not directly referable to the mortgage repayments made by her partner. The court did indicate, however, that a more substantial contribution, clearly freeing a partner to repay the mortgage, would suffice.

Section 37 of the Matrimonial Proceedings and Property Act 1970 does not apply to cohabitants. The position regarding improvements is therefore uncertain. Generally, a person will acquire no beneficial interest in the property of another by expending money or labour on it: *Thomas* v *Fuller-Brown* (1988). Nevertheless the courts have been prepared to infer a common intention to create a beneficial interest where a mistress engaged in heavy and skilled building work to improve the property: *Cooke* v *Head* (1972).

The summary procedure under s. 17 MWPA 1882 (*see* **2** above) is not available to resolve property disputes between cohabitants. Where the beneficial ownership of the family home is in issue, therefore, cohabitants must seek a declaration of trust under s. 30 LPA 1925. Where a dispute relates to personal property or cash, their position will be the same as that of any two individuals in dispute.

Cohabitation will not give rise to a personal right to occupy the family home if it is owned by the other party. Neither does a cohabitant have matrimonial home rights under the FLA 1996. The courts have, however, been prepared to imply a contractual licence to occupy the home in certain circumstances.

> *Tanner* v *Tanner* (1975). A man was unable to regain possession of a house he had purchased for his mistress and two children after the relationship came to an end. The Court of Appeal decided that there was an implied contractual licence entitling the mistress to occupy the property while the children were of school age.

> *Hammond* v *Mitchell* (1992). Waite J confirmed the need for a cohabitant, who is claiming a beneficial interest, to be able to demonstrate the existence of an agreement or understanding based on an express discussion and confirmed by action or, in the absence of such an agreement, whether an intention to share the beneficial interest could be imputed to the parties.

15. Engaged couples

Law Reform (Miscellaneous Provisions) Act 1970 contains provisions relating to engaged couples and what is to happen to their property on termination of the engagement. It allows formerly engaged couples access to the same machinery for resolving disputes as married couples and applies to them the same legal principles.

Section 2(1) extends to formerly engaged couples the same rules of law as apply to spouses for the determination of beneficial interests in property acquired during the engagement. These are the rules discussed above including the presumptions of advancement and resulting trust, where applicable, and the statutory provision relating to improvements contained in s. 37 Matrimonial Proceedings and Property Act 1970.

The Act also deals with gifts. An engagement ring is presumed to be an absolute gift and is not therefore returnable on termination of the engagement. This presumption may be rebutted by proving that the ring was given on condition that it would be returned if the marriage did not take place.

Other gifts between the parties conditional upon the marriage taking place may be recovered, even by the party responsible for terminating the engagement: s. 3(1).

Progress test 8

1. Explain who may use the summary procedure under s. 17 MWPA 1882.

2. What principle governs the ownership of family property?

3. How do spouses and cohabitants establish an interest in their matrimonial or family home?

4. In 1990, M asked F to live with him at his house. When she agreed, M said that, although the house was in his name, 'she should treat the place as her own' and he would transfer it into joint names 'when the time was right'. F only worked for a short time before she was made redundant. She used some of her redundancy pay to refurbish the kitchen but made no other financial contribution to the home. This year, M threw her out because he could no longer stand her laziness. Advise M now that F has made a claim to have an interest in the home.

5. What rights may a wife have in the matrimonial home owned solely by her husband?

6. H and W provided the deposit on their first home jointly, the balance being provided by a mortgage from a building society. The house was in H's sole name because he was the only wage earner. They moved to a new house without further injection of capital. H re-mortgaged the house to the bank to secure his business overdraft. Some years later, H left, W remained. The bank now seek a possession order in default of mortgage repayments. Advise W.

9

Financial relief on termination of marriage

1. Introduction

The courts have wide powers to make financial orders after divorce, nullity and judicial separation, often referred to as ancillary relief. Although ancillary to the divorce proceedings, since the introduction of the 'special procedure', the resolution of property and maintenance matters is probably the most important, and contentious, part of the divorce proceedings for both parties.

Orders may affect the income or the capital of the parties. There are two types of income order: maintenance pending suit and periodical payments, which may be secured or unsecured. There are several orders which provide for the redistribution of capital. The court may make a lump sum order and a transfer of property order. It may order one party to settle property on the other and it may vary an existing settlement. It also has power in certain circumstances to order a sale of property.

It is also appropriate in this chapter to consider the provisions made for family and dependants on the death of a person.

FINANCIAL PROVISION ORDERS

2. Periodical payments orders

The court may order one spouse to make regular payments to the other, usually on a weekly or monthly basis. The application may be made by either party, whether petitioner or respondent, though it is more common for wives to apply when they have children to care for.

A periodical payments order cannot be made until the decree is granted: s. 23(1) MCA 1973. In the case of divorce and nullity that means decree absolute; s. 23(5).

The wording of s. 23 makes it clear that an application for ancillary relief may be made on the granting of the decree or 'at any time thereafter', provided that the applicant has not remarried before lodging the application.

Twiname v *Twiname* (1992). The Court of Appeal allowed a former wife to apply for a lump sum order even though the divorce decree was granted in 1974.

The court may order the payer to give security for the payments: s. 23(1)(b). This means that the payer must transfer property or investments to trustees and execute a deed. The income of the secured fund may then be used to pay the periodical payments. The recipient may resort to the fund (first the income and then the capital) in default of payment.

3. Duration of orders

An order may be backdated to the date of application. Where the applicant is the petitioner, this will usually be the date of the petition, provided that it contained a prayer for ancillary relief. If the respondent is applying, this will usually be the date the respondent filed an answer to the petition or filed an application for ancillary relief where proceedings are undefended and no answer is filed.

An unsecured order can only last for the joint lives of the parties but a secured order may continue after the death of the payer. Both types of order will terminate if the recipient remarries: s. 28(1).

These provisions operate to fix the maximum duration of an order. The court may specify a shorter term and is encouraged to do so by the so-called 'clean break' provisions of s. 25A. Their purpose is to limit financial dependence after divorce or nullity to the shortest possible period which is both just and reasonable. When making a periodical payments order, therefore, the court is now required to consider whether it would be appropriate to limit the order to a period sufficient to enable the recipient to adjust without undue hardship to supporting herself: s. 25A(2).

4. Lump sum orders

Under s. 23(1)(c) the court can order one party to make a cash payment to the other. Only one lump sum order may be made but it may be paid in instalments: *Coleman* v *Coleman* (1972). These may be secured in the same way as periodical payments (s. 23(3)(c)) and payment may be deferred to a future date.

A lump sum order can only be made after decree nisi and may only take effect on decree absolute. Either party may apply and application is made in the same way as for a periodical payments order.

An existing lump sum order, whether payable by instalments or otherwise, will not be affected by the remarriage of the recipient, but a person who has remarried cannot apply for a lump sum order against a former spouse.

A lump sum order can be made for any purpose and it may reduce or exclude periodical payments. However, s. 23(3) specifically provides that it may be used to enable a spouse to meet expenses and liabilities reasonably incurred before application.

PROPERTY ADJUSTMENT ORDERS

5. Transfer of property

Orders for the transfer of property from one spouse to the other are made under s. 24(1)(a). They are commonly made in relation to the matrimonial home but any assets, including reversionary interests in property, may also be transferred in this way. The power extends to property acquired before or after marriage and includes local authority tenancies. The transfer may be made to the spouse, any child of the family or any person for the benefit of such child.

6. Settlement of property

Section 24(1)(b) empowers the court to settle property on another. This power can be used, for example, to set up a trust fund for the benefit of the wife until her death or remarriage and thereafter for the children. It has been most commonly used in relation to the matrimonial home whereby a trust is created for the wife to remain in occupation until the children are grown up, then the property sold and the proceeds divided between the former spouses: *Mesher* v *Mesher* (1980). For a number of reasons, these orders have recently fallen out of favour (*see* 8 below).

7. Variation of settlement

The court may vary the terms of any antenuptial or post-nuptial settlement made for the benefit of the spouses and/or the children of the family: s. 24(1)(c). It may also extinguish or reduce either party's interest under such a settlement. The term 'settlement' has received a wide and generous interpretation by the courts.

E v *E* *(Financial Provision)* (1990). The matrimonial home was purchased by the husband's father and settled on discretionary trusts for the benefit of the spouses and their children. When the marriage broke down, the father-in-law, who was a trustee, rejected the wife's claim to an interest in the property. The court removed him as trustee and varied the trust to provide a lump sum of £250,000 for the benefit of the wife and children.

Brooks v *Brooks* (1995). The House of Lords confirmed that a pension scheme entered into by the husband, which allowed him to make provision for a pension for his spouse, was capable of being a post-nuptial settlement, which could be varied by the court to give the former wife an immediate annuity and a pension in the future.

8. Orders for sale

The court has power to order the sale of specified property on or after making an order for secured periodical payments, a lump sum or property adjustment: s. 24A. The order can be made after decree nisi (in the case of divorce or nullity) but cannot take effect until decree absolute: s. 24A(3).

An order for sale may relate to any property in which either party has an interest in possession or reversion, including the proceeds of sale. Rule 2.64(3) Family Proceedings Rules 1991 enables the court to order possession of property which it has ordered to be sold, thus preventing one party from seeking to frustrate the terms of the order by refusing to vacate the property. The order may have conditions imposed, for example that it be offered for sale to a specified person or persons or that the order not take effect until the expiration of a specified period.

The power to make an order for sale is essentially ancillary to the power to order capital or secured provision. It may be used to enable a spouse to satisfy a capital order or to enforce an order already made but not complied with.

THE NEW PROVISIONS OF THE FAMILY LAW ACT 1996

9. The new provisions of the FLA 1996

When the FLA 1996 comes into effect, the principles relating to financial orders are substantially changed. Schedule 2 of the FLA 1996 amends the MCA 1973 to provide that

(a) In the case of divorce or separation, an order about financial provision may be made under that Act *before a divorce order or separation order is made, but*

(b) to retain the position under the Act where marriages are annulled.

Section 9 deals with arrangements for the future and provides that on application for a divorce order there must be produced one of the following:

(a) A *court order* dealing with financial arrangements.

(b) A *negotiated agreement* as to the financial arrangements.

(c) A *declaration by both parties* that they have made their arrangements.

(d) A *declaration by one of the parties* that there are no arrangements to be made, e.g. because the party has significant assets and needs no support or the other party has no assets.

There are four exemptions to s. 9, contained in Schedule 1:

(a) Application to the court is frustrated because the other party has delayed in complying with the requirements of the court or has otherwise been obstructive, or, for reasons beyond both parties' control, the court has been prevented from obtaining the information it requires.

(b) No agreement is likely to be made because of illness, etc. and delay would be detrimental to a child or prejudicial to the applicant.

(c) No agreement because the other party cannot be contacted.

(d) Applicant has an occupation or non-molestation order, agreement is unlikely and delay would be detrimental or prejudicial.

There is no power to make any order before the statement of marital breakdown has been filed so a spouse in need of financial help will have to apply under the DPMCA 1978 (see Chapter 6). There is already a number of pilot schemes in operation under the Practice Direction: Ancillary Relief Procedure Pilot Scheme [1997] 2FLR 304. The intention is to reduce delay, facilitate settlements and reduce costs. The process involves a full and detailed disclosure in Form E (already unpopular with some practitioners) and a direct referral by the District Judge ('unless it is not appropriate in the circumstances') to a Financial Dispute Resolution appointment. The objective is to 'reduce the tension which inevitably arises in matrimonial and property disputes'. The court will expect parties to make offers and proposals, to respond and give proper consideration to them and 'to use their best endeavours to reach agreement on relevant matters in issue before them.'

THE GUIDELINES FOR DETERMINING ANCILLARY RELIEF

10. The statutory guidelines

Section 25 of the MCA 1973 (as amended by the MFPA 1984) gives guidance to the court in deciding whether and, if so, how to exercise its powers:

(a) The court must have regard to all the circumstances of the case but give first consideration to the welfare while a minor of any child of the family under 18 years: s. 25(1).

(b) The court must have particular regard to the specified matters listed in s. 25(2).

(c) The court must consider and apply the 'clean break' provisions of s. 25A as appropriate.

The court is required to consider all the circumstances but give first but not *paramount* consideration to the welfare of any minor children of the family.

> *Suter* v *Suter and Jones* (1987). The original order met the full cost of mortgage repayments in respect of the family home. Whilst this ensured that the children had a roof over their heads, the trial judge had not taken into account the fact that the wife's cohabitant could make a contribution to household expenses, thus relieving the husband. The Court of Appeal reduced the husband's periodical payments accordingly.

11. Matters taken into account

Whilst the court is required to consider all the circumstances, the Act lists specific matters which must be taken into account. These are found in s. 25(2):

(a) *The income, earnings capacity, property and other financial resources which each of the parties to the marriage has or is likely to have, including in the case of earning capacity any increase in that capacity which it would in the opinion of the court be reasonable to expect a party to the marriage to take steps to acquire.*

The court is concerned with the actual income of the parties and their potential income, where any earning capacity is not fully exploited. Earnings will obviously be taken into account, including overtime. A spouse who chooses to take a low-paid job for personal reasons, when there is clear evidence that more could be earned elsewhere, may be penalised.

Hardy v *Hardy* (1981). The court fixed periodical payments at a level commensurate with the husband's potential rather than actual earnings.

Williams (LA) v *Williams (EM)* (1974). In contrast, the unemployed husband had been ordered to pay periodical payments on the basis that he ought to have found work. On appeal, the court laid great weight on the findings of the DSS that he was not voluntarily out of work.

In *Attwood* v *Attwood* (1968) the court held that a wife's earning capacity should only be taken into account if it is reasonable to expect her to work and it may be unreasonable to expect her to work because of her age, her absence from the job market or the responsibilities of caring for young children. These factors may also be relevant where she does work.

M v *M (Financial Provision)* (1987). The court accepted that a wife's earning capacity as a secretary would inevitably be low after 20 years of marriage and virtual absence from the job market.

Leadbeater v *Leadbeater* (1985). The husband suggested that a 47-year-old wife retrain in the use of modern office equipment in order to boost her earning capacity, but the court held this was unreasonable.

Daubney v *Daubney* (1976). 'Property and other financial resources' includes all capital assets, welfare benefits and even damages for personal injuries.

The court can take into account money or property which a spouse is likely to inherit and assets acquired after separation.

Schuller v *Schuller* (1990). The wife inherited a flat and some £4,000 from a friend after she had separated from her husband, but these assets were still taken into account in deciding the size of the lump sum the husband should be required to pay.

If a spouse has a new partner, his or her financial resources may only be taken into account insofar as they relieve a spouse from certain financial obligations which might otherwise have to be met. However, the court cannot make an order which either directly or indirectly requires a new partner to support the applicant and children of the first family.

(b) *The financial needs, obligations and responsibilities which each of the parties to the marriage has or is likely to have in the foreseeable future.*
Obligations and responsibilities often require the court to balance the needs of a spouse's old and new families.

In *Delaney* v *Delaney* (1990) the Court of Appeal accepted that an ex-husband was entitled to balance his future aspirations for a new life against his responsibilities to his former family.

If a husband takes on unreasonable obligations, however, the court will not be so generous.

> *Slater* v *Slater* (1982). The court disregarded the cost of maintaining an expensive country house which the husband had chosen to occupy when he could have lived less extravagantly elsewhere, and the substantial travel expenses incurred in choosing to live a long way from his work.

Case law shows that in relation to 'needs', there are no absolute standards beyond the minimum level of bed and board. Nevertheless, the courts have been more than willing to accept that the ex-wife of a wealthy man may have greater needs than the wife of a poorer man.

> *Leadbeater* v *Leadbeater* (1985). The wife had enjoyed a lavish lifestyle during a four-year marriage. Nevertheless, the court rejected her need for a three-bedroomed house and £20,000 to furnish it and provided instead for a two-bedroomed house, £10,000 to furnish it plus a small car and £6,500 per year for household and private expenses.

In *Preston* v *Preston* (1982) the court held that needs are 'reasonable requirements'. The husband had capital assets of £2.3m and an income of £40,000 per year. The court considered it reasonable for the wife to have a home worth up to £300,000 and a further cash sum of £600,000.

In *Gojkovic* v *Gojkovic* (1990), the court held that there was no ceiling on a spouse's reasonable needs. A wife who had built up a successful hotel business with her husband was awarded £1.3m to enable her to acquire a new hotel of her own.

(c) *The standard of living enjoyed by the family before the breakdown of the marriage.*

The previous standard of living of the parties is now just one of the factors to be taken into account by the court, losing the greater importance it held before 1984; a dependent spouse had a right to a 'reasonably decent' standard of living where the parties had been married for some time: *M* v *M* (*Financial Provision*) (1987).

In marriages of shorter duration, the courts have taken into account not only the applicant's lifestyle during the marriage but the way the applicant lived beforehand.

> *Attar* v *Attar* (1985). The wife had been an air stewardess earning £15,000 p.a. before she married a millionaire. The marriage lasted only six months and she was awarded a £30,000 lump sum.

(d) *The age of each party to the marriage and the duration of the marriage.*
Age of itself is not important, but it has relevance to other factors, such as earning capacity and financial needs. Younger spouses are more likely to be able to work and/or resume careers and their circumstances lend themselves to clean break orders, whereas elder spouses, particularly wives, are more likely to need ongoing maintenance: see *M* v *M* (*Financial provision*) (1987).

As to the effects of the duration of the marriage, see *Attar* v *Attar* (above).

(e) *Any physical or mental disability of either of the parties to the marriage.*
There is no reported case law relating to this section, probably because a disability will usually affect the earning capacity of a spouse and his or her needs.

(f) *The contributions which each of the parties has made or is likely in the foreseeable future to make to the welfare of the family, including any contribution by looking after the home or caring for the family.*
This provision recognises that a spouse who looks after the home and children contributes as much to the welfare of the family as a husband or wife who works. This is in sharp contrast to the considerations taken into account by the court in deciding whether a spouse has a proprietary interest in the home during the subsistence of the marriage (see Chapter 8).

In much the same way the court will take into account a wife's contribution, often unpaid, to the husband's business. In *Gojkovic* v *Gojkovic* (1990) and *Conran* v *Conran* (1997) substantial lump sums were awarded in recognition of such contribution. In the former case, the award was calculated on the cost of the acquisition of a new hotel business for the wife to run, but the arrival at the figure in *Conran* is less clear.

(g) *The conduct of each of the parties,* **whatever the nature of the conduct and whether it occurred during the marriage or after the separation of the parties or dissolution or annulment of the marriage,** *if that conduct is such that it would in the opinion of the court be inequitable to disregard it.*
The words in bold were added by the FLA 1996 on the insistence of some MPs who thought that conduct was not sufficiently taken into account. How much difference it will make in practice is yet to be seen.

When it is 'inequitable to disregard' conduct was considered in *Wachtel* v *Wachtel* (1973). The Court of Appeal held that the conduct of the parties was only relevant to ancillary relief applications where it was 'both obvious and gross'. Such conduct could affect not only the court's exercise of its discretion to make an order but also the amount of any order made.

Conduct under this head must amount to more than the usual petty acts and squabbles which might be expected on marital breakdown.

Kyte v *Kyte* (1987). The wife actively assisted her depressed husband in a suicide attempt with a view to inheriting and setting up home with her lover. A lump sum of £14,000 was reduced to £5,000 on appeal.

Evans v *Evans* (1989). The husband was discharged from an existing periodical payments order following the wife's conviction for incitement to murder him.

Leadbeater v *Leadbeater* (1985). The court held that it was not inequitable to disregard the wife's multiple adultery as the husband's conduct had been equally as bad.

Following the decision in *Kokosinski* v *Kokosinski* (1980), it would seem that the court may also take 'good' conduct into account. In that case the court considered it inequitable to disregard the wife's exemplary conduct during many years of cohabitation prior to a short marriage. It was impossible to take her contribution into account under s. 25(1)(f) as it occurred before marriage and s. 25(1)(g) was therefore used to support a claim to the family business.

(h) *In the case of proceedings for divorce or nullity of marriage, the value to each of the parties of any benefit (for example, a pension) which, by reason of the dissolution or annulment of the marriage, that party will lose the chance of acquiring.*
The right to share in a spouse's pension entitlement is a valuable benefit which is lost on divorce or annulment. The loss will obviously be greater where the parties are approaching retirement age after a long marriage.

Following the decision of the House of Lords in *Brooks* v *Brooks* (1995) s. 166 of the Pensions Act 1995 amended the MCA 1973 by removing the words 'in the foreseeable future' from the original wording of paragraph **(a)** above and specifically directing the courts to give full consideration to pension rights in addressing paragraphs **(a)** and **(h)**.

Thus, the court can take into account any pension benefits which have accrued to the parties, irrespective of the length of time before the pension becomes payable, and may order the trustees or managers of the scheme to pay part of the pension and/or lump sum to the other (ex)spouse. This is called 'earmarking' and it appears to be left entirely to the court's discretion whether to make an order and, if so, for how much.

There has been considerable criticism of this provision and, in response, the Government produced a Green Paper in September 1996 entitled *The Treatment of Pensions on Divorce*. Since then the present Labour Government has announced a wholesale review of pension provision and this particular area is likely to be in an unsatisfactory state for some time to come.

12. The clean break

Even before the clean break provisions were given statutory authority in 1984, the courts had considered such settlements. In *Minton* v *Minton* (1979), Lord Scarman said: 'The object of modern law [was] to encourage each party to put the past behind them and to begin a new life which is not overshadowed by the relationship which has broken down'. The clean break provisions introduced in the MFPA 1984 were intended to achieve this.

Section 25A(1) imposes a duty on the court, when it has decided to exercise its powers to make property and financial orders in favour of a party to the marriage, to consider whether it would be appropriate to do so in a way which will terminate financial obligations between the parties as soon after decree as the court considers just and reasonable.

Where the court decides to make a periodical payments order, it must consider whether it would be appropriate to limit those payments to a period sufficient to enable the recipient to adjust without undue hardship to the termination of financial dependence on the other party: s. 25A(2).

When making a fixed-term order, the court is given power under s. 28(1A) to direct that no application may be made for the order to be extended.

> *Hedges* v *Hedges* (1991). The Court of Appeal made a periodical payments order, limited in duration to 18 months, to enable a wife in a short, childless marriage, to obtain a better-paid job.

If the court order does not include a specific prohibition on seeking an extension of a time-limited order, a party cannot be prevented from seeking such an extension: *Richardson* v *Richardson* (1994). In that case, it had clearly been agreed that there would be a clean break and the wife would not apply for an extension. However, the order did not contain a specific prohibition. HELD She could apply for, and indeed got, an extension to the term.

If the court considers that no continuing obligation to maintain should be imposed on either party, it may dismiss all applications for periodical payments and direct that no further applications may be made: s. 25A(3).

> *Waterman* v *Waterman* (1989). The judge at first instance made a periodical payments order limited to five years. He also barred the wife from seeking an extension. The marriage had been short and the wife was relatively young. However, the child was only five and it was impossible to predict with certainty that the wife would be able return to work when he was ten. The Court of Appeal, therefore, varied the order by removing the prohibition on extension.

M v *M (Financial Provision)* (1987). The court doubted whether a 47-year-old wife would be able to support herself after five years, or any other period for that matter, and it was unjust to expect her to do so after a 20-year marriage. A clean break was not appropriate.

Where there are no capital assets and a spouse is dependent on State benefits, the court cannot apply the clean break provisions in isolation. It must also consider the public interest in ensuring that the burden of maintenance is not passed on to the State. Clearly there are two principles of public policy at stake here and in each case the court must strike a balance between them in order to achieve a just result. In *Ashley* v *Blackman* (1988) he was an artist who just made enough from his sales to support himself and his second family. His former wife lived on State benefits but there had been numerous applications for variation. HELD This was 'a classic instance' for applying the clean break. No humane society could tolerate a divorced couple of limited means 'remaining manacled to each other' even in the interests of saving the public purse.

Where neither the recipient nor the State is likely to benefit from periodical payments, the court may approve a clean break even where there are no capital assets. In *Seaton* v *Seaton* (1986), for example, the husband had suffered a disabling stroke. His only income was a State disability pension and he was cared for by his parents. In due course it was expected that he would enter residential care. The court felt that periodical payments by the wife would have no effect on the husband's life as he had no significant needs to be met. A clean break order was therefore made with immediate effect.

Where a spouse is on State benefit, the court must ensure that the clean break order does not impose a maintenance burden on the State.

The CSA 1991 has made clean breaks more difficult for families with children, other than the more wealthy, because the Agency will impose a maintenance assessment on the absent parent irrespective of any capital settlement. In addition, s. 107 of the Social Security Administration Act 1992 now allows the Department to recover benefits paid to a person from their former spouse. Previously, payments could only be recovered during the subsistence of the marriage.

Putting these principles into practice does not always produce predictable results. There is no clearly accepted formula to determine the amount of periodical payments or capital provision. Whilst the court can make a range of orders in relation to the matrimonial home, the actual orders made in any given case are not consistent. However, certain formulae have received judicial approval from time to time, and certain orders have fallen into, then out of, favour.

13. Quantum

Historically, the 'one-third rule' provided a starting point for calculation of a wife's entitlement to both maintenance and capital assets. More recently, the courts have been prepared to recognise its usefulness as a starting point for calculation: *Wachtel* v *Wachtel* (1973).

When applied to periodical payments, a wife could expect to receive payments which will bring her income up to one third of the spouses' joint income. But it must take into account tax liability, housing costs and the availability of welfare benefits: *Furniss* v *Furniss* (1982), *Stockford* v *Stockford* (1982).

The 'one-third rule' presupposes that a spouse will receive at least one third of the capital assets and separate provision for the children. If a wife is to receive a larger share of the capital assets, it may be necessary to reduce periodical payments and vice versa.

The 'one-third rule' is no more than a starting point for calculation. The court must assess the net effect of the order and is unlikely to make an order which would reduce the payer below subsistence level (*Shallow* v *Shallow* (1978)). In practice, therefore, the actual needs and requirements of the parties are likely to carry just as much weight with the court as the entitlement to a notional one third.

Also, the level of financial support required to be provided by an absent parent under the CSA 1991 will mean the level of periodical payments for a spouse will inevitably be reduced.

An alternative method of calculation based upon the needs of the applicant rather than a fixed proportion of the assets was formulated in the case of *Duxbury* v *Duxbury* (1987). The so-called 'Duxbury principle' requires the court to award a cash sum which would produce enough to meet the recipient's needs for life. Accountants and investment consultants were consulted and a computer program used to determine the lump sum which would achieve the desired result.

It is the need to predict such matters accurately which limits the application of the Duxbury principle. Thus in *B* v *B* (1990) Ward J described it as a 'useful tool' but stressed that the court retained a wide discretion under s. 25 and had to remember that future events were unpredictable. A wife might therefore be entitled to a larger sum than one that merely covered her needs.

In *F* v *F* (*Ancillary Relief; Substantial Assets*) (1995) Thorpe J held that a simple Duxbury calculation was not appropriate for a 36-year-old mother of three who had only been married seven years. Having had produced to him refined Duxbury calculations he also held that it should be recognised that income requirements would fall in later years and the graph of expenditure is a declining one. He went on to base his assessment on s. 25 needs and reasonable requirements and awarded the wife various sums totalling in all around £9 million.

In *Conran* v *Conran* (1997) similar considerations were applied and the wife was awarded £10.25 million, the largest sum awarded in ancillary proceedings in this country. Part of the award also recognised the 'substantial contribution' made by the wife in building up the husband's business empire but, even so, the sum total was considerably less than one-third of the husband's wealth.

14. The matrimonial home

The considerations referred to in Chapter 8 concerning occupation and ownership of the matrimonial home have no application on termination of marriage. The courts' only considerations are those contained in s. 25 MCA 1973.

Therefore, the court can make a lump sum order whereby one spouse will lose all interest in the property but will receive a cash payment from the other, often raised by way of mortgage on the property.

If the remaining spouse cannot make an immediate lump sum payment, this may be deferred and the spouse who leaves will usually be given a charge over the property. In *Knibb* v *Knibb* (1987), for example, the property was transferred to the wife but she was required to execute a charge in favour of her husband for 40% of any future net proceeds of sale, and he could enforce his security on the wife's death, remarriage or if she voluntarily decided to move.

Alternatively, the matrimonial home could be transferred outright to one spouse, usually the wife, and periodical payments are reduced to a minimum or dismissed altogether. This leaves the husband with more income to meet his future housing needs and provides the wife with a home which she could not otherwise have purchased. Although popular in the 1980s, the impact of the CSA 1991 and the changes in social security rules make it difficult to carry out in practice.

The court may order an immediate sale, but is unlikely to do so where there are young children. Their needs are probably best met by use of a settlement order.

The most common settlement order is the Mesher Order. This is an order for the sale of the property and division of the proceeds, postponed during the dependency of the children. It preserves the property as a capital asset for both parties and as a family home. In *Mesher* v *Mesher* (1980) the

107

husband intended to remarry. There was a substantial equity in the matrimonial home and the wife wished to continue living there with the nine-year-old child of the family. The court ordered that the property be held on trust for sale in equal shares until the child reached the age of 17 years. The wife was to pay all the outgoings except the mortgage repayments which the parties were to bear equally.

Mesher orders were very common at one time but for a number of reasons they have now fallen out of favour. It is said that they create uncertainty and simply postpone the evil day when the property has to be sold. A husband will usually have secured alternative accommodation by that time, but the wife may have insufficient resources to rehouse herself. She and the children may be unable to move to new accommodation while the trust remains alive unless special provision is made in the order.

The Martin Order is another form of settlement. Unlike the Mesher order it allows one spouse, usually the wife, to remain in the property as long as she wishes. It is more appropriate where the parties are older and one spouse has secured alternative accommodation. In *Martin (BH)* v *Martin (BW)* (1977), the husband had obtained council accommodation. A sale of the property and division of the proceeds would not enable the wife to rehouse herself. The property was therefore settled on the wife for life or until she remarried or chose to move. It was then to be sold and the proceeds shared equally between the parties.

In *Bateman* v *Bateman* (1979), a similar order was made but the wife was entitled to receive only one quarter of the proceeds and this was to go to her children if the sale was triggered by her death.

15. Financial provision for children

The court may make orders for periodical payments, lump sums and property adjustment in respect of any children of the family. A child of the family is defined by s. 52(1) MCA 1973 and has the same meaning as it does in the DPMCA 1978. It is:

(a) A child of both parties to the marriage *and*

(b) Any other child, not being a child who has been placed with those parties as foster parents by a local authority or voluntary organisation, who has been treated by both of those parties as a child of the family.

The power to make financial provision orders in favour of children does not depend on the outcome of the proceedings. An order may be made before the granting of the decree and from time to time thereafter: s. 23(2)(a), s. 23(4).

The question of maintenance for the natural child or children will normally be dealt with under the CSA 1991, which is outside the court's jurisdiction, but an application may still be made to the court for a lump sum and/or property adjustment order for the benefit of the child, and financial provision orders for 'non-qualifying' children.

The following orders can be made against either party to the marriage in respect of children of the marriage:

(a) Periodical payments secured or unsecured: s. 23(1)(d)(e).

(b) Lump sum orders: s. 23(1)(f).

(c) Property adjustment orders: s. 24(1)(a)(b).

(d) Antenuptial or post-nuptial settlements may also be varied for a child's benefit: s. 24(1)(c).

As with orders between spouses, the court is given guidance as to how it should exercise its discretion to make financial and property orders in favour of a child of the family.

The court must have regard to all the circumstances of the case but give first consideration to the welfare while a minor of any child of the family under 18 years: s. 25(1).

The court must in particular have regard to;

(a) The financial needs of the child.

(b) The income, earning capacity (if any), property and other financial resources of the child.

(c) Any physical or mental disability of the child.

(d) The manner in which the child was being, and in which the parties to the marriage expected the child to be, educated or trained.

(e) The considerations mentioned in s. 25(2)(a), (b), (c) and (e) in relation to spouses (*see* **10** above).

Because of the wide definition given to the term 'child of the family', an order may be made against a party who is not the child's natural parent. When contemplating such an order it must have regard to the factors listed in s. 25(4) in addition to the matters listed above:

(a) Whether the party against whom the order may be made has assumed any responsibility for the child's maintenance and, if so, to what extent, on what basis and for how long.

(b) Whether in assuming or discharging such responsibility, the party did so knowing that the child was not their own.

(c) The liability of any other person to maintain the child.

16. Duration

An adult child is not expected to look to his or her parents for support unless there are special circumstances justifying this. The court cannot therefore make a financial provision order or a transfer of property order in favour of a child who has attained the age of 18 years.

Periodical payments, whether secured or otherwise, cannot continue beyond the child's 17th birthday, unless the court considers that in the circumstances the child's welfare requires the order to be extended to the child's 18th birthday (s. 29(2)).

These age limits do not apply if:

(a) The child is, or will be, or if an order is made would be, receiving instruction at an educational establishment or undergoing training for a trade, profession or vocation, whether or not the child is also, or will also be, in gainful employment *or*

(b) There are special circumstances which justify the making of an order: s. 29(3).

Whatever the age of the child, an unsecured periodical payments order will cease on the death of the payer: s. 29(4).

VARIATION AND CONSENT ORDERS

17. Consent orders

It has already been noted that spouses may regulate their own affairs by agreement on marital breakdown (*see* 6:7). An agreement embodied in a consent order can achieve a final settlement.

Once the terms of agreement are embodied in a court order they derive their legal effect from the order and not the prior agreement: *Thwaite* v *Thwaite* (1981).

The court has power to make a consent order on the basis of prescribed information which the parties must furnish: s. 33A MCA 1973. It is clearly most important that the court has all the relevant information and an order may be set aside if this is not the case.

Jenkins v *Livesey (formerly Jenkins)* (1985). The wife agreed to accept the transfer of the matrimonial home in full settlement of all financial claims against her husband. The day before a consent order was made in these terms, she became engaged. Three weeks after the order she remarried. The order was set aside because of her failure to disclose her intention to remarry.

As a direct consequence of *Jenkins*, new rules relating to consent applications were introduced. It is now necessary to lodge with every consent application a minute of the order sought and detailed information relating to both parties, including financial resources, commitments and any present intention to remarry or cohabit.

18. Variation and discharge of orders

The court has power to vary or discharge any of the following orders; it may also suspend or revive any provision in the orders (s. 31(1)):

(a) An order for maintenance pending suit.

(b) Any periodical payments order, whether for a spouse or child.

(c) Any secured periodical payments order, whether for a spouse or child.

(d) Any order for payment of a lump sum by instalments, whether for a spouse or child.

(e) Any order for settlement of property (s. 24(1)(b)) or variation of settlement (s. 24(1)(c)(d)) if made on or after a decree of judicial separation;

(f) Any order made under s. 24A(1) for the sale of property.

Periodical payments orders

Most applications for variation relate to periodical payments orders and are prompted by a change in circumstances or the effects of inflation. A spouse who has agreed to accept periodical payments at a certain level is not precluded from seeking variation even if she has undertaken not to do so: *Jessel* v *Jessel* (1979). A nominal order for periodical payments may be varied at any time. Indeed, such orders are usually made to keep alive the recipient's right to apply for variation should her circumstances change.

The court can extend a periodical payments order which is made for a specified term unless the court has made an express direction under s. 28(1A) prohibiting this. Where variation or discharge is ordered, the court may direct that it shall not take immediate effect (s. 31(10)); in this way a payer may be given an opportunity to adjust to the new level of payment. Where discharge rather than variation is ordered, the recipient will have some time to adjust to the loss of support.

The court cannot make a property adjustment order on an application to vary an order for periodical payments in favour of a spouse or child. Formerly, the court could not order a lump sum payment when varying a periodical payments order in favour of a spouse but the FLA 1996 amended that provision and now allows lump sum orders to be made in appropriate circumstances. This does not mean that a spouse may not voluntarily offer a lump sum in return for the discharge of a maintenance order, and the court may properly consider such an offer when exercising its discretion.

In respect to secured orders where the payer dies, either the payer's personal representatives or the recipient may apply for variation, but only with the leave of the court if six months have elapsed since the date on which representation was taken out: s. 31(6). After the six-month period, personal representatives do not have to take into account the possibility of an application for variation when distributing the estate and they will incur no liability if they do so: s. 31(8).

There is no power to vary property adjustment or lump sum orders but there are, however, two limited exceptions to this general rule:

(a) Orders for settlement of property or variation of settlement made on judicial separation may be varied if the decree is subsequently rescinded or the marriage ended by divorce: s. 31(4).

(b) Where a lump sum is payable by instalments, the number and frequency of the instalments may be varied but not the total amount of the order.

Another way in which an order for capital provision may be 'varied' is by application for leave to appeal out of time. In *Barder* v *Barder (Caluori Intervening)* (1987) the House of Lords stated four conditions which had to be satisfied if leave was to be granted in such cases:

(a) The fundamental assumptions upon which the order was based had been negated by a change in circumstances.

(b) The change had occurred relatively soon after the order was made.

(c) Application for leave was made promptly.

(d) The grant of leave would not unfairly prejudice third parties who had acquired interests for value in the property concerned.

In *Barder* itself, a husband was granted leave to appeal out of time where the wife had committed suicide five weeks after the court had directed him to transfer the matrimonial home to her. Under the wife's will the property would have gone to her mother.

A party who claims that all the relevant facts were not disclosed when the original order was made may seek to have it set aside: *Jenkins* v *Livesey (formerly Jenkins)* (1985).

In deciding an application for variation, the court must have regard to all the circumstances of the case and must give first consideration to the welfare while a minor of any child of the family under the age of 18 years: s. 31(7).

The circumstances of the case will include any changes in the matters which the court was required to take into account when making the original order, such as changes in income and earning capacity as well as circumstances which may increase or decrease a party's financial needs.

The possibility of achieving a clean break must be considered when an application is made for variation of a periodical payments order. In particular, the court must consider whether it would be appropriate to vary the order so as to limit payments to such period as will be sufficient to enable the recipient to adjust without hardship to the variation: s. 37(1)(a).

Where an application is made for variation of a secured periodical payments order, after the death of the payer, the court must also take into account the changed circumstances resulting from the death: s. 31(7)(b).

FINANCIAL PROVISION ON DEATH

19. Outline of the law of succession

Succession is a subject in its own right and the following section is the barest outline of matters which affect family provision on death.

Any person over the age of 18 and with appropriate mental capacity can make a will, disposing of his or her property on death. The Wills Act 1837 sets out the formal requirements which, in essence, requires the will to be in writing, signed by the person making it (the *testator*) and witnessed by two competent witnesses.

The subsequent marriage of the testator would revoke the will unless made in contemplation of that forthcoming marriage. In 1983 the law was changed to provide that in the event of a subsequent divorce, the ex-spouse would not benefit. Following unsatisfactory interpretation, the Law Reform (Succession) Act 1995 was passed and provides that:

(a) The ex-spouse is deemed to have predeceased the testator for the purposes of appointment of personal representatives: s. 3(a).

113

(b) The ex-spouse is deemed to have predeceased the testator for the purposes of any benefit given by the will to the ex-spouse: s. 3(b).

(c) Any appointment of the ex-spouse as guardian of the testator's children is revoked by the divorce: s. 4.

Until relatively recent times, testators had complete freedom to dispose of their property as they saw fit, even to the exclusion of family and dependants. However, there has been statutory intervention in the form of the Inheritance (Provision for Family and Dependants) Act 1975 (*see* **19** below).

Statistics show that only 33% of married persons make wills and only 19% of cohabitants do so. A person who dies without making a will is said to die *intestate*, and the distribution of the estate is governed by the Administration of Estates Act 1925. The distribution depends on who are the surviving relatives.

If the intestate is survived by a spouse and children, then (contrary to popular belief) the estate is distributed as follows:

(a) The surviving spouse takes all the personal chattels, which includes furniture, clothing, jewellery, paintings and motor cars (to whatever value).

(b) The spouse is given a 'statutory legacy' which is varied from time to time by the Secretary of State, and currently stands at £125,000. The legacy also carries interest at 4% from the date of death until payment.

(c) If there is any money remaining, one half is held on trust to pay the income to the spouse for life and, on his or her death, to divide the capital equally between the children. The other half is divided between the children immediately on the intestate's death.

The Act also provides that, if any child predeceases the intestate leaving issue, such issue take their parent's share and, if more than one, equally between them. If a child predeceases without issue, his or her share lapses and goes to the other children.

If the intestate dies leaving a spouse, no issue but parents or brothers and sisters then:

(a) The spouse takes the chattels as before.

(b) The statutory legacy is increased to £200,000.

(c) The spouse takes half the residue *absolutely*; the other half goes to the parents, or if they have predeceased to the brothers and sisters equally.

If there is a surviving spouse but no other relatives as above, the spouse takes the estate absolutely.

There may be a problem with the matrimonial home which is not specifically dealt with by the Act. Schedule Two, para. 5(2) of the Intestates Estates Act 1952 gives the spouse power to require the personal representatives to appropriate to him or her any dwelling house in which the surviving spouse was resident at the date of the intestate's death. The spouse must give notice within 12 months of the intestate's death and the value is ascertained at the date of appropriation. If that value is greater than the spouse's share, money may be added by the spouse to make up the difference.

If there is no surviving spouse then the intestate's estate is held for the benefit of:

(a) The issue; or if none,

(b) The parents; if none,

(c) Brothers and sisters or their issue; if none,

(d) Half brothers and half sisters or their issue; if none,

(e) Grandparents; if none,

(f) Uncles and aunts or their issue; if none,

(g) Half uncles and half aunts or their issue; if none,

(h) The estate goes to the crown as *bona vacantia*.

20. The Inheritance (Provision for Family and Dependants) Act 1975

Under this Act, the court has some powers to interfere with the testamentary freedom of a testator if he or she has failed to make reasonable provision for a person who falls into the category of dependant (see below). In addition, if the rules of intestacy do not adequately provide for someone in these categories, they still may apply for financial provision out of the estate. References to sections in this part are references to the 1975 Act unless otherwise stated.

In order to qualify, the applicant must fall into one of six categories listed in s. 1(1). They are:

(a) *The wife or husband of the deceased.* The marriage must be subsisting at the date of death but can include void or voidable marriages which have not been annulled.

(b) *Former spouse of the deceased who has not remarried.* In *Re Fullard* (1981) the Court of Appeal stated that the number of cases which it would be appropriate to bring should be small bearing in mind the extensive powers of the courts under MCA 1973 and, unless there had been a dramatic change in circumstances, applications should be discouraged.

(c) *A child of the deceased.* The head includes legitimated and adopted children, children of unmarried parents but not an adopted child claiming on a natural parent. There must be some degree of dependancy. Thus, applications by adult, able-bodied children will succeed in only the most exceptional circumstances (*Re Coventry* (1980)).

(d) *A person treated by the deceased as a child of the family.* This has the same meaning as in the MCA 1973.

(e) *Any person who immediately before the death of the deceased was being maintained wholly or partially by the deceased.*

This particular subsection has received further clarification, both from the Act itself and also judicial interpretation:

(i) Section 1(3) states that a person is 'maintained' if the deceased '...otherwise than for full and valuable consideration, was making a substantial contribution in money or money's worth 'towards the reasonable needs of that person'.

(ii) What constitutes a substantial contribution will depend on circumstances, for example providing board and lodging for a sister (*Re Wilkinson* (1978)); the provision of a flat, car, £15,000 in shares, and furs and jewellery for a mistress (*Malone* v *Harrison* (1979)).

(iii) Valuable consideration has caused the courts some problems of interpretation, but the case of *Bishop* v *Plumley* (1991) seems to have established a common sense approach to interpretation. In that particular case, the nursing care provided by the applicant, though of great value, was regarded as being part of 'the mutuality of the relationship.'

(iv) In *Re Beaumont* (1980) Megarry VC held that 'immediately before death' should take into account the 'general arrangements between the parties ... not the actual perhaps fluctuating variation of it which existed before death.' Thus, the female partner could claim even though the male partner had been in hospital for some weeks prior to his death.

(f) *Cohabitants.* This category was added by the Law Reform (Succession) Act 1995 and applies to deaths after 31 December 1995. An application may be made by anyone living with the deceased as ' husband and wife' for the two years immediately preceding the death of the deceased. It will still be necessary to establish a degree of dependance.

21. Reasonable provision

In order for a claim to be successful, the deceased must have failed to have provided reasonable provision, judged on an objective basis. The question is simple: has the dependant received reasonable provision out of the estate? There are two standards:

(a) *The surviving spouse.* She or he is deemed to be entitled to such provision as it would be reasonable in all the circumstances for a spouse to receive 'whether or not that provision is required for his or her maintenance': s. 1(2)(a). The level is expected to be that awarded on divorce under the MCA 1973.

(b) *The maintenance standard.* All other applicants are entitled to such financial provision as it would be reasonable in all the circumstances of the case for the applicant to receive for maintenance: s. 1(2)(b). Maintenance means enabling the applicant to 'discharge the cost of his daily living at whatever standard is appropriate to him' (*per* Browne-Wilkinson in *Re Dennis* (1981)).

22. Matters to be taken into consideration

Section 3(1) lays down criteria which are almost identical to those contained in MCA 1973, bearing in mind a spouse has died as opposed to being divorced. The matters are:

(a) *The financial needs and resources of the applicant, any other applicant and the beneficiary.*

(b) *Obligations and responsibilities of the deceased towards the applicant and any beneficiary.*

(c) *The size and nature of the estate.*

(d) *Any physical or mental disability of the applicant or beneficiary.*

(e) *Any other matter including the conduct of the applicant.*

In addition to the above, there are guidelines which only apply to particular categories of applicant:

(a) *Surviving spouse*

　　(i) The age of the applicant and the duration of the marriage
　　(ii) The contribution made by the applicant to the welfare of the family
　　(iii) The provision the applicant might reasonably have expected to

receive if, on the day the deceased died, the marriage had been terminated by divorce.

Re Besterman (1984). The deceased and his wife married in 1958 when he was 54 and she was 42. On his death in 1976, his net estate was worth £1.5 million. He left personal chattels and an income of £3,500 per annum to his widow and the rest of his estate to Oxford University. HELD The wife should receive £378,000 from the estate. She would probably have received considerably more than the testamentary gifts under the MCA 1973 and there were no other beneficiaries to consider.

(b) *Former spouse*
The same standards as apply to spouses apply to former spouses, but there must be exceptional circumstances to make a successful application: *Re Fullard* (1981).

(c) *Child of the deceased*
The courts are expected to take into account the manner in which the applicant was being or might be educated or trained: *Re Coventry* (1980), *Re Jennings* (1994).

(d) *Child of the family*
In addition to the above considerations, the court must take into account:

(i) Whether the deceased had assumed responsibility for the applicant's maintenance and if so to what extent and for how long.
(ii) Whether in assuming responsibility the deceased knew the child was not his own *and*
(iii) The liability of anyone else to maintain the applicant.

In *Re Callaghan* (1985) the applicant was 35 when his mother married his step-father but he treated the applicant as a child of the family and he looked after step-father during his last illness. The latter died intestate leaving £31,000. HELD The applicant was able to show an exceptional relationship, most of the deceased's estate derived from the applicant's mothers estate and he was therefore awarded £15,000

(e) *Dependant of the deceased*
The extent and basis on which the deceased assumed responsibility for the maintenance of the applicant and the length of time for which he discharged that responsibility.

Re Beaumont (1980) was an example where the evidence showed that the parties pooled their resources only to the extent that they were able to live together without either assuming responsibility for the other.

Jelley v *Iliffe* (1981) is an example of the court, in this case the Court of Appeal, taking a more liberal interpretation.

(f) *Cohabitants*

Additional considerations to those set out above are:

(i) The age of the applicant and the length of time they lived as husband and wife or in the same household.

(ii) The contribution made by the applicant to the deceased's family.

Progress test 9

1. What factors do the court take into account when arriving at a financial settlement on divorce?

2. Explain the range of orders available to the court in divorce proceedings.

3. What matters must the court consider in deciding whether a clean break order is appropriate?

4. How will the FLA 1996 affect ancillary relief proceedings?

5. H and W have been married for four years. W's daughter from a previous relationship has always lived with them. H left the matrimonial home to live with his girlfriend, who is pregnant by him. H claims that he only embarked on his affair in retaliation for W's previous promiscuity. For this reason H refuses to pay anything to W and her daughter, despite the fact that he has a well-paid job and W is claiming state benefit.

   Advise H as to his potential liability for financial provision for both W and her daughter.

6. Explain the devolution of property on the death of an intestate.

7. D lived with his disabled son, A, until two months before his death. They had a violent quarrel and D went to stay at the flat, owned by D but occupied by his mistress S, with whom he had had a relationship for 12 years. S had a child by D who was at boarding school, the fees being paid by D. In the last few days of his life, D made a will leaving his entire fortune of £1m to charity. Advise D and S. How, if at all, would your advice differ if D had died intestate?

PART THREE

Children

10

Introduction to the Children Act 1989

1. Introduction

Lord Mackay LC described the Children Act 1989 (which came into force on 14 October 1991) as: 'The most far-reaching reform of child law in living memory'.

The CA 1989 reforms much of the relevant public and private law but it is not completely comprehensive and some knowledge of the earlier law is still essential.

2. Welfare principle

Under s. 1, the welfare of the child is 'paramount', and not merely 'first and paramount' as before. The CA 1989 sets out a 'check list' of matters to be taken into account when arriving at any decision concerning the child's welfare. The primary and continuing responsibility for that welfare is given to parents, and the State, when involved, is to act as their partner. This principle applies in all proceedings concerning children, whether private or public.

There is a need to avoid harmful delays, in litigation or otherwise (s. 1(2)). Whichever court has jurisdiction, they are required to draw up timetables to expedite the hearing of children's issues. Finally, there is the 'non-intervention principle.' Under s. 1(5), the court should make no order unless it would be better than no order at all.

In B v B (1993), the maternal grandmother applied for a residence order which the magistrates refused under s. 1(5) on the basis that there was no risk of the child's removal because the mother had agreed that the child should remain with the grandmother. This was overruled on appeal: the grandmother would be able to authorise matters relating to the child's schooling; the child herself wanted it in order to bring some stability to her life; and there was no guarantee that the mother would not change her mind.

3. The private law

'Parental rights'are replaced by 'parental responsibilities' (s. 3). The significance of this is that these responsibilities continue throughout childhood and do not terminate by the parent ceasing to live with the child, e.g. because of a divorce. The old orders of 'custody' are therefore inappropriate, because they could give care and control to one parent alone. The courts are now empowered under s. 8 to grant residence orders, which settle with whom and where the child shall live, but the parents continue to have parental responsibility for the child, jointly with a person with a residence order.

Access orders are replaced by contact orders, which are wider in scope than simple visiting rights. The father ceases to be the 'natural guardian' of his legitimate children (s. 2(4)), and the legal standing of a father of non-marital children is improved by giving him the opportunity to acquire parental responsibility by agreement with the mother or by court order: s. 4.

4. Public law

Local authorities now have to obtain legal parental 'powers' by court order, not voluntarily by administrative resolution, and there is one ground only, that the child is suffering, or is likely to suffer, significant harm: s. 31. This means the child is not getting the care reasonably expected from a parent, or the child is beyond parental control. Judicial challenge to decisions of local authorities over those in their care is enhanced, as is emergency protection for children thought to be in danger.

Although previously popular with local authorities, wardship is now available to them only in the most exceptional circumstances: s. 100. It is considered that the ranges of orders available under the CA 1989 are sufficient to meet any circumstances that a local authority is likely to encounter.

5. Jurisdiction

There is a three-tier court system under the Act, as implemented by the Children (Allocation of Proceedings) Order 1991, SI 1991, No 1677:

(a) A Family Proceedings Court (part of the magistrates jurisdiction) which has specially trained justices drawn from the 'family panels'.

(b) The County Courts with divorce jurisdiction will continue with it, but some will be divorce courts for administrative purposes only and for cases which can be heard by the district judge. 'Family hearing centres' will hear contested private law s. 8 applications, adoptions and injunctions in domestic violence and matrimonial proceedings. Some of these are designated 'care centres' which will hear public law cases transferred from the family proceedings courts.

(c) The High Court.

These three courts will have concurrent jurisdiction: any of them can make a s. 8 order in any 'family proceedings'. The term is defined to include proceedings under Parts I, II and IV of the CA 1989 (s. 8(3)) but also a wide range of other proceedings in which issues relating to children are likely to arise (s. 8(4)). The court can make orders:

(a) In proceedings which relate to parental responsibility, guardianship and care and supervision orders.

(b) In divorce, nullity and judicial separation proceedings.

(c) In proceedings for financial relief between spouses under the MCA 1973 or the DPMCA 1978.

(d) In adoption proceedings.

(e) In proceedings relating to domestic violence and the occupation of the matrimonial home under the FLA 1996 Part IV.

(f) When exercising the inherent jurisdiction of the High Court in relation to children, usually in wardship proceedings.

Most public law cases must be heard in the magistrates court, but there will be a free choice for private law cases. Cases of exceptional complexity or importance will be transferred. Many orders will be made in the course of divorce proceedings.

Progress test 10

1. What are the fundamental principles of the CA 1989?

2. Outline the changes made to both the private law and the public law in relation to children's matters.

3. Which court's have jurisdiction in CA 1989 matters, and in what proceedings?

11

Children and parents

1. Who is a parent?

Important consequences flow from parenthood but with medical advances in the area of human-assisted reproduction, it is not always easy to determine parentage.

When a child is born to married parents, the husband is presumed to be the father unless disproved by evidence to the contrary. When a child is born outside of marriage, paternity must be proved, unless admitted, before the responsibilities and obligations of fatherhood may be assumed or imposed. The legal principles for determining legitimacy are still important as they determine the status of parents and the legal remedies available to them.

LEGITIMACY

2. Legitimacy

Under common law it was vital to determine whether a child was legitimate or illegitimate, the latter suffering a number of legal disadvantages. These included the inability to inherit parents' property and no right to claim maintenance or other financial support.

However, by a gradual process of statutory reform the disadvantages were removed and the Family Law Reform Act 1987 effectively abolished the remaining distinctions. Section 1 of the Act provides, as a general principle, that references to any relationship between two people shall be construed without regard to whether or not the father or mother of either of them have been married to each other at any time. In the absence of contrary intention this principle applies to all legislation and statutory instruments which postdate the implementation of s. 1 on 1 April 1989. Although no longer appropriate to call a child 'legitimate' or 'illegitimate', it is still necessary to find out whether a child is born of married or unmarried parents because, under the CA, married fathers are automatically given certain rights which unmarried fathers are denied. The rights may be acquired but only by agreement or court order.

3. Determining parentage

Where a child's parents are married at the time of conception or birth, the child is presumed to be the legitimate issue of that marriage and they will be the legal parents.

This presumption is rebuttable, for example, by proof that the husband was away from the wife at the relevant time: *Preston-Jones* v *Preston-Jones* (1951).

Under s. 26 of the Family Law Reform Act 1969 the standard of proof necessary to rebut the presumption of legitimacy is the balance of probabilities. Under s. 20(1), the court may order scientific tests in any civil proceedings in which the paternity of any person is in issue. A person over the age of 16 cannot be tested without their consent, but if a person refuses to consent to a scientific test or otherwise fails to comply with a direction, the court may draw whatever inferences seem proper in the circumstances: s. 23(1). If the person is under 16, consent must be given by the person with care and control.

Recent scientific advances have meant significant changes to the way in which tests are carried out. At one time a blood test was the only method of testing and it could only show with certainty that a particular male could not be the father of the child. Otherwise, it simply proved that the father was in the right blood group and could possibly be the father. Now, with the use of DNA profiling or 'genetic fingerprinting', it is possible to prove paternity with greater certainty using tests carried out on blood and other bodily samples such as saliva, semen and hair roots.

Children of unmarried parents are legitimated by the subsequent marriage of their parents, provided that the father is domiciled in England and Wales at the date of the marriage: s. 2 Legitimacy Act 1969. Such children will be treated as the children of married parents from the date of marriage and their position will be largely the same as that of a child of married parents with two exceptions.

Children of voidable marriages are legitimate and their status is unchanged by a decree of nullity since it does not operate retrospectively. They will always be treated as the children of married parents, therefore, unless the presumption of paternity is successfully rebutted by the husband.

127

Children of void marriages are treated as the children of married parents if at the time of insemination or conception both or either of their parents reasonably believed the marriage to be valid: s. 1 Legitimacy Act 1976.

CHILDREN BORN BY HUMAN-ASSISTED REPRODUCTION

4. Children born by AIH or AID or embryo donation

Medical science has made it possible to assist with reproduction in a number of ways. It has been necessary to clarify the legal status of children born as a result of artificial insemination by husband or donor and also those born as a result of egg or embryo donation.

A child born during marriage as a result of artificial insemination with the husband's own semen (AIH) is treated as the child of married parents and the husband will be the legal father.

Where the birth results from artificial insemination by a donor (AID), a presumption of legitimacy is imposed by statute and may only be rebutted on proof that the husband did not consent to the artificial insemination of his wife: s. 27 Family Law Reform Act 1987. The child will therefore be treated as the child of married parents provided that it is born in England and Wales. However this provision is not retrospective. Thus a child born by AID before s. 27 came into force is illegitimate.

The Human Fertilisation and Embryology Act 1990 extends s. 27 to cover egg or embryo donation. Thus a woman who gives birth after genetic donation will be the child's legal (but not biological) mother and, if she is married, the child will also be the child of the husband unless he did not consent to the treatment.

Section 28 further provides that, where an unmarried couple undergo such treatment, the male partner will be the father of the child provided that the couple sought treatment together.

SURROGACY

5. Surrogacy

A surrogacy arrangement is one where a woman carries and gives birth to a child for the benefit of another. The most common arrangement is for the surrogate mother to be artificially inseminated by the male partner of the commissioning parents, but it can also be done by implanting the surrogate mother with genetic materials from both commissioning parents. In either case, the child's mother will be the surrogate mother. If she is married and her husband has consented to the arrangement, he will be the legal father of the child.

If the commissioning parents wish to become the legal parents, they may apply for a parental order under s. 30 of the Human Fertilization and Embryology Act 1990.

The following conditions must be complied with:

(a) The commissioning parents must be married.

(b) The application must have been brought within six months of the birth.

(c) The child must already be living with the surrogate parents.

(d) The natural mother and the legal father (if known) must consent to the order.

(e) No money other than reasonable expenses must have changed hands.

Re MW (Adoption: Surrogacy) (1995). The court approved a payment of £7,500 to the surrogate mother.

If a surrogate mother refuses to hand a child over after the birth the commissioning parents have few remedies. Surrogacy contracts are unenforceable in law: s. 1A Surrogacy Arrangements Act 1985.

The commissioning parents may be able to seek a residence order under the CA 1989 but the courts have shown a reluctance to intervene once a child has bonded with the surrogate mother: Re P (Minors) (Wardship Surrogacy) (1987).

PARENTAL RESPONSIBILITY

6. Introduction

The concept of parental responsibility is fundamental to child care law. It means all the rights, duties, powers, responsibility and authority which by law a parent of a child has in relation to the child and its property: s. 3(1) CA 1989. The term represents a move away from the concept of parental rights to a more realistic recognition of the parental role.

The CA 1989 does not attempt to list the parental rights and duties which are recognised in law, as it was felt that these were bound to change at various stages in a child's life to meet differing needs and circumstances. It is useful to look at some of the matters which the common law addressed before the CA 1989 was implemented.

7. Parental rights, duties and powers

(a) *Care and control.* To wilfully neglect, abandon or ill-treat a child is the criminal offence of 'cruelty to a child' under the Children and Young Persons Act 1933, s. 1, and it is also an offence to remove a child from the 'lawful control' of a parent by virtue of the Child Abduction Act 1984 (*see* Chapter 13).

(b) *To provide education.* Although the Education Act 1944 has imposed some statutory regulation, parents still have the right to choose between private or state education and theoretically a choice of schools within the state system.

(c) *The duty to maintain and not to neglect the child.* The common law only requires the fairly basic provision of shelter, food and clothing. However, when parents live apart, the absent parent can be called upon to make a quite substantial contribution to the child's maintenance under the CSA 1991 (*see* Chapter 7).

(d) *Discipline.* A parent has the right to inflict reasonable and moderate corporal punishment. What constitutes *reasonable* will always be a question of fact but clearly a parent needs to take into account the age and under-standing of the child, whether his or her rules are reasonable and whether the punishment is in proportion to the 'offence'. Corporal punishment cannot be carried out in state schools, and local authority children's homes.

(e) *Choice of religion.* This is generally determined by the parents but there is no positive duty as such to provide religious education. The courts rarely disturb a child's settled faith unless it is likely to cause the child harm. The CA 1989, s. 22(5) requires that 'due consideration' be given to the child's religious views.

(f) *The right to administer a child's property:*

(g) *The right to appoint a testamentary guardian* to act *in loco parentis* on the death of a parent.

(h) *The right to consent to medical treatment* for a child under the age of 16 (*see* 8 below).

(i) *The right to determine a child's surname.* A child of married parents will usually take the father's surname, a child of unmarried parents usually takes the mother's. If there is a dispute, the issue may have to be resolved by the court. If a residence or care order is made, the child's name cannot be changed without the consent of all having parental responsibility.

(j) *The right to bring or defend legal proceedings* on a child's behalf either as an adult 'next friend' as plaintiff or as an adult 'guardian *ad litem*' when a defendant.

This is not intended to be an exhaustive list.

THE 'GILLICK' CASE AND 'GILLICK COMPETENCE'

8. The 'Gillick' case

In the landmark judgments in the case of *Gillick v West Norfolk and Wisbech Area Health Authority and the DHSS* (1986), the House of Lords recognised that children have the ability to make decisions for themselves below the statutory age limits and that there is a shift from the philosophy of parents' rights to childrens' rights.

The case was concerned with the question of medical treatment and, in particular, the provision of contraceptive treatment to girls under the age of 16. Mrs Gillick was the mother of girls under 16 and sought a declaration that guidance given by the DHSS on the subject of contraception was wrong. The House of Lords found against Mrs Gillick by a majority if 3:2.

The judgments had a much wider impact than the narrow issue of contraceptive treatment. Their Lordships ruled that if a child had sufficient intelligence and understanding, and the maturity to comprehend the nature of the decision, then parental rights yielded to the right of the child to make his or her own decisions. Lord Scarman also said that 'parental rights are derived from parental duty and exist only so long as they are needed for the protection of the person and property of the child'.

There are no age limits laid down, but if a child does have such intelligence, understanding and maturity, it is said that the child is 'Gillick competent'. This shift in emphasis is continued by the CA 1989 which refers to 'parental responsibility' rather than parental rights, though there is little reference in the Act to 'Gillick competence'as such.

9. Subsequent developments to Gillick principles

In *Re R (A Minor)(Medical Treatment)* (1992) psychiatrists wanted to administer drugs to a 15-year-old girl who had a history of mental disorder.

Although the Court of Appeal found that she was not Gillick competent, Lord Donaldson went on to say that, even if she were, she would not be able to refuse consent, as opposed to give consent in the Gillick case, and her wishes could be overridden by anyone with parental responsibility and especially the court.

In *Re W (A Minor) (Medical Treatment)* (1992) Lord Donaldson reaffirmed his judgment in a case involving a 16-year-old anorexic girl who refused treatment. He wanted to provide doctors with a 'flack jacket' so that, as long as someone with authority consented, the doctor would be able to administer treatment without fear of litigation.

This approach was followed in *Re K W and H (Minors) (Medical Treatment)* (1993) where Thorpe J held that 'the law is perfectly clear ... where more than one person has power to consent, only refusal by *all* having that power will veto'. But in the subsequent case of *Re E (Minor) (Wardship)* (1993) where a boy of 15 and his parents, who were all devout Jehovah's witnesses, *all* refused life-saving blood transfusions, the court intervened and ordered treatment.

There is no doubt that in the decade since Gillick, the Court of Appeal have adopted a very narrow and restrictive interpretation of that judgment.

OBTAINING PARENTAL RESPONSIBILITY

10. Who has parental responsibility?

If a child's parents are married to each other at the time of its birth, they will each have parental responsibility for it: s. 2(1) CA 1989. Parents continue to share parental responsibility even after divorce, subject to the provisions of s. 8 (see Chapter 13).

Any presumption the law may make about a child's parentage may be rebutted. Thus, if it can be proved that the mother's husband is not the father of her child, he will not be treated as a parent for the purposes of the CA 1989.

If parents are not married to each other at the time of birth the mother alone will have parental responsibility, although the father may acquire it in one of two ways:

(a) By making a parental responsibility agreement with the child's mother in the prescribed form under s. 4(1)(2) *or*

(b) By a parental responsibility order made by a court under s. 4(1).

Once he acquires parental responsibility, whether by agreement or court order, an unmarried father may only lose it by court order on the application of the child or someone with parental responsibility: s. 4(3).

In the case of *Re C (Minors) (Parental Responsibility)* (1992) the test to be applied to determine whether an unmarried father should be granted a parental responsibility order was as follows: 'Has the father by his conduct during and since the association shown sufficient commitment to the children to justify giving the father a legal status equivalent to that which he would have enjoyed if the parties had been married, due attention being paid to the fact that a number of his parental rights would, if conferred on him, be unenforceable under current conditions?'

This approach was followed subsequently by the Court of Appeal in *Re H (A Minor) (Parental Responsibility)* (1993).

In *Re S (A Minor) (Parental Responsibility)* (1995) it was confirmed that the object of an order is to give the father status, it did not interfere with day-to-day care.

Certain other individuals or statutory agencies may acquire parental responsibility for a child, in most cases as a consequence of a court order. Where parental responsibility is acquired in this way, it will be lost if the order is discharged.

A guardian who takes over responsibility for a child on the death of a parent gets parental responsibility under s. 5(6).

An adoption order will give adoptive parents parental responsibility. It will also extinguish the parental responsibility held by natural parents, and anyone else who has parental responsibility as a consequence of a court order: s. 12 Adoption Act 1976.

If a person has a residence order under s. 8, and that person is not the child's parent or guardian, he or she will acquire parental responsibility while the residence order remains in force: s. 12(2).

Parental responsibility is also given to local authorities who have a care order (s. 33(3)) and anyone with an emergency protection order under s. 44(4). In the earlier case, this will only be for the duration of the order.

11. Exercising parental responsibility

Parental responsibility may be held by more than one person at a time: s. 2(5). In such circumstances each may act alone in meeting that responsibility, except in situations where the law requires the consent of more than one person in a matter affecting a child: s. 2(7).

To take the most simple example of shared parental responsibility, married parents living with the child may act independently in meeting their parental responsibility. They do not need to consult each other and one parent does not have a right of veto against the other. In the event of a dispute between them, the court may make an order under s. 8 (*see* Chapter 13).

Having parental responsibility does not entitle a person to act in a manner incompatible with any order made under the Act: s. 2(8).

A person does not lose parental responsibility for a child simply because responsibility is also acquired by another: s. 2(6). An unmarried mother will share parental responsibility with the child's father if a parental responsibility agreement is made or if the court makes a parental responsibility order under s. 4. A parent and a non-parent may share parental responsibility if the court makes a residence order in favour of the non-parent.

Parental responsibility cannot be transferred or surrendered: s. 2(9). It is not always possible, however, for a person to meet that responsibility at all times. He or she may therefore arrange for someone else to do so on their behalf. The person caring for the child will not acquire parental responsibility but will have power to do whatever is reasonable in all the circumstances to safeguard or promote the child's welfare: s. 3(5). This power is given to any person who has care of a child but does not have parental responsibility for it. It does not allow a carer to act in a way which conflicts with the Act or any court order made under it, but otherwise enables the carer to do whatever is necessary for the child's safety and well-being. That being said, it is difficult to imagine a doctor agreeing to medical treatment, for example, with the consent of a baby-sitter who may find him or herself in a position of having s. 3(5) powers.

Progress test 11

1. In the event of dispute, how may parentage be established ?

2. Consider how far, if at all, legitimacy is an important issue in children's matters.

3. Who are parents of children born by human-assisted reproduction?

4. H and W discovered that W was unable to conceive. W's sister S agreed to have a child in return for £30,000 to cover her expenses and the cost of giving up her hairdressing business during pregnancy. S was artificially inseminated using H's sperm. After the birth, S refuses to hand over the child to H and W. Advise them.

5. What are the principles laid down by the House of Lords in *Gillick* with regard to the upbringing of a child?

6. To what extent, if any, have these principles been undermined by the Court of Appeal?

7. What rights and duties do parents have in respect of their children?

8. What is parental responsibility and who has, or may, acquire it?

9. How can parental responsibility be delegated to another?

10. G, aged 15, is pregnant by her schoolboy lover and wishes to have an abortion. Her parents have deeply held religious objections to abortion and are prepared to bring up their future grandchild themselves. Advise them.

12

Resolution of disputes

1. Introduction

The CA 1989 provides a range of remedies, available to parents and others, which can cover almost any aspect of a child's upbringing, not just disputes which arise between parents during and after marital breakdown. Wardship, as part of the High Court's *parens patriae* jurisdiction, can provide similar remedies.

FUNDAMENTAL PRINCIPLES

2. The welfare principle

The welfare of the child must be the court's paramount consideration whenever it determines any question relating to a child's upbringing or the administration of its property or the application of any income arising from it: s. 1(1).

In *J v C* (1970), Lord MacDermott outlined precisely what is meant by treating the child's welfare as the paramount consideration:

'... a process whereby, when all the relevant facts, relationships, claims and wishes of parents, risks, choices and other circumstances are taken into account and weighed, the course to be followed will be that which is most in the interests of the child's welfare as that term has now to be understood.'

By making the child's welfare the paramount consideration the law ensures that all other factors are judged by reference to how they affect or are likely to affect the child. The court is not concerned with parental conduct or to exhibit a preference for one life-style as opposed to another.

In *Re R (Custody (Minors))* (1986), the court decided that a father's criminal record and dependence on alcohol were relevant factors since they affected his ability to look after his children.

136

Re D (1977). The court thought that placement with a homosexual father would expose the child to the possibility of sexual advances by other male visitors to the home.

In *C* v *C (Custody Appeal)* (1991) the trial judge at first instance took a more liberal approach and awarded custody to a lesbian mother who was living with another woman. The Court of Appeal considered this judgment to be 'plainly wrong'. It stated that a child's welfare was more likely to be promoted by adherence to the moral standards generally accepted in the society in which it was living. In our society the norm is for children to be brought up in a home with a father, mother and siblings. In deciding where a child's welfare lies, it is of great importance to consider which parent is able to offer the nearest approach to that norm.

In disputes between natural parents and third parties the general principle applied by the courts is that a child is best brought up by a natural parent unless this can be shown to endanger its welfare in some way (per Lord Templeman in *Re K D (A Minor) (Ward: Termination of Access)* (1988)).

THE WELFARE CHECKLIST

3. The welfare checklist

Section 1(3) gives the courts a checklist of factors to be taken into account in opposed applications to make, vary or discharge orders under s. 8. The court is to have particular regard to:

(a) *The ascertainable wishes and feelings of the child (in the light of his age and understanding).*
Although the courts are required to give consideration to the child's wishes, they are not limited to listening to 'Gillick competent' children. Indeed, research has shown that court welfare officers will consult with children of quite tender years, sometimes as young as five. In *M* v *M (Transfer of Custody)* (1987), the Court of Appeal said that the trial judge was wrong to ignore the strong views of a 12-year-old girl. However, in *Re P (Minors: Wardship)* (1992) Lady Butler-Sloss said that, although the child's wishes would be taken into account, the court were not bound by them and should depart from them where their future welfare required it. She was speaking in a case concerning boys aged 11 and 13.

(b) *His physical, emotional and educational needs.*
One of the best summaries of the matters which need to be addressed

137

under this heading can be found in a judgment of Hardie-Boys J in the New Zealand case of *Walker* v *Walker and Hanson*. He said:

> '... it includes material welfare, both in the sense of adequacy of resources to provide a pleasant home ... and standard of living, and in the sense of adequacy of care to ensure good health and personal pride. Material considerations ... are secondary matters. ... More important are stability and security, loving and understanding, care and guidance ... warm relationships [are] essential for the full development of the child.'

In *B* v *B (Custody)* (1985) the father was found to be an excellent carer of his three-year-old child, who had been emotionally distressed in a short stay with mother. The judge at first instance ordered that the child should live with mother as father was under a 'moral duty' to come off State benefits and find work. HELD by the Court of Appeal: That was plainly wrong; the welfare of the child was the question and that required the child to be with father.

(c) *The likely effect on him of any change in his circumstances.*
In *D* v *M (Custody Appeal)* (1983) the Court of Appeal HELD that continuity of care was important to a child's sense of security, particularly in the early years.

The importance of the status quo was emphasised by the House of Lords in *J* v *C* (1970). A 10-year-old Spanish boy had lived with English foster parents since the age of three. In wardship proceedings, his Spanish parents applied for his return on the grounds that a child's welfare was best served by being with his parents. The House of Lords HELD that, to all intents and purposes, the child was English and evidence suggested that he was unlikely to adjust to, and integrate with, the Spanish way of life. His removal from a settled and happy environment would damage his emotional stability and happiness and the parent's appeal was dismissed.

(d) *His age, sex, background and any relevant characteristics.*
There is no longer a presumption that one parent be preferred to another on the grounds of a child's particular age: *Re S (Minor: Custody)* (1991). However, in *Brixey* v *Lynas* (1996), a Scottish case, the House of Lords said there would need to be strong and cogent evidence to remove a young child from his or her mother.

Section 22(5) requires local authorities to take into account 'religious persuasion, racial origin and cultural and linguistic background' when considering a placement for a child.

(e) *Any harm which he has suffered or is at risk of suffering.*
If the harm is, or is likely to be, significant, this may trigger the involvement of the local authority (*see* Chapter 15).

(f) *How capable his parents, and any other relevant person, may be of meeting his needs.*
The most obvious 'other relevant person' is a step-parent with whom the child resides. The important factor for the court to consider is the relationship between them.

(g) *The range of powers available to the court under the Act.*
This will include the power to order welfare reports or, if the child has to attend court, the ability to relax the rules of evidence.

4. The non-intervention principle

The court cannot make an order under the Act unless it considers that this would be better for the child than making no order at all: s. 1(5). This is sometimes referred to as the non-intervention principle. It reflects the underlying philosophy that legal intervention should be permitted only where necessary in the interests of the child.

Where the arrangements give no cause for concern and the parents are not in dispute there will be no need for the court to make an order of any sort. Both parents will retain parental responsibility and either may seek a s. 8 order if they subsequently disagree on any matter relating to the child's upbringing. However, there will be circumstances where a court order is necessary, such as where the child's carer does not have parental responsibility: *B v B (A Minor) (Residence Order)* (1992).

By virtue of s. 1(2), the court must have regard to the general principle that any delay in determining a question which relates to a child's upbringing is likely to prejudice that child's welfare. To this end s. 11 requires the court to draw up a timetable in s. 8 proceedings so that the case may proceed without delay.

SECTION 8 ORDERS

5. Section 8 orders

Under s. 8 of the CA 1989, the court has power to make the following orders relating to a child and his upbringing:

(a) A **residence order** which is an order settling the arrangements to be made as to the person with whom a child is to live.

(b) A **contact order** which is an order requiring the person with whom the child lives, or is to live, to allow the child to visit or stay with the person named in the order, or for that person and the child otherwise to have contact with each other.

(c) A **prohibited steps order** which is an order that no step which could be taken by a parent in meeting his or her parental responsibility for a child, and which is of a kind specified in the order, shall be taken by any person without the consent of the court.

(d) A **specific issue order** which is an order giving directions for the purpose of determining a specific question which has arisen, or which may arise, in connection with any aspect of parental responsibility for a child.

These orders deal comprehensively with matters formerly requiring access orders, injunctions, custody and custodianship orders and other remedies previously available under various statutory provisions now repealed. They can only be made with respect to children under the age of 16, unless there are exceptional circumstances: s. 9(7).

A s. 8 order may be made for a specified period; it may impose conditions on those it affects and it may contain directions as to how it shall be carried out: s. 11(7). In *Re O (Minor) (Imposition of Conditions)* (1995) the Court of Appeal were prepared to attach conditions to a residence order. It approved arrangements that the mother should send photos of the child to the father every three months, send him progress reports from nursery school, inform him of significant illness and send medical reports and accept delivery of cards and presents.

There is no presumption that one parent is better suited to care for a child by reason of gender, and the old idea that young children and girls approaching puberty should be with their mothers was rejected by the Court of Appeal in *Re S (Minor: Custody)* (1991). However, in *Re W (A Minor) (Residence Order)* (1992) the Court of Appeal did indicate that there was a rebuttable presumption that a baby's interests were best served by being with its mother. When deciding with whom a child shall live, the court must consider each case on its facts, and exercise its discretion in accordance with the fundamental principles laid down in the CA 1989.

A residence order may be made in favour of more than one person, even if the people concerned live separately: s. 11(4). The order may specify, for example, that the child lives with one parent during term-time and another during the school holidays. However, the courts have disapproved so called 'time sharing' arrangements because of the child's need for a settled home: *Re H (A Minor)* (1993); *Riley v Riley* (1986).

A contact order may cover the usual sort of access arrangement, e.g. personal visits, overnight stays and holidays. It may also provide for other less-personal forms of contact such as letters and telephone calls.

In *Re B (Minors: Access)* (1992) the Court of Appeal said that the power to deprive contact from a parent should not be exercised lightly, even, as in this case, the father's behaviour was 'eccentric and bizarre.'

In *C v C (Child Abuse: Access)* (1988) the alleged abuser of his child was still allowed contact, although under strict supervision.

That being said, research has shown that a substantial number of non-resident parents lose contact within a few years of divorce.

In *Re N (A Minor: Access)* (1992) the court refused to make an order where a teenager implacably refused to visit his father, even though his objections were the result of indoctrination and emotional blackmail by the mother.

Specific issue and prohibited steps orders give the courts power to decide particular issues that arise but may not be used as an indirect means of obtaining a residence or contact order: s. 9(5)(a). Thus, the court cannot be asked to make a specific issue order requiring a child to live with a particular person. Nor may the court make a specific issue order for the purpose of regulating occupation of the family home.

In *Re H (Prohibited Steps Order)* (1995) the Court of Appeal held that a prohibited steps order could not be used to achieve the same result as an order for no contact but as the alleged child abuser was not party to the proceedings an order could be made.

6. Making a section 8 order

The court can make a s. 8 order in any family proceedings where a question arises as to the welfare of any child: s. 10(1). The definition of 'family proceedings, can be found in Chapter 10 (10:**5**).

There are three ways in which a s. 8 order may be made:

(a) The court may be asked to make an order in the course of family proceedings: s. 10(1)(a). For example, either party to divorce proceedings can make an application for s. 8 orders.

(b) It may make an order of its own volition in the course of family proceedings, even though no application has been made: s. 10(1)(b). The court may decide, for example, in domestic violence proceedings that the welfare of the child requires it to make s. 8 orders even though the adult parties have not asked for it nor joined the children to the proceedings.

(c) It may be asked to make an order where there are no other proceedings in progress: s. 20.

7. Who may apply?

The CA 1989 creates two categories of applicant for a s. 8 order: those who are entitled to apply and those who may apply only with the leave of the court.

Parents, guardians and any person with the benefit of a residence order fall within the first category: s. 10(4). An unmarried father also falls within this category, whether or not he has parental responsibility.

By virtue of s. 10(5) the following persons are entitled to apply for a residence or contact order, but not a prohibited steps or specific issue order:

(a) Step-parents

(b) Any person with whom the child has lived for at least three years out of the last five

(c) Any person who:

(i) where the child is subject to a residence order, has the consent of each person in whose favour the order is made
(ii) where the child is in care, has the consent of the local authority
(iii) in any other case has the consent of each of those having parental responsibility.

Anyone else may apply for a s. 8 order with the leave of the court.

The court must have regard to the following matters when considering an application for leave (s. 10(9)):

(a) The nature of the proposed application.

(b) The applicant's connection with the child.

(c) Any risk that the proposed application may disrupt the child's life to an extent which is harmful.

(d) Where the child is being looked after by a local authority, the authority's plans for the child and the wishes and feelings of the parents.

In *Re A and Others (Minors) (Residence Order: Leave to Apply)* (1992) the Court of Appeal HELD that s. 1(1) did not apply and the court was not therefore required to have regard to the child's welfare as its paramount consideration because the application did not involve issues with regard to the child's upbringing.

A child may, with leave, apply for a s. 8 order but this will only be granted if the court is satisfied that the child has sufficient understanding to make the proposed application: s. 10(8).

When dealing with an application the court may direct that no further applications be made by any person named in the order without the leave of the court: s. 9(14).

A court cannot make a s. 8 order which will last beyond the child's 16th birthday unless there are exceptional circumstances. In such a case the order may continue until the child reaches the age of 18: s. 9(6)(10)(11).

A care order will automatically terminate all existing s. 8 orders. A care order is an order placing a child in the care of a local authority.

8. Effect of orders

A non-parent who obtains a residence order will acquire parental responsibility while the order is in force, although such a person may not consent to the child's adoption or appoint a guardian: s. 12(2)(3).

An unmarried father who obtains a residence order will automatically be granted a parental responsibility order under s. 4 if he does not already have parental responsibility. Unless the court directs otherwise, he will then retain parental responsibility for the child even if the residence order comes to an end.

Although it is possible to grant shared residence orders, the courts have made it clear that they should be granted only in unusual circumstances.

Re H (Shared Residence; Parental Responsibility) (1994) The elder child was not the natural child of the husband but did not find out until these proceedings had commenced. The disclosure caused him considerable distress. The Court of Appeal confirmed the trial judges' shared residence order as it was important that the child had the security and knowledge not only that the husband wished to treat the child as if he were his father but the law gave approval to this position.

9. Wardship

The remedy of wardship as a means of resolving disputes concerning children is not repealed by the CA 1989 but its importance has diminished.

The power to make minors wards of court arises from the *parens patriae* jurisdiction of the High Court and is exercised by the Family Division: s. 1(2) Administration of Justice Act 1970. Wardship effectively vests a form of parental responsibility in the court, although day-to-day care and control may be entrusted to a named individual.

Wardship has great flexibility, which appealed to local authorities as an alternative to care proceedings, pre-CA 1989. It has been used to resolve parental disputes, to control children beyond parental control and even to allow a third party to challenge decisions concerning a child's upbringing.

Re D (A Minor) (1976). A social worker challenged a decision to sterilise.

Some, but not all, of the needs met by wardship are now dealt with by orders under the CA 1989.

Wardship proceedings fall within the definition of family proceedings for the purposes of the CA 1989 (*see* 10:5 above) and the court may therefore make the full range of orders under s. 8, including a residence order.

Prohibited steps and specific issue orders are modelled upon wardship powers. The wardship court may make orders for the recovery of missing children and to prevent unauthorised removal abroad, but equivalent orders may also be made under the provisions of the CA 1989 and Family Law Act 1986, ss. 33, 34 and 37.

Perhaps of more importance is that s. 100 of the CA allows local authorities to make wardship applications in only the most exceptional circumstances. It was said during the passage of the Children Bill that wardship applications would 'whither and die'.

CHILD ABDUCTION

10. Child abduction

Under s. 1 of the Child Abduction Act 1984 it is an offence for a parent or person with a residence order to remove a child under 16 from the United Kingdom without the consent of all other persons with parental responsibility or the leave of the court. It is also an offence for a person without parental responsibility to abduct a child under 16 from the person who has lawful control of that child: s. 2.

Where there is reasonable suspicion that an offence will be committed, the police have power to arrest a parent to prevent abduction. An alternative is to seek CA 1989, s. 8 orders with conditions attached preventing removal from the country.

Passports for children are granted on the application of a person with parental responsibility, and objectors can ask that the Passport Office refuse the issue of one. If there is one in existence, the court may order that it be surrendered.

If there is a real and immediate risk that a child may be removed from the United Kingdom in breach of the Child Abduction Act within the next 48 hours, the police can be asked to institute a port alert. The child's name will then be placed on a stop-list maintained by immigration officials for a period of four weeks and then automatically removed. The port alert may be renewed on further application.

Other statutes also assist in the recovery of abducted children. Under the Family Law Act 1986, orders obtained in one part of the United Kingdom are recognised and enforced in any other part. Thus a residence order obtained in England may be enforced in the courts of Scotland or Northern Ireland.

Part I of the Child Abduction and Custody Act 1985 implements the Hague Convention on Civil Aspects of Child Abduction. It enables a person with parental responsibility living in one country to recover a child under 16 who has been wrongfully removed or retained in another, provided that both countries are signatories to the Convention. A child removed within the preceding 12 months must be returned unless there is a grave risk of physical or psychological harm or the child objects. If the child has been away for more than a year its return may not be ordered if it has settled into its new surroundings.

Part II of the 1985 Act implements the European Convention on Recognition and Enforcement of Decisions Concerning the Custody of Children. It enables a person who has obtained a residence or contact order in this country to secure its recognition and enforcement in any other state which is a signatory to the Convention. Where the child was removed within the preceding six months, the child's return is likely to be sanctioned. Where a longer period has elapsed, circumstances have changed or the child's return would be incompatible with the fundamental principles of family law in the state concerned, the order may not be enforced.

If a child has been taken to a country outside the United Kingdom which is not a party to either of these two Conventions, then the deprived parent has no alternative but to start proceedings in the country concerned.

Progress test 12

1. Name and distinguish the orders which may be made under s. 8 of the CA 1989.

2. Who is entitled to apply for a s. 8 order?

3. How is parental responsibility limited when a residence order is in force?

4. Outline the matters contained in the checklist in s. 1(3) of the CA 1989.

5. H and W married in 1987. They adopted twins, B and G, then aged five, in 1988. H and W separated in 1995, when H went to live in Spain. He

returned in 1997 and is unhappy that W is living with the children at the house of C, her boyfriend. H wants the children to live with him, W wants them to stay with her and C. B wants to live with his newly found natural mother and G wants to go and live with her boyfriend who is aged 17.

Discuss the position of all the parties. Would your opinion change if C were female, not male?

6. How has the inherent jurisdiction of the High Court in wardship been restricted by the CA 1989?

7. What steps may a parent take to prevent a child's removal abroad?

13

Local authorities and the family

1. Introduction

Local authorities, and in some circumstances the National Society for the Protection of Cruelty to Children, are given statutory responsibilities for 'children in need'. These range from the provision of accommodation to taking the child into care. They may apply to the court for a child assessment order where there is cause to suspect that a child is suffering or likely to suffer significant harm. There is power to make an emergency protection order to secure a child's removal from home in the short term. Finally, a care order or a supervision order may be made where long-term protection is required.

SCOPE OF LOCAL AUTHORITY DUTIES

2. Role of the local authority

The CA 1989 requires local authorities to provide services for children so that wherever possible they may be brought up within their own families. Section 17(1) imposes a duty on every local authority:

(a) To safeguard and promote the welfare of children within their area who are in need *and*

(b) So far as is consistent with that duty, to promote the upbringing of such children by their families by providing a range and level of services appropriate to those children's needs.

The duty only applies to children 'in need,' defined by s. 17(10) as a child:

(a) who is unlikely to achieve or maintain, or to have the opportunity of achieving or maintaining, a reasonable standard of health or development without the provision of services by a local authority under Part III of the Act *or*

(b) whose health or development is likely to be significantly impaired or further impaired, without the provision of such services *or*

(c) who is disabled. A child is disabled if blind, deaf or dumb or suffers from a mental disorder of any kind or is substantially or permanently handicapped by illness, injury or congenital deformity: s. 17(11).

The CA specifies certain services which local authorities must provide for children in need. The importance of these matters is often overlooked: they were included in the Act as measures which would hopefully prevent the instigation of care proceedings. They are set out in Part III of the Act and Schedule 2, Part I and include:

(a) Appropriate day care provision for under-fives (s. 18(1)).

(b) Appropriate after-school and holiday activities for school age children (s. 18(5)).

(c) Services at home including advice, guidance and counselling; occupational, social, cultural or recreational activities; home help including laundry facilities; transport or assistance with travel expenses in order to use any services provided and assistance with holidays (Schedule 2, paragraph 8).

In addition local authorities are required to provide family centres as appropriate for the use of all children within their area and not just children in need (Schedule 2, paragraph 9). A family centre is a general term which can be applied to a broad range of facilities which may include playgroups, community centres and therapeutic facilities where trained professionals carry out intensive casework with damaged families.

Services may be provided to the child or to any member of the child's family with a view to safeguarding or promoting the child's welfare. 'Family' in this context has a broad meaning. It includes any person with parental responsibility for a child and any other person with whom the child has been living.

3. Provision of accommodation

It is not always possible for children to be looked after at home even with local authority support. CA 1989, s. 20(1) imposes a duty on local authorities to provide accommodation for any child in need within their area who appears to require accommodation as a result of.

(a) there being no person who has parental responsibility *or*

(b) the child being lost or having been abandoned *or*

(c) the person who has been caring for it being prevented (whether or not permanently and for whatever reason) from providing suitable accommodation or care.

There is additional duty under s. 20(3) to provide accommodation for children in need aged 16 or 17 years whose welfare the authority considers is likely to be seriously prejudiced if they do not provide accommodation.

Local authorities have a discretion to provide accommodation to any child within their area if they consider that this would safeguard or promote the child's welfare: s. 20(4). Such accommodation may be provided even though a person with parental responsibility for the child is able to provide accommodation.

Before providing accommodation, the local authority must so far as is reasonably practicable ascertain the child's wishes regarding the provision of accommodation and give due consideration (having regard to the child's age and understanding) to such wishes of the child: s. 20(6)

Local authorities are also required to give due consideration to the child's religious persuasion, racial origin and cultural and linguistic background: s. 22(5).

When finding a placement for an accommodated child, a local authority must first consider placing it with a parent or person with parental responsibility. If this is not possible a placement with a relative, friend or person otherwise connected with the child should be sought unless in either case this would not be reasonably practicable or consistent with the child's welfare: s. 23(6). If children have to be placed with foster parents or in children's homes, the Act requires that as far as possible accommodation should be near to the child's home and siblings be accommodated together: s. 23(7). Accommodation for disabled children should not be unsuitable for their needs: s. 23(8).

An accommodated child is not a child in care. The local authority does not acquire parental responsibility for it although it has a duty to safeguard and promote its welfare while looking after it: s. 22(3).

A person with parental responsibility may remove a child from accommodation provided by or on behalf of a local authority at any time without giving notice: s. 20(8). Furthermore, a local authority may not provide accommodation for a child under s. 20 against the wishes of any person

149

who has parental responsibility for the child and is willing and able to provide or arrange accommodation: s. 20(7).

A local authority cannot refuse to return a child on the request of a person with parental responsibility. If it wishes to retain the child an application must be made for an emergency protection order or a care order and the relevant statutory grounds must be satisfied.

CARE AND SUPERVISION ORDERS

4. Care and supervision orders

The fundamental principles laid down in s. 1 of the CA 1989 apply to applications for care orders, but not to emergency protection or child assessment orders as these are only short-term remedies. There is only one way in which a child may be placed under the care or supervision of a local authority and that is to satisfy the 'Threshold Criteria' laid down by s. 31 of the CA 1989, that is:

(a) that the child concerned is suffering, or is likely to suffer, significant harm *and*

(b) that this is attributable to:

   (*i*) the care given, or likely to be given, if the order were not made, not being what it would be reasonable to expect a parent to give *or*
   (*ii*) the child's being beyond parental control.

A care or supervision order may therefore be made where a child has actually suffered significant harm or where there is good reason to anticipate this. An application may be made to remove a child from home or to prevent its removal from local authority accommodation if the child is living there on a voluntary basis.

The term 'harm' is defined by s. 31(9) as 'ill treatment or the impairment of health or development'.

Development means 'physical, intellectual, emotional, social or behavioural development'.

Health means 'physical or mental health' and 'ill treatment' includes sexual abuse and forms of ill treatment which are not physical: s. 31(9).

The House of Lords in *Re M (a Minor) (Care Order: Threshold Conditions)* (1994) HELD that if the child has suffered significant harm, the relevant date at the time of disposal of the application is the date when the local authority initiated protective measures and subsequent events could be regarded as a continuation of the process. In this case, a very young child had witnessed the murder of his mother by his father, who was sentenced to life imprisonment. By the time of this appeal, the arrangements for the child had been settled to everyone's approval other than the father's but the threshold had been crossed and their Lordships felt able to impose a care order confirming the existing arrangements.

In *Re H (Sexual Abuse: Standard of Proof)* (1996) the House of Lords (by a majority of 3:2) held that 'likely harm' meant a real possibility of harm based on the evidence, using the civil standard of proof, i.e. the balance of probabilities.

'Harm' has already been widely interpreted: in *Re O (A Minor) (Care Order: Education Procedure)* (1992) Ewbank J held that regular non-attendance at school could lead to a care order, rather than an education supervision order because the child had clearly suffered significant harm by not attending school.

Even if the threshold criteria are met, they still only impose a minimum level for intervention. The court must still be satisfied that an order will be better for the child than no order at all (s. 1(5)) and it may use its power to make a s. 8 order instead of the care or supervision order sought.

The paramount consideration in any decision is the welfare of the child and the factors mentioned in the checklist in s. 1(3) must be taken into account (*see* 12:3).

Only a local authority or the NSPCC may apply for a care or supervision order. The court can only make an order in respect of a child under the age of 17, or 16 if married. An application can be made independently or in the course of other family proceedings in the same way as other CA orders.

In *Re B (Care or Supervision Order)* (1996) Holman J took the opportunity to review the authorities which had established criteria for making a care order as opposed to a supervision order. The situation is that:

(a) A care order could be made even if all the parties agreed that the child could continue living at home: *Re T (A Minor) (Care or Supervision Order)* (1994).

(b) A care order can be made even if the local authority was only seeking a supervision order, because the power to remove a child in emergency are significantly stronger under a care order.

(c) Under a care order, responsibility is with the local authority whereas under a supervision order the duty is with the parent.

In the instant case, the judge ruled that a care order was a more serious order and should only be made if the stronger order was necessary for the protection of the child.

5. Effect of care orders

A care order gives a local authority parental responsibility for a child subject to certain limitations: s. 33(3)(a). It may not:

(a) Cause a child to be brought up in a different religion to that of its family *or*

(b) Appoint a guardian *or*

(c) Consent to its adoption.

While a child is in care, no one may cause the child to be known by a new surname or remove the child from the United Kingdom without the consent of every person with parental responsibility or the leave of the court. This does not apply to absences of less than one month. Local authority foster parents may therefore take a foster child on a short holiday abroad without parental consent.

A local authority will share parental responsibility with parents while a care order is in force, but the authority has power to control what the parents may or may not do: s. 33(3)(b). This power may only be exercised where necessary to 'safeguard or promote the child's welfare': s. 33(4). Effectively, the local authority will control where the child lives and other important matters even though it does have a duty to consult parents and take their wishes and feelings into account: s. 22(4)(5).

Before making a care order a court must consider the arrangements which the local authority have made, or propose to make, for contact with the child, and must invite the parties to comment on those arrangements: s. 34(11). In fact, there is a duty to allow the child reasonable contact with its parents, any guardian and anyone else responsible for its care under the terms of a court order immediately before the care order was made: s. 34(1). This will include an unmarried father (whether or not he has parental responsibility) and anyone previously granted a residence order or care and control of the child in wardship proceedings.

If a local authority considers for any reason that contact may be bad for a child, it may in an emergency refuse to allow it for up to seven days. After this it must apply to the court for authority to refuse contact: s. 34(4). In dealing with such an application, the welfare of the child is, of course, the court's paramount consideration and the court is permitted to review the local authority's long-term plans for the child in reaching its decision: *Re B (Termination of Contact: Paramount Consideration)* (1993).

Re D and H (Care: Termination of Contact) (1997). The Court of Appeal re-emphasised that the local authority care plan should command the greatest respect and consideration from the court. The lower court had made an order terminating contact in conflict with the local authority plan. HELD The better course was to give the local authority leave to apply under s. 34(4) to terminate contact when it felt the time was right to do so in accordance with the care plan.

The House of Lords in *Birmingham City Council and Others* v *H (A Minor)* (1994) HELD that where an application is made under s. 34(1) for an order terminating contact, the welfare principle applies to the child and not to the mother even if the mother is herself a child within the meaning of the Act.

6. Duration

A care order will last until the child's 18th birthday unless it is brought to an end sooner. It is automatically discharged by adoption or the making of a residence order. It may also be discharged by a court on the application of the child, any person with parental responsibility for the child or the local authority itself: s. 39(1).

7. Supervision orders

A supervision order places a child under the supervision of a local authority or, in certain circumstances, a probation officer. A supervisor is not given parental responsibility but it is his or her duty to advise, assist and befriend the child. The supervisor must also take steps to give effect to the order and must consider whether to apply for discharge or variation if the order is not complied with or is no longer necessary. The court may include various conditions in a supervision order. The child or the person looking after it may be required to comply with the supervisor's directions to participate in specified activities. The court may include a direction for medical or psychiatric examination or treatment.

A supervision order may be varied or discharged on the application of the child, any person with parental responsibility for it, or the supervisor: s. 39(2).

To some extent, a supervision order lacks teeth. The only way to enforce it is for the local authority to apply for a care order. The protection of the child is the decisive factor when the court decides whether to make a supervision or care order: *Re D (A Minor) (Care or Supervision Order)* (1993); *Re K (Care or Supervision Order)* (1995).

8. Education supervision orders

Separate powers exist where a child of school age is not receiving proper education: s. 36(1). This means efficient full-time education suitable to the child's age, ability, aptitude and any special educational needs s. 36(4).

The court may make an education supervision order on the application of a local education authority: s. 36(1). It will then be the supervisor's duty to advise, assist and befriend the child and its parents so as to secure the child's proper education. An order will initially last for one year but may be extended as often as necessary by up to three years at a time. It will automatically cease when the child reaches school-leaving age.

OTHER ORDERS AND MEASURES

9. Child assessment orders

By virtue of s. 43(i), a local authority or the NSPCC may apply for a child assessment order and the court may make such an order if it is satisfied that:

(a) The applicant has reasonable cause to suspect that a child is suffering, or is likely to suffer, significant harm.

(b) An assessment of the child's health or development, or the way in which it has been treated, is required to enable the applicant to determine whether or not the child is suffering, or likely to suffer, significant harm.

(c) It is unlikely that such an assessment will be made, or be satisfactory, in the absence of a child assessment order.

The order imposes a duty on any person who is in a position to produce the child to produce that child to the person named in the order and to comply with directions relating to the child's assessment as are specified in the order: s. 43(6). A child of sufficient understanding to make an informed decision may refuse to submit to a medical or psychiatric examination or any other assessment: s. 43(8).

The order must specify the nature of the assessment and the date on which it is to begin. It must be completed within seven days unless the court specifies a shorter period. The child cannot be kept away from home overnight unless this is specifically authorised by the court. The applicant does not acquire parental responsibility for the child; this will remain with those previously entitled.

A court can make an emergency protection order instead of a child assessment order if the statutory grounds are met and such order would be more appropriate.

10. Emergency protection orders

Sections 44 and 45 of the CA 1989 allows the court to grant an emergency protection order which gives the applicant wider powers than a child assessment order and is designed for use in different circumstances.

The court may make an order if, but only if, it is satisfied that there is reasonable cause to believe that the child is likely to suffer significant harm if it is not removed to accommodation provided by or on behalf of the applicant or the child does not remain in the place in which it is then being accommodated: s. 44(1)(a).

A court may make an order on the application of a local authority if satisfied that:

(a) The authority is making enquiries under s. 47(1) to ascertain whether it should take any action to safeguard or promote a child's welfare *and*

(b) Those enquiries are being frustrated by the unreasonable refusal of access to the child and the applicant believes that access is required as a matter of urgency: s. 44(1)(b).

The NSPCC is also given the power to apply for an emergency protection order in similar circumstances, that is when it has reasonable cause to suspect significant harm and is denied access to a child: s. 44(1)(c).

The order may last a maximum of eight days and may be extended for a further seven but only if the original applicant was a local authority or the NSPCC.

11. Effects of an emergency protection order

If an emergency protection order is made, it operates to:

(a) Direct that the child be handed over to the applicant *and*

(b) Authorise the removal of the child to accommodation provided by the applicant *and*

(c) Prevent the removal of the child from where it was being accommodated immediately prior to the making of the order: s. 44(4).

Obstruction of the exercise of these powers is a criminal offence: s. 44(5). The order gives the applicant a limited form of parental responsibility; he or she must take only such action as is necessary to safeguard or promote the child's welfare while the order remains in force. Where a child is kept away from home under an emergency protection order the applicant has a duty to return the child as soon as it is safe to do so: s. 44(10).

Sometimes it may be difficult to enforce an emergency protection order or trace a child at risk. In these circumstances the court has a number of additional powers. It may:

(a) Order any person to disclose information about the child's whereabouts: s. 48(1).

(b) Authorise the applicant to enter and search named premises: s. 48(3).

(c) Issue a warrant authorising a police officer to assist in enforcing the order where entry has been refused or access to a child denied: s. 48(9).

The court may also give directions in respect of retaining reasonable contact with the child's parents, anyone with parental responsibility and any person with whom it was living immediately before the order was made: s. 44(13). If this is not desirable for any reason, the court may give directions specifying the contact which is or is not to be allowed between the child and any named person: s. 44(6)(a).

12. Police protection

The police have power to take a child into police protection for up to 72 hours where there is reasonable cause to suspect that the child would otherwise be likely to suffer significant harm: s. 46(1). This is intended to be a short-term remedy and the Act provides for the child to be transferred to local authority accommodation at an early stage. The police are not given parental responsibility, and if the child's continued detention is warranted, the police may apply for an emergency protection order on the local authority's behalf.

13. Guardians *ad litem*

The court has a positive duty to appoint a guardian *ad litem* for the child in most cases unless satisfied that this is not necessary to safeguard the child's interests: s. 41(1). This applies to:

(a) Care proceedings and related applications.

(b) Applications relating to contact under s. 34.

(c) Applications relating to child assessment and emergency protection orders.

(d) Applications for the discharge of care orders or the variation or discharge of supervision orders.

(e) Family proceedings in which the court has made a s. 37 direction and is considering whether to make an interim order.

(f) Applications for residence orders in respect of children who are in care.

The guardian's role is to represent the interests of the child in the proceedings. The guardian is expected to prepare a report for the court and, where necessary, give evidence, and for this purpose is given a right of access to social work records held by the local authority or the NSPCC, as appropriate. However, in *Oxfordshire County Council* v *P* (1995) there were care proceedings in respect of a 12-week-old baby. The mother admitted to the guardian *ad litem* that she had caused injuries to the baby. The guardian went to the police and provided a statement. HELD The guardian should be removed on the grounds of breach of confidentiality.

The guardian may appoint a solicitor for the child and will normally be expected to prepare the child's case with that solicitor. If, however, the child is of an age to give its own instructions and these conflict with those of the guardian, the solicitor must represent the child.

Guardians *ad litem* are selected from panels maintained by local authorities and are usually social workers by training.

Progress test 13

1. What is meant by a child in need?

2. When does a local authority have a duty to provide accommodation for children?

3. What are the threshold criteria for making a care or supervision order?

4. What orders are available to a local authority to enable it to carry out its investigations?

5. What emergency powers are available under the CA 1989 and who may apply them?

6. What is the role of the guardian *ad litem*?

7. H and W have four children under the age of 10. H has serious drug abuse problems. W is the principal wage earner, making a living as a stripper. A

157

neighbour sees her perform at a local club and anonymously telephones the local authority, alleging that the children are 'in grave moral danger.' The local authority want to investigate, but W refuses implacably to let them see the children or to cooperate.

Advise the local authority.

14

Adoption

1. Introduction

Adoption was first introduced into English law in 1926. The modern substantive law is contained in the Adoption Act 1976 (AA 1976) as amended by the CA 1989. References to sections in this chapter are references to sections of the AA 1976 unless otherwise specifically stated.

Adoption means that a child severs all legal relationships with his or her natural parents and replaces them with a new legal relationship with the adoptive parents. An adoption order may contain such terms and conditions as the court thinks fit: s. 12(6). The court could, for example, order that contact be maintained with the child's natural parents or siblings. Adoption proceedings are family proceedings for the purposes of the CA 1989, so the courts are empowered to make s. 8 orders instead of adoption if the court so thinks fit.

THE EFFECTS OF ADOPTION

2. The legal effects of adoption

Section 12 provides that an adoption order gives parental responsibility to the adoptive parents, and any parental responsibility in others, including the natural parents, is extinguished. The adoption order also terminates any orders made under the CA 1989: s. 12(3)(a).

Section 39 provides that, where the adopters are married to each other, the child shall be treated as a legitimate child of the marriage. In any other case, the child will be treated as if born to the adopter in wedlock. In other words, the adopted child shall not be treated as if he or she were illegitimate: s. 39(4).

With regard to the rules of succession, an adopted child is entitled to claim as a natural child of any adoptive parent who dies after 1 January

1976, having made a will on or before that date, unless a contrary intention is expressed. If there is a gift dependant on age, e.g. 'To my eldest child', he or she is assumed to have been born on the date of adoption. On the other hand, a gift which is conditional upon attaining a certain age, such as 18 or 21, will vest on the child's actual birthday.

Section 47(1) provides that for the purposes of marriage and the crime of incest, adoption does not affect the prohibited degrees of relationship which result from a child's birth to his or her natural parents. Although an adopted child cannot marry an adoptive parent, he or she is permitted to marry his or her adoptive sister or brother.

A foreign adoptive child acquires the British citizenship of the parent from the date of adoption.

> *Re W (A Minor) (Adoption: Non-patrial)* (1986). HELD An application should be refused if the main motive was to confer citizenship on the child rather than to promote her welfare.

The case also highlighted that in cases involving foreign children, the following should be taken into account:

(a) The applicant should notify the Home Secretary to enable him to be added as a party if he was so minded.

(b) The weight to be attached to s. 6 (*see* 4 below) decreased as the child neared majority.

(c) The court should consider what other orders might serve the welfare of the child which did not affect nationality or immigration issues.

(d) The balance between the welfare of the child and public policy considerations in relation to nationality and immigration.

CONDITIONS OF ADOPTION

3. Access to birth records

On application any adopted person aged at least 18 whose birth record is kept by the Registrar General must be supplied with the information to enable them to obtain a copy of their birth certificate: s. 51(1). Persons adopted before 12 November 1975 must be counselled before being given that information; those adopted after that date only have to be offered the opportunity of counselling. By virtue of s. 51A, the Registrar General must maintain an Adoption Contact Register which enables both adopted persons and their blood relatives aged at least 18 to provide a contact address.

4. Welfare the first consideration

Section 6 provides that in reaching any decision relating to the adoption of a child, the court or an adoption agency must have regard to all the circumstances, first consideration being given to the need to safeguard and promote the welfare of the child throughout childhood. Section 6 also provides that the child's wishes and feelings must be ascertained and due consideration given to them as far as is reasonably practicable, having regard to the child's age and understanding.

The parliamentary debate took a considerable period of time, trying as they did to strike a balance between parental rights to consent to adoption and the child's welfare. It is interesting to note how far society has progressed in the following decade in arriving at the CA 1989 criteria which makes the child's welfare the paramount consideration.

5. Criteria to be satisfied

The person to be adopted must:

(a) be under 18: s. 72(1) *or*

(b) be at least 19 weeks old and have had a home with the applicant at all times during the preceeding 13 weeks, if either applicant is the child's parent, step-parent or relative, or the child was placed with the applicant by an adoption agency or by order of the High Court: s. 13(1). If the applicant does not meet those criteria, then the child must be at least 12 months old and must have had a home with the applicant at all times during the preceding 12 months: s. 13(2), *or*

(c) never have been married *or*

(d) have parental agreement to the adoption: s. 16 *or*

(e) be free for adoption: s. 18.

Although the Act does not differentiate, there are different types of adoption which involve their own particular and peculiar problems and difficulties. The child in question may be a complete stranger to the adopters. For example, recent publicity concerning unwanted children in Eastern European countries led to numbers of English couples making application for adoption.

161

On the other hand, many applications are made by step-parents to adopt their partner's children. In these circumstances, there must be a temptation on the 'absent' parent's part to give agreement to the order, because this relieves that parent of parental responsibility, and more importantly, of liability to pay child support. Conversely, it is more likely that the court will make a s. 8 residence order under CA 1989 so that the child does not sever his or her links with a natural parent.

There is also the question of so-called 'open' adoptions where both the adopters and the natural parents are aware of each other, their circumstances and the process. It can be the most sensitive and helpful way of transferring responsibility for the child. It is not the most attractive procedure where the actual parent is wanting to sever the relationship with the child.

6. Parental agreement

Each parent or guardian of a child must agree unconditionally to the making of an adoption order. The consent must be freely given, with full understanding of what is involved, and whether or not he or she knows the identity of the applicant: s. 16(1)(b).

A parent cannot impose conditions, although the court may do so under the powers given to it by s. 12(6). This could particularly apply to the child's religious upbringing. Section 7 requires adoption agencies to have regard, as far as practicable, to the wishes of the child's parents as to the child's religious upbringing.

Guardian has the same meaning as in CA 1989. An unmarried father is not a 'parent' unless he has been given parental responsibility: s. 72.

A mother's agreement is ineffective if given within six weeks of the child's birth.

7. Dispensing with parental agreement

The court is given power by s. 16(2) to dispense with the agreement of the parent on one of six specified grounds:

(a) *Parent cannot be found or is incapable of giving agreement.*
'Cannot be found' means cannot be found by taking reasonable steps, but it also includes no practical means of communicating with the parents. In *Re R (Adoption)* (1967) the parents lived in a totalitarian country and any attempts to contact them could have put them in danger. HELD They 'could not be found' for the purposes of the Act. It was also held that they were

incapable of agreeing because it was impossible to ask them and they would probably not be permitted to freely consent by the regime.

(b) *Parent unreasonably withholding consent.*
It is obviously reasonable that a parent will want to preserve his or her relationship with the child, so it follows that the fact that adoption is in the child's welfare does not make the withholding of the agreement unreasonable. However, there are circumstances where the withholding of agreement will be so regarded.

> *Re W* (1971). An unmarried mother placed her third child with foster parents, but 18 months later withdrew her agreement to adoption of the child by the foster parents. HELD by the House of Lords: the test to be applied is what a reasonable parent, placed in the situation of the actual parent, would do in all the circumstances of the case. As a reasonable parent would have regard to the child's welfare, that welfare must be a factor in determining reasonableness.

> *Re D* (1977). A wife divorced her husband because of his homosexuality. She had custody of their eight-year-old boy, she remarried and her new husband wanted to adopt him. The natural father refused agreement because he wished to continue contact. He was prepared to give an undertaking that the boy would not be brought into contact with his homosexual friends. HELD by the House of Lords: a reasonable parent, taking an objective view, would inevitably want to protect his son from the risk of exposure to homosexuality. It followed that the father's refusal to consent was unreasonable and therefore his agreement was dispensed with.

There has been considerable judicial argument as to whether s. 6 applies to the test of reasonableness of withholding agreement to adoption. If the objective tests of *Re W* and *Re D* are to be applied, the argument would appear to be purely academic.

The 'reasonable parent' test applies regardless of age. Thus, the views of a teenage mother will be judged against the views of a reasonably mature parent.

(c) *Parent has persistently failed without reasonable cause to discharge his parental duties in relation to the child.*
Parental duties includes a parent's natural and moral duty to show affection, care and interest, and the common law or statutory duty to maintain the child. 'Persistently' has been held to mean permanently and involve a complete abrogation of parental duties.

163

(d) *Parent has abandoned or neglected the child.*

Restrictive interpretations of these words means that abandonment has its criminal interpretation, literally leaving the child on the roadside or on someone's doorstep, and neglected also has the criminal interpretation.

(e) *Parent has persistently ill treated the child.*

There is no decided case on this particular section. The better view is that there must be more than one act but the extent of ill treatment is unclear.

(f) *Parent has seriously ill treated the child.*

This is an alternative to the above section to deal with the absence of persistence but still address ill treatment which cannot be ignored.

FREEING FOR ADOPTION

8. Freeing for adoption

The adoption process is fraught with uncertainty. Potential adopters can never be sure that the natural parents will either give, or withdraw, agreement to the adoption; s. 18 was an attempt to deal with those uncertainties by giving the court power to declare a child free for adoption before proceedings are commenced and even before a child has been placed for adoption. Such an order means that parental agreement is no longer necessary. It is only available on the application of an adoption agency.

Section 18 can only be invoked if the court is satisfied that the parents have freely consented with full understanding or that consent should be dispensed with on the grounds set out in **7** above. However, such agreement can only be dispensed with if the child is placed for adoption or the court is satisfied that such placement is likely.

An application cannot be made unless a parent or guardian consents to the making of the order, or the adoption agency applies for the agreement to be dispensed with, the child being in the agency's care. A local authority is an adoption agency for this purpose if a child is in its care: s. 18(2).

Section 18(7) provides that the court must be satisfied that an unmarried father who does not have parental responsibility has either no intention of applying for it or, if he has, that he would be likely to fail.

The parents or guardians, or those that can be found, have to be given the option of expressing a preference for not being involved in future questions concerning the child's adoption. If they do, they have no right to be informed whether or not an adoption order has been made within 12 months nor to apply for the revocation of a s. 18 order: s. 20.

A freeing order vests parental responsibility in the adoption agency until an adoption order is made and terminates any order made under the CA 1989.

On the face of it, a freeing order assists both agencies and adopters in removing the uncertainties from the process. In practice it has been little used, principally because of delays in the judicial process in making the freeing order.

9. Revocation of a freeing for adoption order

By virtue of s. 20, the natural parent may apply to the court for a s. 18 order to be revoked on the ground that he or she wishes to resume parental responsibility. Such application can only be made within 12 months of the freeing order and the child does not have its home with the person with whom it has been placed for adoption: s. 20(1).

The effect of the revocation of the freeing order is that:

(a) Parental responsibility given to the adoption agency is extinguished: s. 20(3)(a).

(b) Parental responsibility is restored to the natural mother and the father if they were married at the child's birth: s. 20(3)(b).

(c) Any orders or agreements under CA 1989, s. 4 or any court appointment of a guardian are revived. Section 20(3)(A) states that revocation does not revive other CA 1989 orders or maintenance orders or affect any person's parental responsibility during the subsistence of the freeing order.

A slightly more complicated situation recently faced the House of Lords in *Re G (Adoption: Freeing Order)* (1997). The child had been freed for adoption but had not been adopted, but it was accepted that he could not be safely returned to his mother. HELD A revocation order could be made provided that the child's welfare could be protected by other parts of the children legislation. It was hard to accept that parliament intended the child to remain in some form of limbo. The local authority would apply for a care order to which the mother would consent and on that basis the freeing order would be discharged.

WHO MAY ADOPT?

10. Criteria to be met by potential adopters

If a married couple apply, at least one must be domiciled in the UK (s. 14(2)) and must also have a home in England or Wales.

If the applicants are a parent and a step-parent, the former must at least be 18 and the latter aged 21 or over: s. 14(1)(B).

An unmarried person who meets the above domiciliary requirements may apply if they are aged 21 or over: s. 15(1).

A married person over the age of 21 and satisfying the domiciliary requirements may apply if:

(a) His or her spouse cannot be found or, by virtue of the Human Fertilisation and Embryology Act 1990, there is no other parent *or*

(b) The spouses are living apart and the separation is likely to be permanent *or*

(c) The other spouse is incapable of applying for an order by reason of ill health, physical or mental.

If the application is made by the child's natural mother or father alone, an order cannot be made unless the court is satisfied that the other parent is dead, cannot be found or is excluded for some other reason: s. 15(3).

11. Suitability of applicants for an order

The court will not make an adoption order unless the court is satisfied that the adoption agency, or local authority, have had the opportunity to observe the child in the new home environment: s. 13(3).

If no agency has been involved, the applicant must give at least three months notice of intention to apply for an order to the local authority, who are then required to investigate and produce a report to the court on the suitability of the applicant.

Over and above the statutory requirements, adoption agencies will in practice impose additional requirements. For example, babies will only usually be placed with couples below the ages of 35 for the wife and 40 for the husband, and who have been married for three years or more and are infertile. Others are considered for placements of 'special needs children.'

All may be required to undergo medical tests, provide character references and discuss their lifestyles with the adoption agency.

In *Re W (Adoption: Homosexual Adopter)* (1997) the local authority applied for a freeing order as a step to an adoption application by a homosexual. HELD There is no bar, either in law or in public policy, that would prevent an adoption application by a homosexual, either living alone or with a partner.

The last Conservative government were especially critical of the 'political correctness' and rigidity of these procedures and threatened reform if they were to be re-elected.

12. Convention adoptions

Section 17 provides for adoption by persons who are not domiciled in the UK. The section embodies the rules laid down by the 1965 Hague Convention on the adoption of children.

The child to be adopted must be under 18, unmarried and a resident of the UK or a convention country as designated by order of the Secretary of State: s. 72(1).

If the applicants are married, then either:

(a) each of them must be a UK national *or*

(b) a national of a convention country habitually resident in the UK *or*

(c) both must be UK nationals resident in a convention country.

A single applicant must satisfy the requirements of **(b)** and **(c)**
Parental agreement is necessary if the child is a UK national.

13. Proposals for reform

Reform has been under discussion for some time, amid mounting criticism of practice and procedure. Following a number of discussion papers, a White Paper was published and a draft Adoption Bill was presented in 1996. The then government promised legislation 'as soon as parliamentary time allows' but the bill did not survive the 1997 General Election.

The principal changes were aimed at making adoption agencies more accountable and to involve the court in adoption plans at an earlier stage. If an adoption agency cannot reach agreement with the parent, it must apply for a 'placement order' thereby acquiring parental responsibility. Prospective adopters are also to be given parental responsibility. Not surprisingly, the welfare of the child is to be the paramount consideration and this will be the only ground for dispensing with parental agreement.

The bill made provision for step-parents to acquire parental responsibility without severing the legal relationship of the other natural parent.

Progress test 14

1. What is the effect of an adoption order?

2. Who may apply for an adoption order?

3. On what grounds may a parent's agreement be dispensed with?

4. What is a freeing order?

5. M has a history of schizophrenia. She has three children by three different fathers: A, aged 14, B, aged 12, and C, aged 3. The local authority took the children into care two years ago when M was admitted to a mental hospital. Their care plan is that the children should be adopted by their respective foster parents.

   M has now been discharged, wants C to be returned to her and objects to adoption on the grounds that C will lose contact with her siblings.

   Advise M.

6. How would your advice differ if the Adoption Bill 1996 had come into force?

Appendix

Family Law Act 1996

FAMILY LAW ACT 1996

(c 27)

An Act to make provision with respect to: divorce and separations; legal aid in connection with mediation in disputes relating to family matters; proceedings in cases where marriages have broken down; rights of occupation of certain domestic premises; prevention of molestation; the inclusion in certain orders under the Children Act 1989 of provisions about the occupation of a dwelling-house; the transfer of tenancies between spouses and persons who have lived together as husband and wife; and for connected purposes

[4 July 1996]

PART I

PRINCIPLES OF PARTS II AND III

1 The general principles underlying Parts II and III

The court and any person, in exercising functions under or in consequence of Parts II and III, shall have regard to the following general principles—

(a) that the institution of marriage is to be supported;

(b) that the parties to a marriage which may have broken down are to be encouraged to take all practicable steps, whether by marriage counselling or otherwise, to save the marriage;

(c) that a marriage which has irretrievably broken down and is being brought to an end should be brought to an end—

    (i) with minimum distress to the parties and to the children affected;

    (ii) with questions dealt with in a manner designed to promote as good a continuing relationship between the parties and any children affected as is possible in the circumstances; and

    (iii) without costs being unreasonably incurred in connection with the procedures to be followed in bringing the marriage to an end; and

(d) that any risk to one of the parties to a marriage, and to any children, of violence from the other party should, so far as reasonably practicable, be removed or diminished.

PART II

DIVORCE AND SEPARATION

Court orders

2 Divorce and separation

(1) The court may—
- (a) by making an order (to be known as a divorce order), dissolve a marriage; or
- (b) by making an order (to be known as a separation order), provide for the separation of the parties to a marriage.

(2) Any such order comes into force on being made.

(3) A separation order remains in force—
- (a) while the marriage continues; or
- (b) until cancelled by the court on the joint application of the parties.

3 Circumstances in which orders are made

(1) If an application for a divorce order or for a separation order is made to the court under this section by one or both of the parties to a marriage, the court shall make the order applied for if (but only if)—
- (a) the marriage has broken down irretrievably;
- (b) the requirements of section 8 about information meetings are satisfied;
- (c) the requirements of section 9 about the parties' arrangements for the future are satisfied; and
- (d) the application has not been withdrawn.

(2) A divorce order may not be made if an order preventing divorce is in force under section 10.

(3) If the court is considering an application for a divorce order and an application for a separation order in respect of the same marriage it shall proceed as if it were considering only the application for a divorce order unless—
- (a) an order preventing divorce is in force with respect to the marriage;
- (b) the court makes an order preventing divorce; or
- (c) section 7(6) or (13) applies.

4 Conversion of separation order into divorce order

(1) A separation order which is made before the second anniversary of the marriage may not be converted into a divorce order under this section until after that anniversary:

(2) A separation order may not be converted into a divorce order under this section at any time while—
- (a) an order preventing divorce is in force under section 10; or
- (b) subsection (4) applies.

(3)   Otherwise, if a separation order is in force and an application for a divorce order—

    (a) is made under this section by either or both of the parties to the marriage, and

    (b) is not withdrawn,

the court shall grant the application once the requirements of section 11 have been satisfied.

(4)   Subject to subsection (5), this subsection applies if—

    (a) there is a child of the family who is under the age of sixteen when the application under this section is made; or

    (b) the application under this section is made by one party and the other party applies to the court, before the end of such period as may be prescribed by rules of court, for time for further reflection.

(5)   Subsection (4)—

    (a) does not apply if, at the time when the application under this section is made, there is an occupation order or a non-molestation order in force in favour of the applicant, or of a child of the family, made against the other party;

    (b) does not apply if the court is satisfied that delaying the making of a divorce order would be significantly detrimental to the welfare of any child of the family;

    (c) ceases to apply—

        (i)   at the end of the period of six months beginning with the end of the period for reflection and consideration by reference to which the separation order was made; or

        (ii) if earlier, on there ceasing to be any children of the family to whom subsection (4)(a) applied.

Marital breakdown

5   Marital breakdown

(1)   A marriage is to be taken to have broken down irretrievably if (but only if)—

    (a) a statement has been made by one (or both) of the parties that the maker of the statement (or each of them) believes that the marriage has broken down;

    (b) the statement complies with the requirements of section 6;

    (c) the period for reflection and consideration fixed by section 7 has ended; and

    (d) the application under section 3 is accompanied by a declaration by the party making the application that—

        (i)   having reflected on the breakdown, and

        (ii) having considered the requirements of this Part as to the parties' arrangements for the future,

    the applicant believes that the marriage cannot be saved.

(2)   The statement and the application under section 3 do not have to be made by the same party.

(3)   An application may not be made under section 3 by reference to a particular statement if—
(a) the parties have jointly given notice (in accordance with rules of court) withdrawing the statement; or
(b) a period of one year ("the specified period") has passed since the end of the period for reflection and consideration.

(4)   Any period during which an order preventing divorce is in force is not to count towards the specified period mentioned in subsection (3)(b).

(5)   Subsection (6) applies if, before the end of the specified period, the parties jointly give notice to the court that they are attempting reconciliation but require additional time.

(6)   The specified period—
(a) stops running on the day on which the notice is received by the court; but
(b) resumes running on the day on which either of the parties gives notice to the court that the attempted reconciliation has been unsuccessful.

(7)   If the specified period is interrupted by a continuous period of more than 18 months, any application by either of the parties for a divorce order or for a separation order must be by reference to a new statement received by the court at any time after the end of the 18 months.

(8)   The Lord Chancellor may by order amend subsection (3)(b) by varying the specified period.

6   Statement of marital breakdown

(1)   A statement under section 5(1)(a) is to be known as a statement of marital breakdown; but in this Part it is generally referred to as "a statement".

(2)   If a statement is made by one party it must also state that that party—
(a) is aware of the purpose of the period for reflection and consideration as described in section 7; and
(b) wishes to make arrangements for the future.

(3)   If a statement is made by both parties it must also state that each of them—
(a) is aware of the purpose of the period for reflection and consideration as described in section 7; and
(b) wishes to make arrangements for the future.

(4)   A statement must be given to the court in accordance with the requirements of rules made under section 12.

(5)   A statement must also satisfy any other requirements imposed by rules made under that section.

(6)   A statement made at a time when the circumstances of the case include any of those mentioned in subsection (7) is ineffective for the purposes of this Part.

(7)   The circumstances are—
    (a) that a statement has previously been made with respect to the marriage
       and it is, or will become, possible—
       (i)   for an application for a divorce order, or
       (ii)   for an application for a separation order,
    to be made by reference to the previous statement;
    (b) that such an application has been made in relation to the marriage and
       has not been withdrawn;
    (c)   that a separation order is in force.

Reflection and consideration

7 Period for reflection and consideration

(1)   Where a statement has been made, a period for the parties—
    (a) to reflect on whether the marriage can be saved and to have an opportu-
       nity to effect a reconciliation, and
    (b) to consider what arrangements should be made for the future,

must pass before an application for a divorce order or for a separation order may be
made by reference to that statement.

(2)   That period is to be known as the period for reflection and consideration.

(3)   The period for reflection and consideration is nine months beginning with the
fourteenth day after the day on which the statement is received by the court.

(4)   Where—
    (a) the statement has been made by one party,
    (b) rules made under section 12 require the court to serve a copy of the
       statement on the other party, and
    (c)   failure to comply with the rules causes inordinate delay in service,

the court may, on the application of that other party, extend the period for
reflection and consideration.

(5)   An extension under subsection (4) may be for any period not exceeding the
time between—
    (a) the beginning of the period for reflection and consideration; and
    (b) the time when service is effected.

(6)   A statement which is made before the first anniversary of the marriage to
which it relates is ineffective for the purposes of any application for a divorce order.

(7)   Subsection (8) applies if, at any time during the period for reflection and consideration, the parties jointly give notice to the court that they are attempting a reconciliation but require additional time.

(8)   The period for reflection and consideration—
    (a) stops running on the day on which the notice is received by the court; but
    (b) resumes running on the day on which either of the parties gives notice to
       the court that the attempted reconciliation has been unsuccessful.

(9)   If the period for reflection and consideration is interrupted under sub-section (8) by a continuous period of more than 18 months, any application by either of the parties for a divorce order or for a separation order must be by reference to a new statement received by the court at any time after the end of the 18 months.

(10)   Where an application for a divorce order is made by one party, subsection (13) applies if—

(a) the other party applies to the court, within the prescribed period, for time for further reflection; and

(b) the requirements of section 9 (except any imposed under section 9(3)) are satisfied.

(11)   Where any application for a divorce order is made, subsection (13) also applies if there is a child of the family who is under the age of sixteen when the application is made.

(12)   Subsection (13) does not apply if—

(a) at the time when the application for a divorce order is made, there is an occupation order or a non-molestation order in force in favour of the applicant, or of a child of the family, made against the other party; or

(b) the court is satisfied that delaying the making of a divorce order would be significantly detrimental to the welfare of any child of the family.

(13)   If this subsection applies, the period for reflection and consideration is extended by a period of six months, but—

(a) only in relation to the application for a divorce order in respect of which the application under subsection (10) was made; and

(b) without invalidating that application for a divorce order.

(14)   A period for reflection and consideration which is extended under sub-section (13), and which has not otherwise come to an end, comes to an end on there ceasing to be any children of the family to whom subsection (11) applied.

8   Attendance at information meetings

(1)   The requirements about information meetings are as follows.

(2)   A party making a statement must (except in prescribed circumstances) have attended an information meeting not less than three months before making the statement.

(3)   Different information meetings must be arranged with respect to different marriages.

(4)   In the case of a statement made by both parties, the parties may attend separate meetings or the same meeting.

(5)   Where one party has made a statement, the other party must (except in pre-scribed circumstances) attend an information meeting before—

(a) making any application to the court—

(i) with respect to a child of the family; or

(ii) of a prescribed description relating to property or financial matters; or

(b) contesting any such application.

(6) In this section "information meeting" means a meeting organised, in accordance with prescribed provisions for the purpose—

(a) of providing, in accordance with prescribed provisions, relevant information to the party or parties attending about matters which may arise in connection with the provisions of, or made under, this Part or Part III; and

(b) of giving the party or parties attending the information meeting the opportunity of having a meeting with a marriage counsellor and of encouraging that party or those parties to attend that meeting.

(7) An information meeting must be conducted by a person who—

(a) is qualified and appointed in accordance with prescribed provisions; and

(b) will have no financial or other interest in any marital proceedings between the parties.

(8) Regulations made under this section may, in particular, make provision—

(a) about the places and times at which information meetings are to be held;

(b) for written information to be given to persons attending them;

(c) for the giving of information to parties (otherwise than at information meetings) in cases in which the requirement to attend such meetings does not apply;

(d) for information of a prescribed kind to be given only with the approval of the Lord Chancellor or only by a person or by persons approved by him; and

(e) for information to be given, in prescribed circumstances, only with the approval of the Lord Chancellor or only by a person, or by persons, approved by him.

(9) Regulations made under subsection (6) must, in particular, make provision with respect to the giving of information about—

(a) marriage counselling and other marriage support services;

(b) the importance to be attached to the welfare, wishes and feelings of children;

(c) how the parties may acquire a better understanding of the ways in which children can be helped to cope with the breakdown of a marriage;

(d) the nature of the financial questions that may arise on divorce or separation, and services which are available to help the parties;

(e) protection available against violence, and how to obtain support and assistance;

(f) mediation;

(g) the availability to each of the parties of independent legal advice and representation;

(h) the principles of legal aid and where the parties can get advice about obtaining legal aid;

(i) the divorce and separation process.

(10)   Before making any regulations under subsection (6), the Lord Chancellor must consult such persons concerned with the provision of relevant information as he considers appropriate.

(11)   A meeting with a marriage counsellor arranged under this section—
    (a)   must be held in accordance with prescribed provisions; and
    (b)   must be with a person qualified and appointed in accordance with prescribed provisions.

(12)   A person who would not be required to make any contribution towards mediation provided for him under Part IIIA of the Legal Aid Act 1988 shall not be required to make any contribution towards the cost of a meeting with a marriage counsellor arranged for him under this section.

(13)   In this section "prescribed" means prescribed by regulations made by the Lord Chancellor.

9   Arrangements for the future

(1)   The requirements as to the parties' arrangements for the future are as follows.

(2)   One of the following must be produced to the court—
    (a)   a court order (made by consent or otherwise) dealing with their financial arrangements;
    (b)   a negotiated agreement as to their financial arrangements;
    (c)   a declaration by both parties that they have made their financial arrangements;
    (d)   a declaration by one of the parties (to which no objection has been notified to the court by the other party) that—
        (i)   he has no significant assets and does not intend to make an application for financial provision;
        (ii)   he believes that the other party has no significant assets and does not intend to make an application for financial provision; and
        (iii)   there are therefore no financial arrangements to be made.

(3)   If the parties—
    (a)   were married to each other in accordance with usages of a kind mentioned in section 26(1) of the Marriage Act 1949 (marriages which may be solemnized on authority of superintendent registrar's certificate), and
    (b)   are required to co-operate if the marriage is to be dissolved in accordance with those usages,

the court may, on the application of either party, direct that there must also be produced to the court a declaration by both parties that they have taken such steps as are required to dissolve the marriage in accordance with those usages.

(4)   A direction under subsection (3)—
    (a)   may be given only if the court is satisfied that in all the circumstances of the case it is just and reasonable to give it; and
    (b)   may be revoked by the court at any time.

(5)   The requirements of section 11 must have been satisfied.

(6)   Schedule 1 supplements the provisions of this section.

(7)   If the court is satisfied, on an application made by one of the parties after the end of the period for reflection and consideration, that the circumstances of the case are—

(a) those set out in paragraph 1 of Schedule 1,

(b) those set out in paragraph 2 of that Schedule,

(c) those set out in paragraph 3 of that Schedule, or

(d) those set out in paragraph 4 of that Schedule,

it may make a divorce order or a separation order even though the requirements of subsection (2) have not been satisfied.

(8)   If the parties' arrangements for the future include a division of pension assets or rights under section 25B of the 1973 Act or section 10 of the Family Law (Scotland) Act 1985, any declaration under subsection (2) must be a statutory declaration.

Orders preventing divorce

10   Hardship: orders preventing divorce

(1)   If an application for a divorce order has been made by one of the parties to a marriage, the court may, on the application of the other party, order that the marriage is not to be dissolved.

(2)   Such an order (an "order preventing divorce") may be made only if the court is satisfied—

(a) that dissolution of the marriage would result in substantial financial or other hardship to the other party or to a child of the family; and

(b) that it would be wrong, in all the circumstances (including the conduct of the parties and the interests of any child of the family), for the marriage to be dissolved.

(3)   If an application for the cancellation of an order preventing divorce is made by one or both of the parties, the court shall cancel the order unless it is still satisfied—

(a) that dissolution of the marriage would result in substantial financial or other hardship to the party in whose favour the order was made or to a child of the family; and

(b) that it would be wrong, in all the circumstances (including the conduct of the parties and the interests of any child of the family), for the marriage to be dissolved.

(4)   If an order preventing a divorce is cancelled, the court may make a divorce order in respect of the marriage only if an application is made under section 3 or 4(3) after the cancellation.

(5)   An order preventing divorce may include conditions which must be satisfied before an application for cancellation may be made under subsection (3).

(6)   In this section "hardship" includes the loss of a chance to obtain a future benefit (as well as the loss of an existing benefit).

Welfare of children

11   Welfare of children

(1)   In any proceedings for a divorce order or a separation order, the court shall consider—
   (a)   whether there are any children of the family to whom this section applies; and
   (b)   where there are any such children, whether (in the light of the arrangements which have been, or are proposed to be, made for their upbringing and welfare) it should exercise any of its powers under the Children Act 1989 with respect to any of them.

(2)   Where, in any case to which this section applies, it appears to the court that—
   (a)   the circumstances of the case require it, or are likely to require it, to exercise any of its powers under the Children Act 1989 with respect to any such child,
   (b)   it is not in a position to exercise the power, or (as the case may be) those powers, without giving further consideration to the case, and
   (c)   there are exceptional circumstances which make it desirable in the interests of the child that the court should give a direction under this section,

it may direct that the divorce order or separation order is not to be made until the court orders otherwise.

(3)   In deciding whether the circumstances are as mentioned in subsection (2)(a), the court shall treat the welfare of the child as paramount.

(4)   In making that decision, the court shall also have particular regard, on the evidence before it, to—
   (a)   the wishes and feelings of the child considered in the light of his age and understanding and the circumstances in which those wishes were expressed;
   (b)   the conduct of the parties in relation to the upbringing of the child;
   (c)   the general principle that, in the absence of evidence to the contrary, the welfare of the child will be best served by—
      (i)   his having regular contact with those who have parental responsibility for him and with other members of his family; and
      (ii)   the maintenance of as good a continuing relationship with his parents as is possible; and
   (d)   any risk to the child attributable to—
      (i)   where the person with whom the child will reside is living or proposes to live;
      (ii)   any person with whom that person is living or with whom he proposes to live; or
      (iii) any other arrangements for his care and upbringing.

(5)   This section applies to—
    (a) any child of the family who has not reached the age of sixteen at the date when the court considers the case in accordance with the requirements of this section; and
    (b) any child of the family who has reached that age at that date and in relation to whom the court directs that this section shall apply.

Supplementary

12   Lord Chancellor's rules

(1)   The Lord Chancellor may make rules—
    (a) as to the form in which a statement is to be made and what information must accompany it;
    (b) requiring the person making the statement to state whether or not, since satisfying the requirements of section 8, he has made any attempt at reconciliation;
    (c) as to the way in which a statement is to be given to the court;
    (d) requiring a copy of a statement made by one party to be served by the court on the other party;
    (e) as to circumstances in which such service may be dispensed with or may be effected otherwise than by delivery to the party;
    (f) requiring a party who has made a statement to provide the court with information about the arrangements that need to be made in consequence of the breakdown;
    (g) as to the time, manner and (where attendance in person is required) place at which such information is to be given;
    (h) where a statement has been made, requiring either or both of the parties—
        (i)   to prepare and produce such other documents, and
        (ii) to attend in person at such places and for such purposes,
      as may be specified;
    (i) as to the information and assistance which is to be given to the parties and the way in which it is to be given;
    (j) requiring the parties to be given, in such manner as may be specified, copies of such statements and other documents as may be specified.

(2)   The Lord Chancellor may make rules requiring a person who is the legal representative of a party to a marriage with respect to which a statement has been, or is proposed to be, made—
    (a) to inform that party, at such time or times as may be specified—
        (i)   about the availability to the parties of marriage support services;
        (ii) about the availability to them of mediation; and
        (iii) where there are children of the family, that in relation to the arrangements to be made for any child the parties should consider the child's welfare, wishes and feelings;
    (b) to give that party, at such time or times as may be specified, names and addresses of persons qualified to help—

(i)   to effect a reconciliation; or

(ii)   in connection with mediation; and

(c)   to certify, at such time or times as may be specified—

    (i)   whether he has complied with the provision made in the rules by virtue of paragraphs (a) and (b);

    (ii)   whether he has discussed with that party any of the matters mentioned in paragraph (a) or the possibility of reconciliation; and

    (iii) which, if any, of those matters they have discussed.

(3)   In subsections (1) and (2) "specified" means determined under or described in the rules.

(4)   This section does not affect any power to make rules of court for the purposes of this Act.

Resolution of disputes

13 Directions with respect to mediation

(1)   After the court has received a statement, it may give a direction requiring each party to attend a meeting arranged in accordance with the direction for the purpose—

(a)   of enabling an explanation to be given of the facilities available to the parties for mediation in relation to disputes between them; and

(b)   of providing an opportunity for each party to agree to take advantage of those facilities.

(2)   A direction may be given at any time, including in the course of proceedings connected with the breakdown of the marriage (as to which see section 25).

(3)   A direction may be given on the application of either of the parties or on the initiative of the court.

(4)   The parties are to be required to attend the same meeting unless—

(a)   one of them asks, or both of them ask, for separate meetings; or

(b)   the court considers separate meetings to be more appropriate.

(5)   A direction shall—

(a)   specify a person chosen by the court (with that person's agreement) to arrange and conduct the meeting or meetings; and

(b)   require such person as may be specified in the direction to produce to the court, at such time as the court may direct, a report stating—

    (i)   whether the parties have complied with the direction; and

    (ii)   if they have, whether they have agreed to take part in any mediation.

14 Adjournments

(1)   The court's power to adjourn any proceedings connected with the breakdown of a marriage includes power to adjourn—

    (a) for the purpose of allowing the parties to comply with a direction under section 13; or

    (b) for the purpose of enabling disputes to be resolved amicably.

(2)   In determining whether to adjourn for either purpose, the court shall have regard in particular to the need to protect the interests of any child of the family.

(3)   If the court adjourns any proceedings connected with the breakdown of a marriage for either purpose, the period of the adjournment must not exceed the maximum period prescribed by rules of court.

(4)   Unless the only purpose of the adjournment is to allow the parties to comply with a direction under section 13, the court shall order one or both of them to produce to the court a report as to—

    (a) whether they have taken part in mediation during the adjournment;

    (b) whether, as a result, any agreement has been reached between them;

    (c) the extent to which any dispute between them has been resolved as a result of any such agreement;

    (d) the need for further mediation; and

    (e) how likely it is that further mediation will be successful.

Financial provision

15 Financial arrangements

(1)   Schedule 2 amends the 1973 Act.

(2)   The main object of Schedule 2 is—

    (a) to provide that, in the case of divorce or separation, an order about financial provision may be made under that Act before a divorce order or separation order is made; but

    (b) to retain (with minor changes) the position under that Act where marriages are annulled.

(3)   Schedule 2 also makes minor and consequential amendments of the 1973 Act connected with the changes mentioned in subsection (1).

Jurisdiction and commencement of proceedings

19 Jurisdiction in relation to divorce and separation

(1)   In this section "the court's jurisdiction" means—

    (a) the jurisdiction of the court under this Part to entertain marital proceedings; and

    (b) any other jurisdiction conferred on the court under this Part, or any other enactment, in consequence of the making of a statement.

(2)   The court's jurisdiction is exercisable only if—

    (a) at least one of the parties was domiciled in England and Wales on the statement date;

    (b) at least one of the parties was habitually resident in England and Wales throughout the period of one year ending with the statement date; or

    (c) nullity proceedings are pending in relation to the marriage when the marital proceedings commence.

20   Time when proceedings for divorce or separation begin

(1)   The receipt by the court of a statement is to be treated as the commencement of proceedings.

(2)   The proceedings are to be known as marital proceedings.

Intestacy

21 Intestacy: effect of separation

Where—

    (a) a separation order is in force, and

    (b) while the parties to the marriage remain separated, one of them dies intestate as respects any real or personal property,

that property devolves as if the other had died before the intestacy occurred.

Marriage support services

2   Funding for marriage support services

(1)   The Lord Chancellor may, with the approval of the Treasury, make grants in connection with—

    (a) the provision of marriage support services;

    (b) research into the causes of marital breakdown;

    (c) research into ways of preventing marital breakdown.

(2)   Any grant under this section may be made subject to such conditions as the Lord Chancellor considers appropriate.

(3)   In exercising his power to make grants in connection with the provision of marriage support services, the Lord Chancellor is to have regard, in particular, to the desirability of services of that kind being available when they are first needed.

23   Provision of marriage counselling

(1)   The Lord Chancellor or a person appointed by him may secure the provision, in accordance with regulations made by the Lord Chancellor, of marriage counselling.

(2)   Marriage counselling may only be provided under this section at a time when a period for reflection and consideration—

    (a) is running in relation to the marriage; or

    (b) is interrupted under section 7(8) (but not for a continuous period of more than 18 months).

(3)   Marriage counselling may only be provided under this section for persons who would not be required to make any contribution towards the cost of mediation provided for them under Part IIIA of the Legal Aid Act 1988.

(4)   Persons for whom marriage counselling is provided under this section are not to be required to make any contribution towards the cost of the counselling.

Interpretation

24   Interpretation of Part II etc

(1)   In this Part—
"the 1973 Act" means the Matrimonial Causes Act 1973;
"child of the family" and "the court" have the same meaning as in the 1973 Act;
"divorce order" has the meaning given in section 2(1)(a);
"divorce proceedings" is to be read with section 20;
"marital proceedings" has the meaning given in section 20;
"non-molestation order" has the meaning given by section 42(1);
"occupation order" has the meaning given by section 39;
"order preventing divorce" has the meaning given in section 10(2);
"party", in relation to a marriage, means one of the parties to the marriage;
"period for reflection and consideration" has the meaning given in section 7;
"separation order" has the meaning given in section 2(1)(b);
"separation proceedings" is to be read with section 20;
"statement" means a statement of marital breakdown;
"statement of marital breakdown" has the meaning given in section 6(1).

25   Connected proceedings

(1)   For the purposes of this Part, proceedings are connected with the breakdown of a marriage if they fall within subsection (2) and, at the time of the proceedings—
   (a) a statement has been received by the court with respect to the marriage and it is or may become possible for an application for a divorce order or separation order to be made by reference to that statement;
   (b) such an application in relation to the marriage has been made and not withdrawn; or
   (c) a divorce order has been made, or a separation order is in force, in relation to the marriage.

(2)   The proceedings are any under Parts I to V of the Children Act 1989 with respect to a child of the family or any proceedings resulting from an application—
   (a) for, or for the cancellation of, an order preventing divorce in relation to the marriage;
   (b) by either party to the marriage for an order under Part IV;
   (c) for the exercise, in relation to a party to the marriage or child of the family, of any of the court's powers under Part II of the 1973 Act;
   (d) made otherwise to the court with respect to, or in connection with, any proceedings connected with the breakdown of the marriage.

PART IV

FAMILY HOMES AND DOMESTIC VIOLENCE

Rights to occupy matrimonial home

30 Rights concerning matrimonial home where one spouse has no estate, etc

(1) This section applies if—

    (a) one spouse is entitled to occupy a dwelling-house by virtue of—

        (i) a beneficial estate or interest or contract; or

        (ii) any enactment giving that spouse the right to remain in occupation; and

    (b) the other spouse is not so entitled.

(2) Subject to the provisions of this Part, the spouse not so entitled has the following rights ("matrimonial home rights")—

    (a) if in occupation, a right not to be evicted or excluded from the dwelling-house or any part of it by the other spouse except with the leave of the court given by an order under section 33;

    (b) if not in occupation, a right with the leave of the court so given to enter into and occupy the dwelling-house.

(3) If a spouse is entitled under this section to occupy a dwelling-house or any part of a dwelling-house, any payment or tender made or other thing done by that spouse in or towards satisfaction of any liability of the other spouse in respect of rent, mortgage payments or other outgoings affecting the dwelling-house is, whether or not it is made or done in pursuance of an order under section 40, as good as if made or done by the other spouse.

(4) A spouse's occupation by virtue of this section—

    (a) is to be treated, for the purposes of the Rent (Agriculture) Act 1976 and the Rent Act 1977 (other than Part V and sections 103 to 106 of that Act), as occupation by the other spouse as the other spouse's residence, and

    (b) if the spouse occupies the dwelling-house as that spouse's only or principal home, is to be treated, for the purposes of the Housing Act 1985 and Part I of the Housing Act 1988, as occupation by the other spouse as the other spouse's only or principal home.

(5) If a spouse ("the first spouse")—

    (a) is entitled under this section to occupy a dwelling-house or any part of a dwelling-house, and

    (b) makes any payment in or towards satisfaction of any liability of the other spouse ("the second spouse") in respect of mortgage payments affecting the dwelling-house,

the person to whom the payment is made may treat it as having been made by the second spouse, but the fact that that person has treated any such payment as having been so made does not affect any claim of the first spouse against the second spouse to an interest in the dwelling-house by virtue of the payment.

(6)   If a spouse is entitled under this section to occupy a dwelling-house or part of a dwelling-house by reason of an interest of the other spouse under a trust, all the provisions of subsections (3) to (5) apply in relation to the trustees as they apply in relation to the other spouse.

(7)   This section does not apply to a dwelling-house which has at no time been, and which was at no time intended by the spouses to be, a matrimonial home of theirs.

(8)   A spouse's matrimonial home rights continue—
(a)   only so long as the marriage subsists, except to the extent that an order under section 33(5) otherwise provides; and
(b)   only so long as the other spouse is entitled as mentioned in subsection (1) to occupy the dwelling-house, except where provision is made by section 31 for those rights to be a charge on an estate or interest in the dwelling-house.

(9)   It is hereby declared that a spouse—
(a)   who has an equitable interest in a dwelling-house or in its proceeds of sale, but
(b)   is not a spouse in whom there is vested (whether solely or as joint tenant) a legal estate in fee simple or a legal term of years absolute in the dwelling-house,

is to be treated, only for the purpose of determining whether he has matrimonial home rights, as not being entitled to occupy the dwelling-house by virtue of that interest.

31   Effect of matrimonial home rights as charge on dwelling-house

(1)   Subsections (2) and (3) apply if, at any time during a marriage, one spouse is entitled to occupy a dwelling-house by virtue of a beneficial estate or interest.

(2)   The other spouse's matrimonial home rights are a charge on the estate or interest.

(3)   The charge created by subsection (2) has the same priority as if it were an equitable interest created at whichever is the latest of the following dates—
(a)   the date on which the spouse so entitled acquires the estate or interest;
(b)   the date of the marriage; and
(c)   1st January 1968 (the commencement date of the Matrimonial Homes Act 1967).

(4)   Subsections (5) and (6) apply if, at any time when a spouse's matrimonial home rights are a charge on an interest of the other spouse under a trust, there are, apart from either of the spouses, no persons, living or unborn, who are or could become beneficiaries under the trust.

(5)   The rights are a charge also on the estate or interest of the trustees for the other spouse.

(6)   The charge created by subsection (5) has the same priority as if it were an equitable interest created (under powers overriding the trusts) on the date when it arises.

(7)   In determining for the purposes of subsection (4) whether there are any persons who are not, but could become, beneficiaries under the trust, there is to be disregarded any potential exercise of a general power of appointment exercisable by either or both of the spouses alone (whether or not the exercise of it requires the consent of another person).

(8)   Even though a spouse's matrimonial home rights are a charge on an estate or interest in the dwelling-house, those rights are brought to an end by—
    (a) the death of the other spouse, or
    (b) the termination (otherwise than by death) of the marriage,

unless the court directs otherwise by an order made under section 33(5).

(9)   If—
    (a) a spouse's matrimonial home rights are a charge on an estate or interest in the dwelling-house, and
    (b) that estate or interest is surrendered to merge in some other estate or interest expectant on it in such circumstances that, but for the merger, the person taking the estate or interest would be bound by the charge,

the surrender has effect subject to the charge and the persons thereafter entitled to the other estate or interest are, for so long as the estate or interest surrendered would have endured if not so surrendered, to be treated for all purposes of this Part as deriving title to the other estate or interest under the other spouse or, as the case may be, under the trustees for the other spouse, by virtue of the surrender.

(10) If the title to the legal estate by virtue of which a spouse is entitled to occupy a dwelling-house (including any legal estate held by trustees for that spouse) is registered under the Land Registration Act 1925 or any enactment replaced by that Act—
    (a) registration of a land charge affecting the dwelling-house by virtue of this Part is to be effected by registering a notice under that Act; and
    (b) a spouse's matrimonial home rights are not an overriding interest within the meaning of that Act affecting the dwelling-house even though the spouse is in actual occupation of the dwelling-house.

(11) A spouse's matrimonial home rights (whether or not constituting a charge) do not entitle that spouse to lodge a caution under section 54 of the Land Registration Act 1925.

(12) If—
    (a) a spouse's matrimonial home rights are a charge on the estate of the other spouse or of trustees of the other spouse, and
    (b) that estate is the subject of a mortgage,

then if, after the date of the creation of the mortgage ("the first mortgage"), the charge is registered under section 2 of the Land Charges Act 1972, the charge is, for the purposes of section 94 of the Law of Property Act 1925 (which regulates the rights of mortgages to make further advances ranking in priority to subsequent mortgages), to be deemed to be a mortgage subsequent in date to the first mortgage.

(13) It is hereby declared that a charge under subsection (2) or (5) is not registrable under subsection (10) or under section 2 of the Land Charges Act 1972 unless it is a charge on a legal estate.

33   Occupation orders where applicant has estate or interest etc or has matrimonial home rights

(1)   If—
    (a) a person ("the person entitled")—
        (i)   is entitled to occupy a dwelling-house by virtue of a beneficial estate or interest or contract or by virtue of any enactment giving him the right to remain in occupation, or
        (ii) has matrimonial home rights in relation to a dwelling-house, and
    (b) the dwelling-house—
        (i)   is or at any time has been the home of the person entitled and of another person with whom he is associated, or
        (ii) was at any time intended by the person entitled and any such other person to be their home,

the person entitled may apply to the court for an order containing any of the provisions specified in subsections (3), (4) and (5)

(2)   If an agreement to marry is terminated, no application under this section may be made by virtue of section 62(3)(e) by reference to that agreement after the end of the period of three years beginning with the day on which it is terminated.

(3)   An order under this section may—
    (a) enforce the applicant's entitlement to remain in occupation as against the other person ("the respondent");
    (b) require the respondent to permit the applicant to enter and remain in the dwelling-house or part of the dwelling-house;
    (c) regulate the occupation of the dwelling-house by either or both parties;
    (d) if the respondent is entitled as mentioned in subsection (1)(a)(i), prohibit, suspend or restrict the exercise by him of his right to occupy the dwelling-house;
    (e) if the respondent has matrimonial home rights in relation to the dwelling-house and the applicant is the other spouse, restrict or terminate those rights;
    (f) require the respondent to leave the dwelling-house or part of the dwelling-house; or
    (g) exclude the respondent from a defined area in which the dwelling-house is included.

(4)   An order under this section may declare that the applicant is entitled as mentioned in subsection (1)(a)(i) or has matrimonial home rights.

(5) If the applicant has matrimonial home rights and the respondent is the other spouse, an order under this section made during the marriage may provide that those rights are not brought to an end by—

    (a) the death of the other spouse; or

    (b) the termination (otherwise than by death) of the marriage.

(6) In deciding whether to exercise its powers under subsection (3) and (if so) in what manner, the court shall have regard to all the circumstances including—

    (a) the housing needs and housing resources of each of the parties and of any relevant child;

    (b) the financial resources of each of the parties;

    (c) the likely effect of any order, or of any decision by the court not to exercise its powers under subsection (3), on the health, safety or well-being of the parties and of any relevant child; and

    (d) the conduct of the parties in relation to each other and otherwise.

(7) If it appears to the court that the applicant or any relevant child is likely to suffer significant harm attributable to conduct of the respondent if an order under this section containing one or more of the provisions mentioned in subsection (3) is not made, the court shall make the order unless it appears to it that—

    (a) the respondent or any relevant child is likely to suffer significant harm if the order is made; and

    (b) the harm likely to be suffered by the respondent or child in that event is as great as, or greater than, the harm attributable to conduct of the respondent which is likely to be suffered by the applicant or child if the order is not made.

(8) The court may exercise its powers under subsection (5) in any case where it considers that in all the circumstances it is just and reasonable to do so.

(9) An order under this section—

    (a) may not be made after the death of either of the parties mentioned in subsection (1); and

    (b) except in the case of an order made by virtue of subsection (5)(a), ceases to have effect on the death of either party.

(10) An order under this section may, in so far as it has continuing effect, be made for a specified period, until the occurrence of a specified event or until further order.

34 Effect of order under s 33 where rights are charge on dwelling-house

(1) If a spouse's matrimonial home rights are a charge on the estate or interest of the other spouse or of trustees for the other spouse—

    (a) an order under section 33 against the other spouse has, except so far as a contrary intention appears, the same effect against house, persons deriving title under the other spouse or under the trustees and affected by the charge, and

    (b) sections 33(1), (3), (4) and (10) and 30(3) to (6) apply in relation to any person deriving title under the other spouse or under the trustees and affected by the charge as they apply in relation to the other spouse.

(2)   The court may make an order under section 33 by virtue of subsection (1)(b) if it considers that in all the circumstances it is just and reasonable to do so.

35   One former spouse with no existing right to occupy

(1)   This section applies if—
   (a) one former spouse is entitled to occupy a dwelling-house by virtue of a beneficial estate or interest or contract, or by virtue of any enactment giving him the right to remain in occupation;
   (b) the other former spouse is not so entitled; and
   (c) the dwelling-house was at any time their matrimonial home or was at any time intended by them to be their matrimonial home.

(2)   The former spouse not so entitled may apply to the court for an order under this section against the other former spouse ("the respondent").

(3)   If the applicant is in occupation, an order under this section must contain provision—
   (a) giving the applicant the right not to be evicted or excluded from the dwelling-house or any part of it by the respondent for the period specified in the order; and
   (b) prohibiting the respondent from evicting or excluding the applicant during that period.

(4)   If the applicant is not in occupation, an order under this section must contain provision—
   (a) giving the applicant the right to enter into and occupy the dwelling-house for the period specified in the order; and
   (b) requiring the respondent to permit the exercise of that right.

(5)   An order under this section may also—
   (a) regulate the occupation of the dwelling-house by either or both of the parties;
   (b) prohibit, suspend or restrict the exercise by the respondent of his right to occupy the dwelling-house;
   (c) require the respondent to leave the dwelling-house or part of the dwelling-house; or
   (d) exclude the respondent from a defined area in which the dwelling-house is included.

(6)   In deciding whether to make an order under this section containing provision of the kind mentioned in subsection (3) or (4) and (if so) in what manner, the court shall have regard to all the circumstances including—
   (a) the housing needs and housing resources of each of the parties and of any relevant child;
   (b) the financial resources of each of the parties;
   (c) the likely effect of any order, or of any decision by the court not to exercise its powers under subsection (3) or (4), on the health, safety or well-being of the parties and of any relevant child;

(d) the conduct of the parties in relation to each other and otherwise;

(e) the length of time that has elapsed since the parties ceased to live together;

(f) the length of time that has elapsed since the marriage was dissolved or annulled; and

(g) the existence of any pending proceedings between the parties—

    (i) for an under section 23A or 24 of the Matrimonial Causes Act 1973 (property adjustment orders in connection with divorce proceedings etc);

    (ii) for an order under paragraph 1(2)(d) or (e) of Schedule 1 to the Children Act 1989 (orders for financial relief against parents); or

    (iii) relating to the legal or beneficial ownership of the dwelling-house.

(7) In deciding whether to exercise its power to include one or more of the provisions referred to in subsection (5) ("a subsection (5) provision") and (if so) in what manner, the court shall have regard to all the circumstances including the matters mentioned in subsection (6)(a) to (e).

(8) If the court decides to make an order under this section and it appears to it that, if the order does not include a subsection (5) provision, the applicant or any relevant child is likely to suffer significant harm attributable to conduct of the respondent, the court shall include the subsection (5) provision in the order unless it appears to the court that—

(a) the respondent or any relevant child is likely to suffer significant harm if the provision is included in the order; and

(b) the harm likely to be suffered by the respondent or child in that event is as great as or greater than the harm attributable to conduct of the respondent which is likely to be suffered by the applicant or child if the provision is not included.

(9) An order under this section—

(a) may not be made after the death of either of the former spouses; and

(b) ceases to have effect on the death of either of them.

(10) An order under this section must be limited so as to have effect for a specified period not exceeding six months, but may be extended on one or more occasions for a further specified period not exceeding six months.

(11) A former spouse who has an equitable interest in the dwelling-house or in the proceeds of sale of the dwelling-house but in whom there is not vested (whether solely or as joint tenant) a legal estate in fee simple or a legal term of years absolute in the dwelling-house is to be treated (but only for the purpose of determining whether he is eligible to apply under this section) as not being entitled to occupy the dwelling-house by virtue of that interest.

(12) Subsection (11) does not prejudice any right of such a former spouse to apply for an order under section 33.

(13) So long as an order under this section remains in force, subsections (3) to (6) of section 30 apply in relation to the applicant—

(a) as if he were the spouse entitled to occupy the dwelling-house by virtue of that section; and

(b) as if the respondent were the other spouse.

36 One cohabitant or former cohabitant with no existing right to occupy

(1) This section applies if—
   (a) one cohabitant or former cohabitant is entitled to occupy a dwelling-house by virtue of a beneficial estate or interest or contract or by virtue of any enactment giving him the right to remain in occupation;
   (b) the other cohabitant or former cohabitant is not so entitled; and
   (c) that dwelling-house is the home in which they live together as husband and wife or a home in which they at any time so lived together or intended so to live together.

(2) The cohabitant or former cohabitant not so entitled may apply to the court for an order under this section against the other cohabitant or former cohabitant ("the respondent").

(3) If the applicant is in occupation, an order under this section must contain provision—
   (a) giving the applicant the right not to be evicted or excluded from the dwelling-house or any part of it by the respondent for the period specified in the order; and
   (b) prohibiting the respondent from evicting or excluding the applicant during that period.

(4) If the applicant is not in occupation, an order under this section must contain provision—
   (a) giving the applicant the right to enter into and occupy the dwelling-house for the period specified in the order; and
   (b) requiring the respondent to permit the exercise of that right.

(5) An order under this section may also—
   (a) regulate the occupation of the dwelling-house by either or both of the parties;
   (b) prohibit, suspend or restrict the exercise by the respondent of his right to occupy the dwelling-house;
   (c) require the respondent to leave the dwelling-house or part of the dwelling-house; or
   (d) exclude the respondent from a defined area in which the dwelling-house is included.

(6) In deciding whether to make an order under this section containing provision of the kind mentioned in subsection (3) or (4) and (if so) in what manner, the court shall have regard to all the circumstances including—
   (a) the housing needs and housing-resources of each of the parties and of any relevant child;
   (b) the financial resources of each of the parties;

(c)   the likely effect of any order, or of any decision by the court not to exercise its powers under subsection (3) or (4), on the health, safety or well-being of the parties and of any relevant child;

(d)   the conduct of the parties in relation to each other and otherwise;

(e)   the nature of the parties' relationship;

(f)   the length of time during which they have lived together as husband and wife;

(g)   whether there are or have been any children who are children of both parties or for whom both parties have or have had parental responsibility;

(h)   the length of time that has elapsed since the parties ceased to live together; and

(i)   the existence of any pending proceedings between the parties—

   (i)   for an order under paragraph 1 (2)(d) or (e) of Schedule to the Children Act 1989 (orders for financial relief against parents); or

   (ii)   relating to the legal or beneficial ownership of the dwelling-house.

(7)   In deciding whether to exercise its powers to include one or more of the provisions referred to in subsection (5) ("a subsection (5) provision") and (if so) in what manner, the court shall have regard to all the circumstances including—

(a)   the matters mentioned in subsection (6)(a) to (d); and

(b)   the questions mentioned in subsection (8).

(8)   The questions are—

(a)   whether the applicant or any relevant child is likely to suffer significant harm attributable to conduct of the respondent if the subsection (5) provision is not included in the order; and

(b)   whether the harm likely to be suffered by the respondent or child if the provision is included is as great as or greater than the harm attributable to conduct of the respondent which is likely to be suffered by the applicant or child if the provision is not included.

(9)   An order under this section—

(a)   may not be made after the death of either of the parties; and

(b)   ceases to have effect on the death of either of them.

(10)   An order under this section must be limited so as to have effect for a specified period not exceeding six months, but may be extended on one occasion for a further specified period not exceeding six months.

(11)   A person who has an equitable interest in the dwelling-house or in the proceeds of sale of the dwelling-house but in whom there is not vested (whether solely or as joint tenant) a legal estate in fee simple or a legal term of years absolute in the dwelling-house is to be treated (but only for the purpose of determining whether he is eligible to apply under this section) as not being entitled to occupy the dwelling-house by virtue of that interest.

(12)   Subsection (11) does not prejudice any right of such a person to apply for an order under section 33.

(13) So long as the order remains in force, subsections (3) to (6) of section 30 apply in relation to the applicant—

(a) as if he were a spouse entitled to occupy the dwelling-house by virtue of that section; and

(b) as if the respondent were the other spouse.

37 Neither spouse entitled to occupy

(1) This section applies if—

(a) one spouse or former spouse and the other spouse or former spouse occupy a dwelling-house which is or was the matrimonial home; but

(b) neither of them is entitled to remain in occupation—

(i) by virtue of a beneficial estate or interest or contract; or

(ii) by virtue of any enactment giving him the right to remain in occu-pation.

(2) Either of the parties may apply to the court for an order against the other under this section.

(3) An order under this section may—

(a) require the respondent to permit the applicant to enter and remain in the dwelling-house or part of the dwelling-house;

(b) regulate the occupation of the dwelling-house by either or both of the spouses;

(c) require the respondent to leave the dwelling-house or part of the dwelling-house; or

(d) exclude the respondent from a defined area in which the dwelling-house is included.

(4) Subsections (6) and (7) of section 33 apply to the exercise by the court of its powers under this section as they apply to the exercise by the court of its powers under subsection (3) of that section.

(5) An order under this section must be limited so as to have effect for a specified period not exceeding six months, but may be extended on one or more occasions for a further specified period not exceeding six months.

38 Neither cohabitant or former cohabitant entitled to occupy

(1) This section applies if—

(a) one cohabitant or former cohabitant and the other cohabitant or former cohabitant occupy a dwelling-house which is the home in which they live or lived together as husband and wife; but

(b) neither of them is entitled to remain in occupation—

(i) by virtue of a beneficial estate or interest or contract; or

(ii) by virtue of any enactment giving him the right to remain in occu-pation.

(2) Either of the parties may apply to the court for an order against the other under this section.

(3)   An order under this section may—
   (a) require the respondent to permit the applicant to enter and remain in the dwelling-house or part of the dwelling-house;
   (b) regulate the occupation of the dwelling-house by either or both of the parties;
   (c) require the respondent to leave the dwelling-house or part of the dwelling-house; or
   (d) exclude the respondent from a defined area in which the dwelling-house is included.

(4)   In deciding whether to exercise its powers to include one or more of the provisions referred to in subsection (3) ("a subsection (3) provision") and (if so) in what manner, the court shall have regard to all the circumstances including—
   (a) the housing needs and housing resources of each of the parties and of any relevant child;
   (b) the financial resources of each of the parties;
   (c) the likely effect of any order, or of any decision by the court not to exercise its powers under subsection (3), on the health, safety or well-being of the parties and of any relevant child;
   (d) the conduct of the parties in relation to each other and otherwise; and
   (e) the questions mentioned in subsection (5).

(5)   The questions are—
   (a) whether the applicant or any relevant child is likely to suffer significant harm attributable to conduct of the respondent if the subsection (3) provision is not included in the order; and
   (b) whether the harm likely to be suffered by the respondent or child if the provision is included is as great as or greater than the harm attributable to conduct of the respondent which is likely to be suffered by the applicant or child if the provision is not included.

(6)   An order under this section shall be limited so as to have effect for a specified period not exceeding six months, but may be extended on one occasion for a further specified period not exceeding six months.

39   Supplementary provisions

(1)   In this Part an "occupation order" means an order under section 33, 35, 36, 37 or 38.

(2)   An application for an occupation order may be made in other family proceedings or without any other family proceedings being instututed.

(3)   If—
   (a) an application for an occupation order is made under section 33, 35, 36, 37 or 38, and
   (b) the court considers that it has no power to make the order under the section concerned, but that it has power to make an order under one of the other sections.

the court may make an order under that other section.

(4)   The fact that a person has applied for an occupation order under sections 35 to 38, or that an occupation order has been made, does not affect the right of any person to claim a legal or equitable interest in any property in any subsequent proceedings (including subsequent proceedings under this Part).

40   Additional provisions that may be included in certain occupation orders

(1)   The court may on, or at any time after, making an occupation order under section 33, 35 or 36—
    (a)   impose on either party obligations as to—
        (i)   the repair and maintenance of the dwelling-house; or
        (ii)   the discharge of rent, mortgage payments or other outgoings affecting the dwelling-house;
    (b)   order a party occupying the dwelling-house or any part of it (including a party who is entitled to do so by virtue of a beneficial estate or interest or contract or by virtue of any enactment giving him the right to remain in occupation) to make periodical payments to the other party in respect of the accommodation, if the other party would (but for the order) be entitled to occupy the dwelling-house by virtue of a beneficial estate or interest or contract or by virtue of any such enactment;
    (c)   grant either party possession or use of furniture or other contents of the dwelling-house;
    (d)   order either party to take reasonable care of any furniture or other contents of the dwelling-house;
    (e)   order either party to take reasonable steps to keep the dwelling-house and any furniture or other contents secure.

(2)   In deciding whether and, if so, how to exercise its powers under this section, the court shall have regard to all the circumstances of the case including—
    (a)   the financial needs and financial resources of the parties; and
    (b)   the financial obligations which they have, or are likely to have in the foreseeable future, including financial obligations to each other and to any relevant child.

(3)   An order under this section ceases to have effect when the occupation order to which it relates ceases to have effect.

41   Additional considerations if parties are cohabitants or former cohabitants

(1)   This section applies if the parties are cohabitants or former cohabitants.

(2)   Where the court is required to consider the nature of the parties' relationship, it is to have regard to the fact that they have not given each other the commitment involved in marriage.

42   Non-molestation orders

(1)   In this Part a "non-molestation order" means an order containing either or both of the following provisions—

(a) provision prohibiting a person ("the respondent") from molesting another person who is associated with the respondent;

(b) provision prohibiting the respondent from molesting a relevant child.

(2) The court may make a non-molestation order—

(a) if an application for the order has been made (whether in other family proceedings or without any other family proceedings being instituted) by a person who is associated with the respondent; or

(b) if in any family proceedings to which the respondent is a party the court considers that the order should be made for the benefit of any other party to the proceedings or any relevant child even though no such application has been made.

(3) In subsection (2) "family proceedings" includes proceedings in which the court has made an emergency protection order under section 44 of the Children Act 1989 which includes an exclusion requirement (as defined in section 44A(3) of that Act).

(4) Where an agreement to marry is terminated, no application under subsection (2)(a) may be made by virtue of section 62(3)(e) by reference to that agreement after the end of the period of three years beginning with the day on which it is terminated.

(5) In deciding whether to exercise its powers under this section and, if so, in what manner, the court shall have regard to all the circumstances including the need to secure the health, safety and well-being—

(a) of the applicant or, in a case falling within subsection (2)(b), the person for whose benefit the order would be made; and

(b) of any relevant child.

(6) A non-molestation order may be expressed so as to refer to molestation in general, to particular acts of molestation, or to both.

(7) A non-molestation order may be made for a specified period or until further order.

(8) A non-molestation order which is made in other family proceedings ceases to have effect if those proceedings are withdrawn or dismissed.

Further provisions relating to occupation and non-molestation orders

43 Leave of court required for applications by children under sixteen

(1) A child under the age of sixteen may not apply for an occupation order or a non-molestation order except with the leave of the court.

(2) The court may grant leave for the purposes of subsection (1) only if it is satisfied that the child has sufficient understanding to make the proposed application for the occupation order or non-molestation order.

44 Evidence of agreement to marry

(1) Subject to subsection (2), the court shall not make an order under section 33 or 42 by virtue of section 62(3)(e) unless there is produced to it evidence in writing of the existence of the agreement to marry.

(2) Subsection (1) does not apply if the court is satisfied that the agreement to marry was evidenced by—
  (a) the gift of an engagement ring by one party to the agreement to the other in contemplation of their marriage, or
  (b) a ceremony entered into by the parties in the presence of one or more other persons assembled for the purpose of witnessing the ceremony.

45 Ex parte orders

(1) The court may, in any case where it considers that it is just and convenient to do so, make an occupation order or a non-molestation order even though the respondent has not been given such notice of the proceedings as would otherwise be required by rules of court.

(2) In determining whether to exercise its powers under subsection (1), the court shall have regard to all the circumstances including—
  (a) any risk of significant harm to the applicant or a relevant child, attributable to conduct of the respondent, if the order is not made immediately;
  (b) whether it is likely that the applicant will be deterred or prevented from pursuing the application if an order is not made immediately; and
  (c) whether there is reason to believe that the respondent is aware of the proceedings but is deliberately evading service and that the applicant or a relevant child will be seriously prejudiced by the delay involved—
    (i) where the court is a magistrates' court, in effecting service of proceedings; or
    (ii) in any other case, in effecting substituted service.

(3) If the court makes an order by virtue of subsection (1) it must afford the respondent an opportunity to make representations relating to the order as soon as just and convenient at a full hearing.

(4) If, at a full hearing, the court makes an occupation order ("the full order"), then—
  (a) for the purposes of calculating the maximum period for which the full order may be made to have effect, the relevant section is to apply as if the period for which the full order will have effect began on the date on which the initial order first had effect; and
  (b) the provisions of section 36(10) or 38(6) as to the extension of orders are to apply as if the full order and the initial order were a single order.

(5) In this section—
  "full hearing" means a hearing of which notice has been given to all the parties in accordance with rules of court;

"initial order" means an occupation order made by virtue of subsection (1); and

"relevant section" means section 33(10), 35(10), 36(10), 37(5) or 38(6).

46 Undertakings

(1)   In any case where the court has power to make an occupation order or non-molestation order, the court may accept an undertaking from any party to the proceedings.

(2)   No power of arrest may be attached to any undertaking given under subsection (1).

(3)   The court shall not accept an undertaking under subsection (1) in any case where apart from this section a power of arrest would be attached to the order.

(4)   An undertaking given to a court under subsection (1) is enforceable as if it were an order of the court.

(5)   This section has effect without prejudice to the powers of the High Court and the county court apart from this section.

47 Arrest for breach of order

(1)   In this section "a relevant order" means an occupation order or a non-molestation order.

(2)   If—
(a)   the court makes a relevant order; and
(b)   it appears to the court that the respondent has used or threatened violence against the applicant or a relevant child,

it shall attach a power of arrest to one or more provisions of the order unless satisfied that in all the circumstances of the case the applicant or child will be adequately protected without such a power of arrest.

(3)   Subsection (2) does not apply in any case where the relevant order is made by virtue of section 45(1), but in such a case the court may attach a power of arrest to one or more provisions of the order if it appears to it—
(a)   that the respondent has used or threatened violence against the applicant or a relevant child; and
(b)   that there is a risk of significant harm to the applicant or child, attributable to conduct of the respondent, if the power of arrest is not attached to those provisions immediately.

(4)   If, by virtue of subsection (3), the court attaches a power of arrest to any provisions of a relevant order, it may provide that the power of arrest is to have effect for a shorter period than the other provisions of the order.

(5)   Any period specified for the purposes of subsection (4) may be extended by the court (on one or more occasions) on an application to vary or discharge the relevant order.

(6)   If, by virtue of subsection (2) or (3), a power of arrest is attached to certain provisions of an order, a constable may arrest without warrant a person whom he has reasonable cause for suspecting to be in breach of any such provision.

(7)   If a power of arrest is attached under subsection (2) or (3) to certain provisions of the order and the respondent is arrested under subsection (6)—
    (a) he must be brought before the relevant judicial authority within the period of 24 hours beginning at the time of his arrest; and
    (b) if the matter is not then disposed of forthwith, the relevant judicial authority before whom he is brought may remand him.

In reckoning for the purposes of this subsection any period of 24 hours, no account is to be taken of Christmas Day, Good Friday or any Sunday.

(8)   If the court has made a relevant order but—
    (a) has not attached a power of arrest under subsection (2) or (3) to any provisions of the order, or
    (b) has attached that power only to certain provisions of the order,

then, if at any time the applicant considers that the respondent has failed to comply with the order, he may apply to the relevant judicial authority for the issue of a warrant for the arrest of the respondent.

(9)   The relevant judicial authority shall not issue a warrant on an application under subsection (8) unless—
    (a) the application is substantiated on oath; and
    (b) the relevant judicial authority has reasonable grounds for believing that the respondent has failed to comply with the order.

(10) If a person is brought before a court by virtue of a warrant issued under subsection (9) and the court does not dispose of the matter forthwith, the court may remand him.

(11) Schedule 5 (which makes provision corresponding to that applying in magistrates' courts in civil cases under sections 128 and 129 of the Magistrates' Courts Act 1980) has effect in relation to the powers of the High Court and a county court to remand a person by virtue of this section.

(12) If a person remanded under this section is granted bail (whether in the High Court or a county court under Schedule 5 or in a magistrates' court under section 128 or 129 of the Magistrates' Courts Act 1980), he may be required by the relevant judicial authority to comply, before release on bail or later, with such requirements as appear to that authority to be necessary to secure that he does not interfere with witnesses or otherwise obstruct the course of justice.

49   Variation and discharge of orders

(1)   An occupation order or non-molestation order may be varied or discharged by the court on an application by—
    (a) the respondent, or
    (b) the person on whose application the order was made.

(2)   In the case of a non-molestation order made by virtue of section 42(2)(b), the order may be varied or discharged by the court even though no such application has been made.

(3)   If a spouse's matrimonial home rights are a charge on the estate or interest of the other spouse or of trustees for the other spouse, an order under section 33 against the other spouse may also be varied or discharged by the court on an application by any person deriving title under the other spouse or under the trustees and affected by the charge.

(4)   If, by virtue of section 47(3), a power of arrest has been attached to certain provisions of an occupation order or non-molestation order, the court may vary or discharge the order under subsection (1) in so far as it confers a power of arrest (whether or not any application has been made to vary or discharge any other provision of the order).

Transfer of tenancies

53.   Transfer of certain tenancies

Schedule 7 makes provision in relation to the transfer of certain tenancies on divorce etc or on separation of cohabitants.

General

62   Meaning of "cohabitants", "relevant child" and "associated persons"

(1)   For the purposes of this Part—
  (a) "cohabitants" are a man and a woman who, although not married to each other, are living together as husband and wife; and
  (b) "former cohabitants" is to be read accordingly, but does not include cohabitants who have subsequently married each other.

(2)   In this Part, "relevant child", in relation to any proceedings under this Part, means—
  (a) any child who is living with or might reasonably be expected to live with either party to the proceedings;
  (b) any child in relation to whom an order under the Adoption Act 1976 or the Children Act 1989 is in question in the proceedings; and
  (c) any other child whose interests the court considers relevant.

(3)   For the purposes of this Part, a person is associated with another person if—
  (a) they are or have been married to each other;
  (b) they are cohabitants or former cohabitants;
  (c) they live or have lived in the same household, otherwise than merely by reason of one of them being the other's employee, tenant, lodger or boarder;
  (d) they are relatives;
  (e) they have agreed to marry one another (whether or not that agreement has been terminated);

(f) in relation to any child, they are both persons falling within subsection (4); or

(g) they are parties to the same family proceedings (other than proceedings under this Part).

(4) A person falls within this subsection in relation to a child if—
   (a) he is a parent of the child; or
   (b) he has or has had parental responsibility for the child.

(5) If a child has been adopted or has been freed for adoption by virtue of any of the enactments mentioned in section 16(1) of the Adoption Act 1976, two persons are also associated with each other for the purposes of this Part if—
   (a) one is a natural parent of the child or a parent of such a natural parent; and
   (b) the other is the child or any person—
      (i) who has become a parent of the child by virtue of an adoption order or has applied for an adoption order, or
      (ii) with whom the child has at any time been placed for adoption.

(6) A body corporate and another person are not, by virtue of subsection (3)(f) or (g), to be regarded for the purposes of this Part as associated with each other.

63 Interpretation of Part IV

(1) In this Part—
   "adoption order" has the meaning given by section 72(1) of the Adoption Act 1976;
   "associated", in relation to a person, is to be read with section 62(3) to (6);
   "child" means a person under the age of eighteen years;
   "cohabitant" and "former cohabitant" have the meaning given by section 62(1);
   "the court" is to be read with section 57;
   "development" means physical, intellectual, emotional, social or behavioural development;
   "dwelling-house" includes (subject to subsection (4))—
      (a) any building or part of building which is occupied as a dwelling,
      (b) any caravan, house-boat or structure which is occupied as a dwelling, and any yard, garden, garage or outhouse belonging to it and occupied with it;
   "family proceedings" means any proceedings—
      (a) under the inherent jurisdiction of the High Court in relation to children; or
      (b) under the enactments mentioned in subsection (2);
   "harm"—
      (a) in relation to a person who has reached the age of eighteen years, means ill-treatment or the impairment of health; and
      (b) in relation to a child, means ill-treatment or the impairment of health or development;

"health" includes physical or mental health;

"ill-treatment" includes forms of ill-treatment which are not physical and, in relation to a child, includes sexual abuse;

"matrimonial home rights" has the meaning given by section 30;

"mortgagor" and "mortgagee" have the same meaning as in the Law of Property Act 1925;

"mortgage payments" includes any payments which, under the terms of the mortgage, the mortgagor is required to make to any person;

"non-molestation order" has the meaning given by section 42(1);

"occupation order" has the meaning given by section 39;

"parental responsibility" has the same meaning as in the Children Act 1989;

"relative", in relation to a person, means—

(a) the father, mother, stepfather, stepmother, son, daughter, stepson, stepdaughter, grandmother, grandfather, grandson or granddaughter of that person or of that person's spouse or former spouse, or

(b) the brother, sister, uncle, aunt, niece or nephew (whether of the full blood or of the half blood or by affinity) of that person or of that person's spouse or former spouse.

and includes, in relation to a person who is living or has lived with another person as husband and wife, any person who would fall within paragraph (a) or (b) if the parties were married to each other;

"relevant child", in relation to any proceedings under this Part, has the meaning given by section 62(2);

(2) The enactments referred to in the definition of "family proceedings" are—

(a) Part II;

(b) this Part;

(c) the Matrimonial Causes Act 1973;

(d) the Adoption Act 1976;

(e) the Domestic Proceedings and Magistrates' Courts Act 1978;

(f) Part III of the Matrimonial and Family Proceedings Act 1984;

(g) Parts I, II and IV of the Children Act 1989;

(h) section 30 of the Human Fertilisation and Embryology Act 1990.

(3) Where the question of whether harm suffered by a child is significant turns on the child's health or development, his health or development shall be compared with that which could reasonably be expected of a similar child.

(4) For the purposes of sections 31, 32, 53 and 54 and such other provisions of this Part (if any) as may be prescribed, this Part is to have effect as if paragraph (b) of the definition of "dwelling-house" were omitted.

(5) It is hereby declared that this Part applies as between the parties to a marriage even though either of them is, or has any time during the marriage been, married to more than one person.

Index

Adoption 159–67
  access to birth records 160
  child's status 159–60
  freeing for 164
  legal effects 159
  parental agreement 162
  reform, proposals for 167
  rights of succession 161, 166
  welfare principle 161
  who may adopt
    convention orders 167
    criteria 161, 166
    suitability of applicants 166
Adultery
  general considerations 27
  intolerability 28
  living together after 28
  meaning 27
  standard of proof 27–8
Arrangements for the future,
  see Divorce and see Financial relief in
    matrimonial proceedings

Behaviour
  living together after incident 28
  meaning of behaviour 28
  test to be applied 29
Bigamy 7, 15

Capacity
  non-consummation 17
  and see Void and voidable marriages
  to marry 8
Care orders 150–3
  criteria for 150
  duration 153
  effect of 152
  parental contact 152
Child abduction 144–5

Child assessment orders 154
Child of family
  failure to provide reasonable
    maintenance for 66
  meaning 66–7
Child protection law
  care orders, see Care orders
  child assessment orders 154
  education supervision orders 154
  emergency protection orders 155
  guardian ad litem 156
  local authorities, duties of 147–8
  police protection 156
  section 8 orders 151
  supervision orders 153
Child Support Acts 1991–1995 76–81
  absent parent 77
  benefit case 79
  Child Support Agency 76
  clean break following settlement by 80
  departure directions 80–1
  maintenance calculation 77–8
  purpose 76
  qualifying child 76
  refusal to supply information 79
Children
  abduction, see Child abduction
  contact orders 140
  delay in proceedings 123
  dispute resolution 136–45
  domicile of 8
  FLA 1996 protection 48
  financial orders 66–7 108–10
    see also Financial relief in
      matrimonial proceedings
  legitimacy 126, 127
  medical treatment 131–2
  - in need 147
  non-intervention 123

Children *continued*
  parental responsibility, *see* Parental
    responsibility
  prohibited steps orders 140
  residence orders 139
  section 8 orders 139–43
  specific issue orders 140
  wardship 143–4
  welfare principle 123–4, 136–9
  welfare in divorce 35, 43
Cohabitants
  property, *see* Property disputes
  protection from violence *see* Domestic
    violence

Desertion
  absence of consent 31
  absence of good cause 31
  constructive 30
  intention 30
  meaning of 30–1
  resumption of cohabitation 31
  termination of 31
Divorce under the FLA 1996 36–46
  arrangements for the future 41–2
  background to new changes 36
  entitlement to divorce 40
  general principles 37
  information meeting 37
  irretrievable breakdown 41
  marriage counselling 38
  marital breakdown, statement of 39
  mediation 38
  orders preventing divorce 44
  period of reflection and consideration
    39–40
  substantial hardship 44
  welfare of children 43
Divorce under the MCA 1973 26–36
  adultery 27–8
    see also Adultery
  bars to decree nisi 34–5
  behaviour of respondent 28–30
    see also Behaviour
  desertion 30–1
    see also Desertion

  financial relief, *see* Financial relief in
    matrimonial proceedings
  irretrievable breakdown 26
  separation, five years' 33–4
  separation, two years 31–3
  time qualification 26
Domestic violence 47–57
  inherent jurisdiction 55–6
  orders under FLA 1996 Part IV
    associated persons 48
    non-molestation orders 53–4
    occupation orders 49–53
  Protection from Harassment Act 1997
    56
Domicile 8, 22
  of choice 8
  dependent domicile 8
  of origin 8

European Convention on Recognition
  and Enforcement of Decisions
  Concerning the Custody of Children
  145

Family Law Act 1996, *see* Divorce,
  Domestic violence
Financial obligations during marriage
  61–74
  common law duty to maintain 61
  maintenance and separation agree-
    ments 63–4
  orders in family proceedings courts
    failure to provide reasonable
      maintenance 65
    duration 69
    factors to be taken into account
      67
    grounds for application 65–6
    interim orders 69
    lump sum orders 66
    periodical payments orders 66
    variation 70
    voluntary separation orders 68
  orders in High Court and county
    courts
    duration 72

Financial obligations during marriage
  continued
    factors to be taken into account
      72–3
    grounds 71
    lump sum orders 72
    periodical payment orders 71
    variation 73
  public law duty to maintain 62
Financial orders for children
  duration 110
  guidelines 109
  range of orders 109
Financial relief in matrimonial
  proceedings 94–113
  arrangements for the future 97–8
  'clean break' 104–5
  discharge of orders 111–13
  lump sum orders 95
  matters to be taken into account
    99–103
  periodical payments 94
  property adjustment orders 96
  quantum 106
  secured orders 95
  variation of orders 110
Financial provision on death 113–19
  applicants 115–16
  applications for
    child of deceased 118
    child of the family 118
    former spouse 118
    surviving spouse 117
  matters to be considered 117–18
  range of orders 117
  reasonable financial provision 117
  succession, rules of 113–15
Foreign divorce recognition 45–6
Foreign marriage 11
  polygamous 11
  recognition of 11
  child abduction, and 145

General principles of FLA 1996 37
Guardians
  guardian *ad litem* 156–7

parental responsibility of 133
testamentary 133

Hague Convention on Civil Aspects of
  Child Abduction 145

Judicial separation
  ancillary orders 94
  jurisdiction to grant orders 41

Local authority
  and see Child protection law
  accommodation provision 148–50
  care orders, *see* Care orders
  child assessment orders 154
  children in need 147–8
  disabled children 148
  emergency protection orders 155–6
  parental responsibility 133
  section 8 orders and 147
  supervision orders 153
  wardship 143

Marriage
  age of parties 9
  Anglican 9
  annulment, *see* Nullity
  banns 10
  bigamy 7, 15
  capacity 8, 9
  common licence 10
  definition 7
  divorce, *see* Divorce
  foreign marriage, recognition of
    11
  formalities 9
  invalidating defects, *see* Void and
    voidable marriages
  notice 10
  Superintendent Registrar's certificate
    9, 10
  Superintendent Registrar's certificate
    and licence 10
Married Women's Property Acts
  determination of rights 83
  housekeeping allowances 84

Matrimonial home rights
  enforcement 90
  definition 90
  third parties, protection of interest
    against 91
Matrimonial property
  common fund 84
  gifts
    between spouses 85
    wedding presents 85
  housekeeping allowance 84
  joint bank accounts 84
  and see financial obligations during
    marriage
  and see Financial relief in matrimonial
    proceedings
  and see Property disputes
Mental disorder, ground for avoiding
  marriage 20

Non-consummation, *see* Void and
  voidable marriages
Non-molestation injunctions, *see*
  Domestic violence
Nullity of marriage
  approbation 20
    knowledge of defect 21
    time limitation 21
  bars to petition 20–1
  financial relief *see* Financial relief in
    matrimonial proceedings
  foreign element 22–4
  see also Void and voidable marriages

Occupation orders, *see* Domestic
  violence
Orders preventing divorce, *see* Divorce

Parental responsibility 129–34
  adoptive parents, 133
  agreement 132
  application, for 133
  care orders and 152
  Gillick, decision in 131
  guardians 133
  local authorities 133

  married parents 132
  residence orders 133
  unmarried parents 132–3
Parentage, determining 127–9
  DNA profiling 127
  embryo donation 128
  genetic fingerprinting 127
  natural 127
  surrogacy 128–9
  unmarried father 127, 132
Pension rights 103
Period for reflection and consideration,
  see Divorce under FLA 1996
Property adjustment orders
  children 109
  discharge 111–13
  financial relief in matrimonial
    proceedings 96
Property disputes
  common intention 86
    agreement 86
    contribution 86
  constructive trusts 85–6
  implied and resulting trusts 85–8
  matrimonial home rights 89–91
  quantification of beneficial interest 88
  s. 17 MWPA 91
  s. 70 LPA 1925 89
Protection from harassment 56

Residence orders 139

Separation agreements 63–4
Specific issue orders 140

Void and voidable marriages
  void marriages
    bigamous 15
    formal defects 15
    capacity 14
    parties not of opposite sex 15
    potentially polygamous 11
    prohibited degrees 14
  voidable marriages
    duress 18
    lack of consent 18

Void and voidable marriages *continued*
    mental disorder 20
    mistake 19
    non-consummation 16
      incapacity 17
      wilful refusal 17
    respondent's venereal disease 20
    unsoundness of mind 19

Wardship 143–4
    local authorities, and 144
    scope 143
Will
    reasonable provision 117
    revoked by marriage 117